FINANCIAL INSTITUTIONS AND SERVICES

LARGE FINANCIAL INSTITUTIONS

THE "LIVING WILLS" REQUIREMENT AND ECONOMIC ISSUES ASSOCIATED WITH "TOO BIG TO FAIL"

FINANCIAL INSTITUTIONS AND SERVICES

Additional books in this series can be found on Nova's website under the Series tab.

Additional e-books in this series can be found on Nova's website under the e-book tab.

FINANCIAL INSTITUTIONS AND SERVICES

LARGE FINANCIAL INSTITUTIONS

THE "LIVING WILLS" REQUIREMENT AND ECONOMIC ISSUES ASSOCIATED WITH "TOO BIG TO FAIL"

FRANKLIN PIERCE
EDITOR

nova publishers
New York

Library of Congress Cataloging-in-Publication Data

ISBN: 978-1-63482-261-9

Published by Nova Science Publishers, Inc. † New York

CONTENTS

PREFACE

This book reviews the legal structure of the DFA's living will requirements; and examines some of the steps that these institutions might voluntarily take, which, in the view of the FRB and FDIC, would improve their resolvability, including strategic divestiture; legal reorganization; amendment of default trigger provisions of qualified financial contracts; and increasing their long-term, unsecured debt as a proportion of their assets.

Chapter 1 – One of the chief objectives of the Dodd-Frank Wall Street Reform and Consumer Protection Act (DFA) is to promote financial stability within the United States, without the need for emergency governmental assistance to troubled firms. To achieve this goal, the DFA establishes a heightened regulatory regime for certain, generally large "covered financial institutions." A pillar of this heightened regulatory regime is that each covered financial institution must submit "credible" plans to the Board of Governors of the Federal Reserve System (FRB) and the Federal Deposit Insurance Corporation (FDIC) detailing how the firm could be quickly resolved in an orderly fashion under the U.S. Bankruptcy Code or other applicable insolvency regime "in the event of a material financial distress or failure." These resolution plans are commonly referred to as "living wills."

Over 130 institutions have filed at least one resolution plan with regulators. Each of the 11 largest financial firms in the U.S., which each hold more than $250 billion in nonbank assets, has filed at least two resolution plans. However, all 11 of these companies' plans, in spite of the fact that some of them span tens of thousands of pages, have fallen short of the minimum requirements of the DFA's living wills regime in the discretionary view of the FRB and FDIC. The 11 firms' next living wills are due July 2015. If any of these plans is determined to be insufficient, then the FRB and FDIC have expressed their intent "to use their [enforcement] authority under [DFA] section 165(d)," which eventually could include the power to require an institution "to divest certain assets or operations ... to facilitate an orderly resolution...."

This report reviews the legal structure of the DFA's living will requirements, pursuant to both DFA Section 165(d) and the regulations and guidance issued jointly by the FRB and FDIC, and explains the August 2014 joint announcement of the FRB and FDIC regarding the inadequacies of the 2013 living wills filed by the 11 largest, most complex financial institutions in the country. This report also examines some of the steps that these institutions might voluntarily take, which, in the view of the FRB and FDIC, would improve their resolvability, including strategic divestiture; legal reorganization; amendment of default trigger provisions of qualified financial contracts; and increasing their long-term, unsecured debt as a proportion of their assets.

Chapter 2 – The U.S. and global financial systems are the definition of concentrated risk. They are composed of systemically important financial institutions (SIFIs) that are highly leveraged, heavily reliant on wholesale funding, and unduly interconnected. When even one of these institutions fails, its impact on world economies can be devastating.

To mitigate this impact, the Dodd-Frank Act of 2010 requires that each SIFI show itself capable of going through bankruptcy without bringing the economy down with it. This is no simple task, especially when such firms have assets at risk that rival the size of the home country's GDP.

These remarks address the topic of resolution through bankruptcy.

Chapter 3 – This is a Statement of Daniel K. Tarullo, Member, Board of Governors of the Federal Reserve System. Hearing on "Wall Street Reform: Assessing and Enhancing the Financial Regulatory System", before the Senate Committee on Banking, Housing, and Urban Affairs, dated September 9, 2014.

Chapter 4 – This is a Statement of Martin J. Gruenberg, Chairman, Federal Deposit Insurance Corporation. Hearing on "Wall Street Reform: Assessing and Enhancing the Financial Regulatory System" before the Senate Committee on Banking, Housing, and Urban Affairs, dated September 9, 2014.

Chapter 5 – Although "too big to fail" (TBTF) has been a perennial policy issue, it was highlighted by the near-collapse of several large financial firms in 2008. Financial firms are said to be TBTF when policy makers judge that their failure would cause unacceptable disruptions to the overall financial system, and they can be TBTF because of their size or interconnectedness. In addition to fairness issues, economic theory suggests that expectations that a firm will not be allowed to fail create moral hazard—if the creditors and counterparties of a TBTF firm believe that the government will protect them from losses, they have less incentive to monitor the firm's riskiness because they are shielded from the negative consequences of those risks. If so, they could have a funding advantage compared with other banks, which some call an implicit subsidy. S.Con.Res. 8, passed by the Senate on March 22, 2013, and H.Con.Res. 25, as amended and passed by the Senate on October 16, 2013, create a non-binding budget reserve fund that allows for future legislation to address the TBTF funding advantage.

There are a number of policy approaches—some complementary, some conflicting—to coping with the TBTF problem, including providing government assistance to prevent TBTF firms from failing or systemic risk from spreading; enforcing "market discipline" to ensure that investors, creditors, and counterparties curb excessive risk-taking at TBTF firms; enhancing regulation to hold TBTF firms to stricter prudential standards than other financial firms; curbing firms' size and scope, by preventing mergers or compelling firms to divest assets, for example; minimizing spillover effects by limiting counterparty exposure; and instituting a special resolution regime for failing systemically important firms. A comprehensive policy is likely to incorporate more than one approach, as some approaches are aimed at preventing failures and some at containing fallout when a failure occurs.

Parts of the Wall Street Reform and Consumer Protection Act (Dodd-Frank Act; P.L. 111-203) address all of these policy approaches. For example, it created an enhanced prudential regulatory regime administered by the Federal Reserve for non-bank financial firms designated as "systemically important" by the Financial Stability Oversight Council (FSOC) and banks with more than $50 billion in assets. About 30 U.S. bank holding companies and a larger number of foreign banks have more than $50 billion in assets, and the FSOC has designated two insurers (AIG and Prudential) and GE Capital as systemically important. According to the insurer MetLife, FSOC has proposed to designate it as well. In addition, eight banks headquartered in the United States will be assessed capital surcharges under Basel III. H.R. 4881, ordered to be reported by the House Financial Services Committee on June 20, 2014, would place a one-year moratorium on FSOC designations. H.R. 5016, which passed the House on July 16, 2014, would not allow any funds to be used to designate a non-bank as systemically important or as posing a systemic threat to financial stability. S. 2270, as passed by the Senate, and H.R. 5461, as passed by the House, would allow regulators to exempt insurers from bank capital requirements (the "Collins Amendment" to the Dodd-Frank Act).

The Dodd-Frank Act also created a special resolution regime administered by the Federal Deposit Insurance Corporation to take into receivership failing firms that pose a threat to financial stability. This regime has not been used to date, and has some similarities to how the FDIC resolves failing banks. Statutory authority used to prevent financial firms from failing during the crisis has either expired or been narrowed by the Dodd-Frank Act.

In: Large Financial Institutions
Editors: Franklin Pierce

ISBN: 978-1-63482-261-9

Chapter 1

"Living Wills": The Legal Regime for Constructing Resolution Plans for Certain Financial Institutions*

David H. Carpenter

Summary

One of the chief objectives of the Dodd-Frank Wall Street Reform and Consumer Protection Act (DFA) is to promote financial stability within the United States, without the need for emergency governmental assistance to troubled firms. To achieve this goal, the DFA establishes a heightened regulatory regime for certain, generally large "covered financial institutions." A pillar of this heightened regulatory regime is that each covered financial institution must submit "credible" plans to the Board of Governors of the Federal Reserve System (FRB) and the Federal Deposit Insurance Corporation (FDIC) detailing how the firm could be quickly resolved in an orderly fashion under the U.S. Bankruptcy Code or other applicable insolvency regime "in the event of a material financial distress or failure." These resolution plans are commonly referred to as "living wills."

Over 130 institutions have filed at least one resolution plan with regulators. Each of the 11 largest financial firms in the U.S., which each hold more than $250 billion in nonbank assets, has filed at least two

* This is an edited, reformatted and augmented version of a Congressional Research Service publication, No. R43801, dated December 4, 2014.

resolution plans. However, all 11 of these companies' plans, in spite of the fact that some of them span tens of thousands of pages, have fallen short of the minimum requirements of the DFA's living wills regime in the discretionary view of the FRB and FDIC. The 11 firms' next living wills are due July 2015. If any of these plans is determined to be insufficient, then the FRB and FDIC have expressed their intent "to use their [enforcement] authority under [DFA] section 165(d)," which eventually could include the power to require an institution "to divest certain assets or operations ... to facilitate an orderly resolution.... "

This report reviews the legal structure of the DFA's living will requirements, pursuant to both DFA Section 165(d) and the regulations and guidance issued jointly by the FRB and FDIC, and explains the August 2014 joint announcement of the FRB and FDIC regarding the inadequacies of the 2013 living wills filed by the 11 largest, most complex financial institutions in the country. This report also examines some of the steps that these institutions might voluntarily take, which, in the view of the FRB and FDIC, would improve their resolvability, including strategic divestiture; legal reorganization; amendment of default trigger provisions of qualified financial contracts; and increasing their long-term, unsecured debt as a proportion of their assets.

In addition to voluntary measures, there are bills in the 113th Congress that would change how financial institutions are regulated to promote the financial stability of the United States. For example, H.R. 46 and S. 20, the Financial Takeover Repeal Act of 2013, would repeal the DFA in its entirety, including the provisions designed to promote financial stability. H.R. 5421, the Financial Institution Bankruptcy Act of 2014, and a similar bill, S. 1861, the Taxpayer Protection and Responsible Resolution Act, would make changes to the Bankruptcy Code to facilitate the resolution of financial institutions. H.R. 1450/S. 685, the Too Big to Fail, Too Big to Exist Act, would require the Secretary of the Treasury to identify all financial institutions it considers to be "too big to fail," and to "break up [these] entities ... so that their failure would no longer cause a catastrophic effect on the United States or global economy without taxpayer bailout." And H.R. 613, the Systemic Risk Mitigation Act, would among other things, require every bank holding company with $50 billion or more in consolidated assets to hold long-term, subordinated debt of the value of at least 15% of its total consolidated assets. Proponents argue that this could help promote the long-term viability of the firm and, if the firm actually fails, help absorb some of its losses.

INTRODUCTION

One of the chief objectives of the Dodd-Frank Wall Street Reform and Consumer Protection Act (DFA)[1] is to promote financial stability within the United States,[2] without the need for emergency governmental assistance to troubled firms like that provided by the Troubled Asset Relief Program (TARP) in 2008.[3] In fact, the first two titles of the DFA are devoted specifically to that policy objective.

Title I establishes the Financial Stability Oversight Council (FSOC)—a council of financial regulators[4] authorized "to identify risks to the financial stability of the United States that could arise from the material financial distress or failure, or ongoing activities, of large, interconnected [financial institutions]" and generally "to respond to emerging threats to the stability of the United States financial system."[5] Title I also establishes a heightened regulatory regime for domestic bank holding companies with $50 billion or more in consolidated assets, certain foreign banks and foreign bank holding companies with $50 billion or more in total consolidated assets,[6] and certain nonbank financial institutions that are designated by a 2/3 vote of the FSOC as potentially systemically significant. These "covered financial institutions" are subject to, among other things, heightened capital requirements and more restrictive leverage ratios than their smaller, less complex peers.

Additionally, a pillar of this heightened regulatory regime is that each covered financial institution must submit "credible" plans to the Board of Governors of the Federal Reserve System (FRB) and the Federal Deposit Insurance Corporation (FDIC) detailing how the firm could be quickly resolved in an orderly fashion under the U.S. Bankruptcy Code[7] or other applicable insolvency regime[8] "in the event of a material financial distress or failure." These resolution plans are commonly referred to as "living wills." If a covered financial institution fails to submit a "credible" resolution plan in the discretionary view of both the FRB and FDIC, then the company could be subject to enforcement actions, including the compelled divestiture of certain business lines and assets, as a means to foster its resolvability. The DFA does not explicitly define what it means to be "credible," thus providing the FRB and FDIC considerable discretion to implement the living wills regime.

Relatedly, Title II of the DFA[9] establishes a special insolvency regime that could be used if it were determined that the failure or financial distress of a bank or nonbank financial institution[10] poses a systemic threat to the U.S. financial system in spite of the heightened regulatory regime established by DFA, Title I and related financial laws and regulations. The Title II insolvency regime, called Orderly Liquidation Authority (OLA), would be administered by the FDIC.[11] Under OLA, the FDIC generally would have to liquidate the failed firm within five years,[12] and, although public funds could be used initially, the cost of the resolution ultimately is intended to be paid for through the assets of the failed company or, if necessary, post-hoc assessments on surviving covered financial institutions.[13]

A financial firm generally can only be subject to OLA if:

- 2/3 of the FRB and either 2/3 of the Board of Directors of the FDIC, 2/3 of the Securities and Exchange Commission,[14] or the Director of the Federal Insurance Office[15] vote to recommend the appointment to OLA based on a series of statutory standards, including an evaluation of the impact that the company's failure would have on financial stability;[16] and
- the Secretary of the Treasury determines, among other things, that the institution is "in default or in danger of default,"[17] that "the failure of the financial company and its resolution under otherwise applicable Federal or State law would have *serious adverse effects on financial stability* in the United States," and "*no viable private sector alternative is available....* "[18]

In other words, OLA is statutorily structured as a fallback alternative to the normally applicable insolvency regimes, such as the U.S. Bankruptcy Code, and is to be triggered only under extraordinary circumstances.

The living wills regime theoretically could play a crucial role in avoiding the need to employ OLA or some other extraordinary governmental action. This living wills regime requires large, complex, or otherwise systemically significant financial firms, in coordination with federal regulators, to design detailed roadmaps for utilizing—and to modify corporate, contractual, and other legal structures to make it easier to utilize—normal resolution regimes if these firms become insolvent or in danger of default.

Covered financial institutions' initial living wills were required to be submitted in several waves, beginning in July 2012. Over 130 institutions have filed at least one resolution plan with regulators.[19] Each of the 11 largest financial firms in the United States, which each hold more than $250 billion in nonbank assets, has filed at least two resolution plans.[20] **Table 1** sheds some light on the size, make-up, and complexity of these 11 financial institutions. As is discussed in greater detail below, all 11 of these companies' plans, in spite of the fact that some of them span tens of thousands of pages,[21] have fallen short of the minimum requirements of DFA Section 165(d) in the view of the FRB and FDIC.[22] These 11 firms' next living wills are due July 2015. If any of these plans is determined to be insufficient, then the FRB and FDIC have expressed their intent "to use their [enforcement] authority under section 165(d)," which eventually could include the power to require an institution "to divest certain assets or operations ... to facilitate an orderly resolution.... "[23]

This report reviews the legal structure of the DFA's living will requirements, pursuant to both DFA Section 165(d) and the regulations and guidance issued jointly by the FRB and FDIC; explains the August 2014 joint announcement of the FRB and FDIC regarding the inadequacies of the 2013 living wills filed by the 11 largest, most complex financial institutions in the country; analyzes the steps that the FRB and FDIC have suggested that these companies could take to rectify the common shortcomings in resolution plans filed thus far; and discusses the enforcement tools the FRB and FDIC may utilize against firms that fail to submit "credible" resolution plans.

This report focuses on the legal aspects of the DFA living wills regime and how the FRB and FDIC are administering the regime. Policy issues, although raised at times, generally are outside its scope. In particular, this report takes no stance on whether or not the living wills regime, specifically, or DFA, Titles I and II, generally, actually promote financial stability, or whether the steps that the FRB and FDIC have recommended that covered financial institutions take to improve their resolvability would in fact do so.

It also should be noted that this report concentrates on the FRB's and FDIC's interpretation and implementation of the living wills regime because these two regulators are empowered to implement DFA Section 165(d) by law, as it currently exists. Congress, of course, has broad discretion to pass legislation modifying the existing regime. In fact, there are bills in the 113th Congress that would change how financial institutions are regulated to promote the financial stability of the United States. For example, H.R. 46 and S. 20, the Financial Takeover Repeal Act of 2013, would repeal the DFA in its entirety, including the provisions designed to promote financial stability in Titles I and II. On December 2, 2014, the House of Representatives approved H.R. 5421, the Financial Institution Bankruptcy Act of 2014, which would amend the Bankruptcy Code "in order to facilitate the resolution of an insolvent financial institution in bankruptcy." H.R. 5421 appears to be intended to eliminate the need for OLA. A similar bill, S. 1861, the Taxpayer Protection and Responsible Resolution Act, would make changes to the Bankruptcy Code to facilitate the resolution of financial institutions, while also explicitly repealing DFA Title II.

H.R. 1450/S. 685, the Too Big to Fail, Too Big to Exist Act, would require the Secretary of the Treasury to identify all financial institutions it considers to be "too big to fail," and within one year of such designation, "break up [these] entities ... so that their failure would no longer cause a catastrophic effect on the United States or global economy without taxpayer bailout." And as a final example, H.R. 613, the Systemic Risk Mitigation Act, would among other things, require every bank holding company with $50 billion or more in consolidated assets to hold long-term, subordinated debt of the value of at least 15% of its total consolidated assets. As is discussed more fully below, increasing long-term, unsecured debt arguably could help promote the longterm viability of the firm and, if the firm actually fails, help absorb some of its losses.[24]

Table 1.Complexity at First-Wave Resolution Plan Filers

Company	Total Assets* (U.S. Dollars; Billions)	Notional Derivatives* (U.S. Dollars; Billions)	Short Term Funding**	Countries with Operations
Bank of America	$2,171	$55,472	19.4%	>40
Bank of New York Mellon	$401	$1,321	19.0%	35
Barclays***	$2,249	$66,516	25.4%	36
Citigroup	$1,910	$61,753	20.8%	160
Credit Suisse****	$1,005	$58,353	21.2%	>50
Deutsche Bank^	$2,280	$75,420	18.0%	>70
Goldman Sachs	$860	$57,695	26.7%	>50
JPMorgan Chase	$2,520	$68,326	20.3%	>100
Morgan Stanley	$827	$44,135	26.1%	43
State Street Corp.	$282	$1,263	8.3%	29
UBS^^	$1,108	$29,437	9.3%	>50

Source: Table and notes pulled in its entirety with permission and with minor edits for CRS formatting from *Financial Stocks Weekly: Living Wills Become a New Pressure Point on Big Banks*, Keefe, Bruyette & Wood (KBW), at 2, Aug. 25, 2014, available at http://op.bna.com/bar.nsf/id/jbar-9nblk8/$File/kbw.pdf (developed by KBW from company reports, SNL Financial, and KBW Research).

Notes:

* Total assets and notional derivatives based on company disclosures which may differ in accounting convention between countries.

**Shown as a percentage of total liabilities. For U.S. banks, KBW defined short-term funding as fed funds and repurchase agreements, jumbo time deposits, short trading positions, commercial paper, and borrowings with less than one year until maturity.

***Barclays disclosed the 36 countries which make up 90% of revenues. For short-term funding, KBW used select wholesale funding (repos, trading portfolio liabilities, <1 year wholesale debt).

****For Credit Suisse, KBW showed short-term funding as repos, short positions, and short-term borrowings.

^Deutsche Bank data as of the fourth quarter of FY2013. Short-term funding equals wholesale funding (unsecured wholesale funding, asset-backed commercial paper, and capital markets issuance) with a maturity of less than one year, secured funding and shorts, and financing vehicles.

^^Short-term funding includes repos, trading account liabilities, certificates of deposit, commercial paper, other money market paper.

DFA §165(D)—THE "LIVING WILLS" REGIME

DFA Section 165(d) requires certain banks and bank holding companies with greater than $50 billion in assets[25] and nonbank financial institutions designated by the FSOC for heightened prudential regulation by the FRB (together, "covered financial institutions") to submit plans to the FRB and FDIC detailing how the companies would be resolved in an orderly and swift fashion under the Bankruptcy Code (or other applicable insolvency regime) if the companies failed or otherwise suffered significant financial trouble.[26] Pursuant to DFA Section 165(d), the plans must include information about how affiliated insured depository institutions are buffered from the activities of the nonbank subsidiaries of the company; detailed information regarding the company's obligations, liabilities, and assets; a list of the company's significant counterparties; a list of entities with rights to collateral backing the company's existing obligations; a list of any cross-guarantees linked to security agreements; detailed information regarding the company's ownership structure; and "any other information that the [FRB and FDIC] jointly require by rule or order."[27] Section 165(d) also requires each covered financial institution to provide periodic reports on "the nature and extent to which the company has credit exposure to other [covered financial institutions]" and other such institutions have with it.[28]

The FRB and FDIC are required to review the resolution plan submissions,[29] in a process that FRB Chairman Janet Yellen stated is "intended to be iterative."[30] If the FRB and FDIC *jointly* determine that a submitted resolution plan "is not credible or would not facilitate an orderly resolution of the company under [traditional insolvency regimes]," then the regulators must inform the relevant company of the plan's shortcomings and require the company to submit a modified plan within a specified time.[31]

The DFA does not explicitly define the term "credible." Thus, the FRB and FDIC have considerable discretion in determining whether a particular living will "is not credible or would facilitate an orderly resolution" of a covered financial institution given its unique business model, legal structure, assets, liabilities, etc.

If a covered company fails to submit a credible plan within the allotted timeframe, then the FRB and FDIC may jointly place limits on the company's operations and activities, or subject them to heightened liquidity, capital, or leverage standards until resolution plans that meet statutory requirements are submitted. Additionally, if a covered company fails to submit a credible resolution plan within two years of being subject to such heightened standards or restrictions, then the FRB and FDIC are authorized to compel the company to divest certain business lines and assets, as a means to foster its resolvability.[32]

FRB AND FDIC JOINT REGULATIONS

On November 1, 2011, the FRB and FDIC issued final regulations to implement DFA Section 165(d).[33] The regulations establish various economic conditions that resolution plans should assume;[34] establish the form that resolution plans should take;[35] specify the timeframes in which living wills must be filed;[36] and provide greater clarity as to what covered bank and nonbank financial institutions must include in their plans,[37] the process by which resolutions plans will be reviewed by the FRB and FDIC,[38] and how DFA Section 165(d) and the regulations will be enforced.[39]

Assumptions

The regulations require that, in devising their resolution plans, covered financial institutions should take into account the same "baseline, adverse, and severely adverse economic conditions" that are established by the FRB for implementing the annual stress tests performed by the companies in accordance with DFA Section 165(i).[40] This requirement prevents covered financial institutions from developing living wills exclusively predicated on the potentially overly optimistic presumption that the rest of the market and the economy as whole will be functioning normally even while one or more covered financial institutions are being forced to liquidate because of financial trouble. The resolution plans also are prohibited from relying upon "the provision of extraordinary support by the United States or any other government to the covered company or its subsidiaries.... "[41]

Form

Pursuant to the regulations, the resolution plans must be separated into two distinct sections—one that will be made available to the public and a second that generally will be treated as confidential.[42] The public section of a living will should have an executive summary that provides an overview of the company's business that includes such information as its consolidated financial statements, a list of its principal officers, descriptions of its resolution planning processes and related governing structure, and descriptions of its hedging and derivatives activities.[43] Whether or not the information in and materials used to create resolution plans will be treated as confidential[44] is determined by the FRB's Rules Regarding Availability of Information,[45] the FDIC's Disclosure of Information Rules,[46] and the Freedom of Information Act (FOIA).[47] In accordance with those rules, covered companies may apply to regulators to have certain information in their living wills to be treated as confidential.[48]

Thus far, the full living will submissions for many covered financial institutions are thousands, if not tens of thousands, of pages long.[49] The public sections of resolution plans, which are the only portions that have not been treated as confidential, typically are between 15 and 35 pages long.[50]

Information

The regulations detail the information[51] that living wills should include, with emphasis not just on the covered parent company, but also its "material entities," "critical operations," and "core business lines."[52] In addition to an executive summary, living wills should provide:

- a "strategic analysis" of—
    - the assumptions the covered company used to develop the plan;

  - a "[r]ange of specific actions to be taken by the covered company to facilitate a rapid and orderly resolution ... ";
  - the company's financial needs and available resources in both normal times and times of severe stress;
  - steps that the company would take to limit the impact on the U.S. financial system upon the collapse of a Material Entity, Core Business Line, or Critical Operation;
  - time frames in which the company would be able to implement the various components of its resolution plan; and
  - the current fair market value of its Critical Operations, Core Business Lines, and other important assets.[53]
- an account of how resolution planning is woven into the covered company's corporate structure, including a list of the senior management responsible for supervising the company's resolution planning;[54]
- a description of the steps the company has taken to strengthen its resolution plan since its last filing;[55]
- a detailed accounting and mapping of the company's legal organization, including the "location, jurisdiction of incorporation, licensing, and key management associated with each material legal entity";[56]
- a detailed accounting of the company's consolidated and unconsolidated balance sheets, liabilities, pledged collateral, important hedging activities, significant counterparties and how the failure of those counterparties likely would impact the covered company, and important off-balance-sheet exposures;[57] and
- any additional information regarding "interconnections and interdependencies ... that, if disrupted, would materially affect the funding or operations of the covered company."[58]

Filing Deadlines, Regulatory Review, and Enforcement

The regulations establish a staggered schedule for the approximately 130 covered financial institutions' initial living will submissions. Covered institutions with more than $250 billion of consolidated nonbank assets were required to file their initial plans by July 1, 2012.[59] There were 11 of these "first-wave filers."[60] Four covered institutions holding between $100 and $250 billion in nonbank assets were required to submit their first living wills one year later—July 1, 2013.[61] The remaining approximately 115 covered institutions had until December 31, 2013, to make their initial submissions.[62]

Covered financial institutions must submit a living will at least once every year, generally by the anniversary date of their initial submission.[63] However, the FRB and FDIC may jointly require plans be submitted more frequently[64] and, with proper notice, may require a plan to be submitted earlier than the regular due date[65] or may provide an extension for submission.[66] The regulators may compel covered institutions to provide updates on specified aspects of filed resolution plans, as well.[67] Covered companies also generally must provide the FRB and FDIC notice and an explanation of "any event, occurrence, change in conditions or circumstances, or other change that results in, or could reasonably be foreseen to have, a material effect on the [company's] resolution plan ... ," within 45 days of such occurrence.[68]

Within 60 days of receiving a living will, the FRB and FDIC are to inform each covered institution if its submission is "informationally incomplete" and what information is needed to enable regulators to effectively review the plan.[69] Upon such notification, the covered company generally will have 30 days to submit all necessary information.[70]

The regulations also provide that covered institutions that are notified by the FRB and FDIC that their living wills are not "credible" generally will have 90 days to submit a modified plan that details the changes that were made to rectify the deficiencies cited by the regulators, as well as explanations for why the company thinks the revised plan actually would "facilitate an orderly resolution of the covered company under the Bankruptcy Code."[71] If the FRB and FDIC impose heightened capital, liquidity, or leverage requirements or limits on activities or operations on a covered company for submitting a revised resolution plan that does not fit within the regulators' deadline or does not adequately address the noted deficiencies, those heightened standards or limitations will remain in effect until a living will has been submitted that the regulators consider credible.[72]

The regulations reiterate that a failure to submit a credible plan within two years of the regulators' determination to impose heightened standards or activity restrictions could lead to the FRB and FDIC forcing the company to "divest[] of such assets and operations [as are] necessary to facilitate an orderly resolution."[73]

Further, in consultation with the FDIC, the FRB may exercise any of the enforcement powers provided under 12 U.S.C. §1818 against a covered financial institution that fails to comply with the living wills regime.[74] Section 1818's broad and flexible enforcement powers include the authority to issue cease and desist orders, issue prompt corrective actions, and assess civil money penalties.[75]

The DFA does not establish an appeals process specifically for the living wills regime. Disagreements regarding the enforcement of the living wills regime between a covered financial institution and the FRB and FDIC, like with other enforcement-related contentions, more often than not will be resolved informally through the iterative supervisory process.[76] However, if matters cannot be settled informally, a covered financial institution could avail itself of the formal hearing and judicial review process that generally applies to depository institutions, bank holding companies, and certain foreign banks and foreign bank holding companies.[77]

INITIAL SUBMISSION OF PLANS BY "FIRST-WAVE FILERS" AND REGULATORY RESPONSE

The 11 first-wave filers submitted their initial living wills to the FRB and FDIC by the July 1, 2012, deadline. The 11 companies are Bank of America, Bank of New York Mellon, Barclays, Citigroup, Credit Suisse, Deutsche Bank, Goldman Sachs, JPMorgan Chase, Morgan Stanley, State Street Corp., and UBS. The regulators did not make any official determinations regarding whether or not particular first-wave plans were "informationally incomplete" or not "credible." Instead, the regulators publicly responded in April 2013 by issuing a joint guidance document "to provide further clarification, guidance and direction" for how the 11 covered companies should develop their 2013 plans.[78] The regulators also provided the companies an additional three months to submit their 2013 plans, by adjusting the deadline from July 1 to October 1, 2013.[79]

The guidance stipulates that the executive summaries should include "concise descriptions of the key elements" of the firm's general resolution strategy.[80] The strategic analysis portion of the livings wills should consist of a more detailed narrative that is bolstered and substantiated by data and other information in appendixes.[81] Where relevant, the narrative should provide citations to specific provisions of appendixes. Each narrative also must at a minimum address five important obstacles to resolvability that the FRB and FDIC have identified.[82] These five obstacles are

1) contending with several, potentially competing, resolution regimes;
2) the impact of the covered financial institution's actions or inactions on self-interested ring fencing by administrators of foreign resolution regimes and the company's counterparties;
3) reliance on third parties and affiliates for the provision of important services and operations, and the potential for matters outside of the covered financial institution's control to disrupt those services and operations;
4) disruptions caused by the actions of the covered institution's counterparties, such as a counterparty's unilateral ability to increase margin requirements, close-out, liquidate, or net derivative contracts upon the covered financial institution's default; and
5) the illiquidity of the covered company's Material Entities and its impact on their ability to maintain Critical Operations.[83]

The guidance further elaborates on the assumptions that covered companies are and are not permitted to make in the development of their living wills. In addition to not being permitted to assume financial assistance from the United States or a foreign government, for instance, the guidance states that covered companies also should not assume they will be able to acquire unsecured financing just before default, such as debtor-in-possession financing as part of a Chapter 11 bankruptcy plan.[84]

2013 Resolution Plans by the 11 First-Wave Filers

In light of the guidance, each of the 11 first-wave filers submitted its second living will by the October 1, 2013, deadline. Some of these documents span more than 10,000 pages.[85] In spite of their girth, however, on August 5, 2014, the FDIC and FRB publicly announced that each of these living wills failed to establish sufficient plans for the companies' resolutions.[86] The regulatory agencies noted that some improvements were made from the firms' original submissions in 2012, but that each of the plans submitted in 2013 had various deficiencies, which were specified in individualized letters delivered to each company.[87] Although each firm had unique issues, the FRB and FDIC noted that problems with the 2013 living wills had two common characteristics. The resolution plans:

> (i) [made] assumptions that the agencies regard as unrealistic or inadequately supported, such as assumptions about the likely behavior of customers, counterparties, investors, central clearing facilities, and regulators, and (ii) the[y] fail[ed] to make, or even to identify, the kinds of changes in firm structure and practices that would be necessary to enhance the prospects for orderly resolution.[88]

The agencies are requiring the companies to take a number of steps to get their living wills into compliance with DFA Section 165(d). These actions include

- simplifying the companies' business structures and legal organizations;
- modifying derivatives, commodities, and other "qualified financial contracts" (QFCs)[89] to provide a temporary stay from a counterparty's rights to terminate the contracts when a covered financial institution enters an insolvency proceeding;
- strengthening internal operations, including the ability to produce documents and other necessary information for implementing a resolution in a timely manner; and
- establishing the ability to maintain necessary operations during a resolution.[90]

As a result of shortcomings in the resolution plans, the FDIC went so far as to issue an official determination that all 11 of the 2013 plans are "not credible and do not facilitate an orderly resolution under the U.S. Bankruptcy Code." Had the FRB voted to make the same determination, the regulators would have established the predicate condition for exercising their Section 165(d) enforcement powers. Instead, the FRB "determined that the 11 banking organizations must take immediate action to improve their resolvability and reflect those improvements in their 2015 plans."[91]

All of the companies are expected to submit living wills that the FRB and FDIC consider "credible" by July 1, 2015. If any fail to file adequate plans by then, the FRB's and FDIC's joint statement on August 5 indicates that the regulators intend to exercise their authority under Section 165(d) to "impose more stringent capital, leverage, or liquidity requirements, or restrictions on the growth, activities, or operations of the company" until robust resolution plans are submitted. As previously mentioned, if a covered company fails to rectify its living will within two years of the regulators imposing "more stringent" standards, the FRB and FDIC would have the power to compel the companies to divest certain business lines and assets.[92] This divestiture power is in addition to the FRB's general enforcement tools under 12 U.S.C. Section 1818.[93]

Initial Submissions for Covered Financial Institutions with Less than $250 Billion in Nonbank Assets and Regulatory Response

After reviewing the initial resolution plans of the covered financial institutions that were not among the first-wave filers, which were due on July 1, 2012, the FRB and FDIC did not publicly indicate that any of the resolution plans were out of compliance with the Dodd-Frank Act, at least to a degree that would warrant exercising Section 165(d) enforcement powers. The regulators, however, provided each of these firms "with guidance, clarification and direction for their second resolution plans."[94]

In a joint press release, the regulators indicated that they had established three different standards of resolution plans of varying degrees of sophistication. The regulators informed each covered financial institution as to the standard with which it must comply based on their determination of the firm's complexity and the extent of its operations within the United States.

More than 30 firms with less than $250 billion in nonbank assets, but which have relatively complex operations, must submit full resolution plans akin to those of the first-wave filers. An intermediate group of approximately 25 covered financial institutions will be allowed to submit "tailored plans" using a model template that the regulators issued publicly along with the joint press release.[95] The model template establishes a series of statements to be answered and provides a consistent order by which information may be presented.[96] The remaining covered financial institutions, which the FRB and FDIC have determined have only limited domestic operations, may meet their Section 165(d) responsibilities by building off of their original filings and submitting living wills that discuss "material changes to their initial plans as well as actions taken to strengthen the effectiveness of their initial plans."[97]

Steps 11 First-Wave Filers Could Take to Enhance Resolvability, as Recommended by the FRB and FDIC

In light of the fact that the FRB and FDIC have indicated that the 11 first-wave filers' living wills are lacking, this report examines some of the steps that these institutions might voluntarily take, which, in the discretionary views of the FRB and FDIC, would improve their resolvability. Although this report focuses on the legal issues associated with living wills, it should be noted that implementing the changes discussed below could result in increased administrative, regulatory, and market costs. Due to the fact that some of these steps would help address the common deficiencies noted by the regulators and because some of the first-wave filers are such dominant players in certain markets, some of these steps, if implemented, could lead to industrywide changes. Consequently, some of the changes designed to eliminate risks to the U.S. financial system that policy makers explicitly chose to limit to the largest, most complex financial firms in the country, have the potential to indirectly impact smaller companies, including community banks.

Strategic Divestiture

One notable way that the FRB and FDIC have indicated covered financial institutions could improve their resolvability would be to engage in strategic divestiture to simplify operations. This approach would seem to be what some policy makers and commentators have described as "breaking up the big banks."[98] While it would seem that the divestiture of significant portions of an institution's business so as to dramatically reduce its overall size could increase resolvability, size is only one of many factors that might affect a firm's resolvability. Other potential strategies include divestiture of foreign assets or particular products that are not adequately hedged or that carry concentrated risk exposure, as are discussed below.

Divestiture of Foreign Assets and Entities

One potential strategy could be to sell off smaller, nonessential entities that are organized and operating in foreign countries.[99] Focusing on this type of divestiture would not only reduce the institution's size and complexity, but would have the added benefit of reducing the institution's geographical footprint and potentially the number of foreign insolvency regimes with jurisdiction over aspects of the covered financial company. As is indicated in **Table 1**, each of the 11 first-wave filers is spread over at least 29 different countries, with two operating in more than 100. If these covered financial institutions failed, they likely would have assets in each of those countries that could be subject to insolvency regimes specific to those countries. As previously mentioned, contending with multiple insolvency regimes is also one of the five obstacles that the FRB and FDIC specifically have told the 11 first-wave filers should address in their resolution plans.[100] FDIC Vice-Chairman Thomas M. Hoenig has explained:

> Countries have their own laws, courts, and regulatory environment. Contracts enforceable in one country might not be so in another. Depositor preference, wholesale funding arrangements, derivatives, and repurchase agreements often are treated differently among countries when a firm enters bankruptcy.[101]

Reducing the number of countries of operation and the extent of operations within countries could help improve a covered financial institution's resolvability by, for example, reducing the coordination burdens of multiple insolvency regimes cooperating on the proper allocation of assets and treatment of creditors and, relatedly, the incentive of administrators of those regimes from engaging in self-interested "ring-fencing" of the failed institution's assets. Ring-fencing, in this context,[102] refers to an insolvency regime administrator freezing the transfer of assets[103] held by an affiliate of a failed institution that are located within the jurisdiction of the administrator so that those assets may be used to pay off domestic creditors, potentially at the expense of creditors located in other jurisdictions. Ring-fencing can lead to an inefficient allocation of the failed firm's assets, inconsistent treatment among creditor classes, and cutting the flow of cross-border funds that may be needed to maintain certain Critical Operations.[104]

The FDIC in recent years has been active in entering memoranda of understanding (MOU) with administrators of these cross-border insolvency regimes establishing ground rules regarding how the administrators of the cross-border insolvency regimes will interact and coordinate with each other if a multinational financial institution went into default.[105] While the FDIC's actions are potentially beneficial, it may be difficult to reach agreements with every relevant country. Even to the extent that MOU are entered into, they generally are not legally enforceable, and thus essentially rely on voluntary cooperation, which might be lacking in the midst of financial tumult.[106]

Divestiture Based on Risk

Another possible focus could be the divestiture of particular products or economic sectors that are viewed as insufficiently hedged or carry unusually concentrated risk exposure. For example, in the run-up to the "Great Recession," American International Group (AIG) was on one-side of a significant portion of the overall market for certain credit default swap derivative products linked to mortgage assets, through which AIG essentially was insuring the performance of mortgage-backed securities.[107] When the mortgage market crashed, AIG faced large margin calls and payouts on these mortgage-related derivatives products, which, according to the Financial Crisis Inquiry Commission, played a major role in the company's near collapse and its need for extraordinary assistance from the Federal Reserve.[108] In theory, going through the process of developing a living will could alert a covered financial institution's internal risk managers, as well as regulators, to significant concentrations akin to AIG's mortgage-related credit default swaps. This, in turn, could provide an impetus to divest the products to reduce concentration exposures to more reasonable, less risky levels in the view of internal risk managers or regulators.

Legal Reorganization

Where divestiture is not a viable or an attractive option, a covered financial institution might focus on reorganizing or restructuring to reduce its complexity or interconnectedness.

Domestic Reorganization

One type of restructuring that FDIC Chairman Gruenberg has highlighted is to align business areas with legal organizations. This could mean transferring the legal interests in interconnected business lines to a single subsidiary to serve as an intermediate holding company.[109] The goal of the Chairman's suggestion is to improve resolvability by, for example, creating a more transparent and rational organization. It also could ease the company's ability to maintain necessary operations during the resolution process. When assessing a legal restructuring strategy, covered financial institutions might place a particular focus on aligning certain Material Entities and Core Operations within distinct legal structures to help buffer them from financial losses originating in other parts of the conglomerate. Taking these steps also likely would increase directors', management's, and the regulators' understanding of the covered financial institution's legal structure and help reduce its complexity and interconnectedness.

To further address the regulators' concerns, the covered financial company could have policies in place intended to ensure that each intermediate holding company is sufficiently capitalized to absorb some potential losses by the subsidiaries in the intermediate holding company. Companies could take additional steps to implement policies by which the intermediate holding company would formally serve as a "source of strength"[110] for its subsidiaries and which generally would prohibit other portions of the covered financial institution from guaranteeing the liabilities of entities within the intermediate holding company structure.[111] Contracts with counterparties and affiliates could memorialize these policies. This could help avoid the need for the parent holding company to serve as a source of strength for its dozens or, in some instances, hundreds of subsidiaries, which do not conduct Core Operations and are not Material Entities.[112]

The creation of incorporation and contractual barriers within each intermediate holding company arguably could help reduce the likelihood that financial distress within the intermediate holding company and its subsidiaries would spread into other parts of the covered financial institution, and vice-versa. This potentially could reduce the likelihood that the financial stress would pose material risk to the whole covered financial institution.[113]

For example, virtually all of AIG's credit default swaps that were linked to mortgage-backed securities were issued by one subsidiary, AIG Financial Products (AIG FP). According to the Financial Crisis Inquiry Commission, AIG FP's ability to issue those credit default swaps was aided by the fact that the AIG parent holding company guaranteed their performance.[114] Had AIG FP been organized within an intermediate holding company and prohibited from entering credit default swaps that were guaranteed by the parent holding company, counterparties may have been more reticent to purchase credit default swaps from AIG FP. This in turn might have reduced AIG FP's exposure and concentration in the market while simultaneously diminishing the risk to AIG (the parent holding company) when the credit default swaps went sour.

Foreign Reorganization

In a slightly different context that shares many parallels with the living wills regime, the FRB issued final regulations[115] requiring certain foreign banking organizations[116] to establish one or more U.S.-based intermediate holding companies. These intermediate holding companies must hold virtually all[117] of the ownership interests of the conglomerate's U.S.-based financial subsidiaries. Some of the policy justifications for these regulations were to reduce the risk of a firm's cross-border activities to the financial stability of the U.S., help eliminate a "fractured organizational structure that can reduce the effectiveness of attempts ... to manage [] risks," and improve the resolvability of U.S-based subsidiaries within U.S. resolution regimes.[118] Similarly, the FRB noted that, to the extent that unusual circumstances prevent a foreign banking organization from transferring all ownership rights of its U.S.-based subsidiaries to the intermediate holding company, then "the [FRB] expects to require passivity commitments or other supervisory agreements to limit the exposure to and transactions between the U.S. intermediate holding company and the U.S. subsidiary that remains outside of the U.S. intermediate holding company."[119]

It appears that some foreign covered financial institutions are indeed taking some of these reorganization steps. UBS, for example, announced on September 29, 2014, that it was restructuring by creating a parent holding company as a beginning step in a plan to eventually separate much of its banking activities into a distinct banking subsidiary and to establish a U.S.-based intermediate holding company through which it would conduct most of its U.S.-based activities.[120] The company explained the purpose for the restructuring in this way:

> the establishment of a holding company is a significant step in a series of envisaged changes to UBS's legal structure that are intended to substantially improve its resolvability in response to evolving industry-wide "too-big-to-fail" requirements. ... After the setup of the holding company, further anticipated changes extending into 2016 include the establishment of a banking subsidiary in Switzerland (by mid-2015) and a US Intermediate Holding Company (by mid-2016).[121]

Legally restructuring in the ways described above likely would result in costs to covered financial institutions. There would be administrative and legal costs associated with reorganizing the firm, transferring ownership rights, establishing board and risk management oversight of the intermediate holding company, and potentially in the amendment and redrafting of contracts. Transferring capital from other portions of the covered financial institution to the intermediate holding company could impact compliance with minimum capital standards in effect in the U.S. or other regulatory jurisdictions and may result in negative tax consequences.[122] The borrowing costs of intermediate holding companies or other subsidiaries that are subject to contractual or other legal barriers to receiving financial support from the parent also might be higher than they would if there was an explicit guarantee by the parent.[123] There also is the possibility that, even if contracts between intermediate holding companies and their counterparties explicitly state that the parent covered financial institution does not guarantee the performance of specific contracts or the financial stability of certain subsidiaries, counterparties might presume the parent would choose to do so in practice to avoid legal and reputational harms of default.[124] Similarly, the market forces that arguably would make the reorganizations described above beneficial may break down if market participants believe that emergency governmental assistance would be provided if a covered financial institution's subsidiaries defaulted and the parent was unable to cover the losses.[125]

Amending Default Trigger Provisions in Qualified Financial Contracts

Another step that the FDIC and FRB are promoting to help improve covered financial institutions' resolvability is for covered financial institutions to voluntarily modify the standard terms in derivatives, securities, commodities, and other financial contracts to give covered financial institutions and administrators of insolvency regimes greater control over the netting, close-out, and settlement of such contracts upon the covered financial institution triggering a default provision.[126] One possible change could be to contractually provide for a brief "stay" on a counterparty's ability to enforce its rights under the contract, akin to the FDIC's power as receiver under OLA[127] and as a conservator or receiver for insured depository institutions under the Federal Deposit Insurance Act (FDI Act).[128] The special but disparate treatment of derivatives, securities, and other financial contracts under the Bankruptcy Code, on the one hand, and the FDI Act and OLA, on the other, are discussed in detail below.

Modifying the standard terms of these contracts potentially could improve the resolvability of covered financial institutions. First, it would ensure that the contracts are treated the same in a standard bankruptcy process as they are in the special insolvency regimes administered by the FDIC, which would mean that the impact on parties to these contracts would more likely be the same regardless of which insolvency regime a covered financial institution is subject. It also could increase the likelihood that cross-border financial contracts would be treated uniformly by insolvency regimes in other countries, although complete uniformity would likely require statutory and regulatory changes, as well. As is discussed more fully below, it appears that a significant number of global financial institutions are voluntarily taking steps to modify many of these contracts to provide a temporary stay from counterparties' ability to exercise default trigger rights when a financial institution enters bankruptcy or another insolvency regime.

Separately from the issue of modifying these financial contracts, FDIC Vice Chairman Thomas M. Hoenig has suggested that some covered financial institutions should reduce their overall exposure to these contracts.[129] **Table 1** illustrates that most of the 11 first-wave filers have notional derivatives exposures exponentially larger than their total consolidated assets.

Overview of the Treatment of Qualified Financial Contracts under the Bankruptcy Code

A "stay" is a power by which creditors are, at least temporarily, barred from pursuing their claims against a defaulting entity. As one commentator explains:

> Stays permit the resolution authority [the time to] collect and validate claims, to determine the best way to dispose of assets in an orderly, non-fire-sale manner, and to treat all like-priority creditors equally. Stays prevent creditor runs and keep contracts in force—the counter party is bound by the contract; claims on the insolvent firm remain pending; and collateral may usually not be liquidated. This facilitates the coordination of creditor claims.[130]

The U.S. Bankruptcy Code establishes a general stay automatically upon petitioning for bankruptcy.[131] However, the Code provides a number of exceptions to the automatic stay, including for certain "qualified financial contracts (QFCs)"i.e., securities contracts, commodity contracts, forward contracts, repurchase agreements, swap agreements, and netting arrangements.[132] It is especially common for financial institutions to be parties to QFCs, making special protections provided for them all the more important in case of a financial institution's insolvency.

Additionally, the Bankruptcy Code provides trustees, who administer bankruptcy liquidations, the authority to avoid (i.e., claw-back or reverse) certain transfers (subject to certain limitations[133]) made by debtors shortly before a bankruptcy petition is filed.[134] The purpose of this avoidance power is to facilitate the equitable distribution of the bankruptcy estate's assets among credit classes and to limit the "race to the courthouse" problem.[135] However, most QFCs are exempt from this general avoidance power.[136]

These so-called "safe-harbor protections" for QFCs were established, in part, to suppress the negative repercussions of a financial institution's bankruptcy on global financial markets—in other words to reduce systemic risk.[137] These safe harbors provide counterparties with the power to terminate or liquidate the collateral[138] held against the contracts and net or setoff each party's positions subsequent to a troubled firm filing a bankruptcy petition.[139] These legal constructs are explained by two prominent economists this way:

> Close-out and netting consist of two separate but related rights, often combined in a single contract: 1) the right of a counterparty to unilaterally terminate contracts under specified conditions (close-out), and 2) the right to offset amounts due at termination of individual contracts between the same counterparties when determining the final obligation [(netting)].[140]

Almost all QFCs have close-out and netting provisions that are triggered by an act of default, including the institution filing for bankruptcy, even if the contract itself is still performing. Some scholars argue that these provisions have the potential to exacerbate the financial condition of ailing firms and to deplete their assets.[141] For example, debtors of the Lehman Brothers bankruptcy estate estimated that, just prior to the bankruptcy petition being filed, they were a party to around 930,000 QFCs. Of those nearly 1 million contracts, approximately 733,000 were terminated within about three months of Lehman Brothers filing its bankruptcy petition.[142] It appears that, in the vast majority of the QFCs that were terminated, the non-Lehman counterparties were "in the money"—that is, Lehman owed money to the counterparty.[143] Those counterparties that held collateral against their QFCs were able to terminate the contracts and keep the collateral as settlement of their claims.[144] QFCs that were not collateralized could be closed-out and overall positions could be netted. The counterparties were then able to seek a claim as unsecured creditors of the bankruptcy estate.[145] Harvey Miller, the lead attorney for the Lehman Brother bankruptcy, testified before a Subcommittee of the House Judiciary Committee, that Lehman's counterparties' unilateral authority to terminate, close-out, and net QFCs "caused a massive destructive value for Lehman."[146]

Overview of the Treatment of Qualified Financial Contracts Under the FDIC' s Receivership Regimes

Whereas the general rule for a corporate liquidation under the Bankruptcy Code is the implementation of the automatic stay to provide time to ensure that similarly situated creditors are treated equally, the FDIC as receiver is more likely to further the statutory objectives of the FDI Act and OLA by maintaining much of the company's operations. For example, when acting as a receiver under the FDI Act, the FDIC generally will ensure that consumers continue to have access to FDIC-insured consumer deposits in order to achieve its primary goal of protecting insured deposits "at the least possible cost to the Deposit Insurance Fund."[147] Although it has never exercised the authorities before, the FDIC has indicated that maintaining a failed firm's Critical Operations would be a major strategy of resolution under OLA as a means to promote financial stability, which is the overarching purpose of OLA.[148] To reach these ends, the FDIC is empowered with greater flexibility to manage the QFCs of a troubled depository under the FDI Act or a nondepository financial institution under OLA than is available under the Bankruptcy Code.[149]

Notably, the FDIC, as receiver, is empowered with the authorities of the failed firm's directors, management, and shareholders. The FDIC also under certain circumstances may transfer, repudiate, and avoid the QFCs of a troubled depository or nondepository financial institution. It may employ those powers during the imposition of a temporary stay in which counterparties are prohibited from exercising their rights to terminate QFCs, liquidate collateral, and net their overall positions with the failed firm solely because the FDIC has been appointed its conservator or receiver. Such a stay would remain in place until the counterparties are notified of a transfer of the QFC or until 5:00 p.m. of the business day after the appointment of the receiver.[150] Only after this temporary stay are counterparties free to exercise rights to net, terminate, or liquidate under such contracts.[151]

During this stay, the FDIC is permitted to transfer QFCs to other financial institutions as long as certain notice requirements are met. In exercising this authority, the FDIC must either transfer all QFCs with a particular party and its affiliates to a single financial institution, or it may not transfer any of them.[152]

The FDIC, as receiver under the FDI Act and OLA, also may repudiate certain contracts if allowing performance would be "burdensome" and "disaffirmance or repudiation ... will promote the orderly administration of the institution's affairs."[153] The FDIC may only repudiate QFCs, however, if it repudiates all QFCs with a particular counterparty and its affiliates.[154] In other words, the FDIC must either repudiate all QFCs with a particular party and its affiliates, or it may not repudiate any of them.

Finally, in contrast to QFCs being completely exempt from the avoidance power under the Bankruptcy Code,[155] the FDIC as conservator or receiver may avoid (i.e., reverse or claw-back) property transferred pursuant to a QFC when the transfer was performed with the "actual intent to hinder, delay, or defraud" the FDIC, or the failed company or its creditors.[156]

Analysis of Strategy to Amend the Default Trigger Provisions in Qualified Financial Contracts

The temporary stay for QFCs under both the FDI Act and OLA gives the FDIC a brief period of time to determine how to most effectively and economically exercise its transfer, avoidance, and repudiation powers and to assess whether requisite legal conditions for employing those powers exist. For example, the FDIC might choose to transfer performing QFCs to different financial institutions to obviate the unnecessary and inefficient process of a counterparty terminating the QFC with the failed firm and then seeking to re-establish virtually the same contract in the private market with a different financial institution to stand in the shoes of the failed firm.

This temporary stay is in stark contrast to the blanket exception from the automatic stay for netting, terminating, and liquidating QFCs under the Bankruptcy Code. Modifying QFCs to provide covered financial institutions in default or their insolvency regime administrators with the same powers as the FDIC as receiver under OLA or the FDI Act arguably could reduce the financial strain on an insolvent covered financial institution, as well as its many counterparties.[157]

On the other hand, providing the FDIC with the discretion on whether to transfer or repudiate QFCs arguably could increase uncertainty in financial markets because it may be difficult to predict how the FDIC will exercise that discretion.[158] This uncertainty could incentivize a covered financial institution's counterparties to exercise default trigger rights prior to the FDIC stepping in (or the company filing a petition for bankruptcy), thus hastening and exacerbating the covered financial institution's financial duress. If the FDI Act and OLA were amended so as to treat QFCs under those regimes the same as they are under the Bankruptcy Code, there is a strong likelihood that counterparties to a failed firm would decide whether or not to terminate, close-out, and net QFCs based on whether not they would be "in the money."

In October 2014, 18 of the world's largest financial institutions, working through the International Swaps and Derivatives Association, Inc. (ISDA) announced an agreement in principal to voluntarily amend a significant portion of the industry's over-the-counter (i.e., those that are negotiated privately between parties rather than being traded on public exchanges) swaps contracts to allow for a temporary stay from counterparties' ability to terminate, liquidate, and accelerate the contracts when one of the other participating financial institutions enters a resolution process.[159] The agreement, called the ISDA Resolution Stay Protocol,

> essentially enables adhering counterparties to opt into certain overseas resolution regimes via a change to their derivatives contracts. While many existing national resolution frameworks impose stays on early termination rights following the start of resolution proceedings, these stays might only apply to domestic counterparties trading under domestic law agreements, and so might not capture cross-border trades.[160]

Approximately 90% of the over-the-counter derivatives market will be covered by the ISDA Resolution Stay Protocol when it is implemented by the initial 18 companies, but that market share is expected to increase as additional institutions join.[161] The 18 firms also agreed to work with their regulators as they implement similar temporary stays through regulations in the United States and other jurisdictions. The companies expect to finalize the terms of the Protocol in November, which will go into effect at the beginning of 2015. The initial participating financial institutions include the domestically based Bank of America Merrill Lynch, Citigroup, Goldman Sachs, JP Morgan Chase, and Morgan Stanley.[162] The FDIC and FRB expressed their support of the ISDA Resolution Stay Protocol in a joint press release.[163]

Increasing Long-Term, Unsecured Debt

Another step that representatives of the FDIC and FRB have indicated would be beneficial to the resolution of a covered financial institution is for these institutions to increase their long-term, unsecured debt as a proportion of their risk-weighted assets.[164] This policy also is being proposed by the Basel Committee on Banking Supervision[165] and the Financial Stability Board[166] to apply globally to systemically important financial institutions.

There has been a significant amount of focus on the role that minimum capital requirements can have on reducing the likelihood that covered financial companies will fail.[167] Capital requirements are not intended to completely eliminate a financial institution's risk of default.[168] In order to effectively serve as financial intermediaries for their customers and to keep financial markets functioning, financial institutions typically fund their loans and other assets through liabilities (e.g., customer deposits). As a result, there always will be some risk that the capital held by a financial institution will not be enough to cover its losses.[169]

According to the FDIC and FRB, long-term unsecured debt has several benefits over secured and short-term unsecured debt in an insolvency proceeding. First, holders of long-term, unsecured debt are more likely to be willing to accept haircuts and otherwise restructure their claims in a resolution. Secured creditors in an insolvency proceeding generally are protected up to the value of the collateral underlying their claim against the insolvent company.[170] Thus, they have little incentive to voluntarily take a haircut or accept less than the value of the underlying collateral.

Second, it is often the case that long-term debt better aligns the market interests of the covered financial institution with debt holders, as compared with short-term and secured debt. Secured debt holders, because they are generally protected up to the full value of the underlying collateral, generally do not have a strong incentive to ensure that covered financial institutions are managed for long-term stability.[171] Similarly, short-term debt holders of a covered financial institution are more likely to only be concerned about the financial strength of covered financial institutions through the life of the debt. On the other hand, long-term, unsecured debt holders are more likely to have an interest in the long-term stability of the covered financial institution because they generally are going to be low priority claimants in a resolution proceeding. Consequently, if a covered financial institution fails, the long-term, unsecured creditors likely will be absorbing its losses.[172] As a result, part of the consideration into whether or not to extend long-term, unsecured credit to a covered financial institution is the company's long-term viability. If a covered financial institution's long-term financial health is questioned, it likely will have difficulty obtaining longterm unsecured credit at a reasonable cost. Additionally, short-term debt could be hard to rollover in a stressed environment. A firm that is heavily reliant upon short-term debt may be less stable during a market downturn than one that relies more on long-term debt.[173] (**Table 1** lists the short-term funding as a percentage of total liabilities of the 11 first-wave filers.)

FRB Governor Daniel K. Tarullo has explained it this way:

> While minimum capital requirements are designed to cover losses up to a certain statistical probability, in the even less likely event that the equity of a financial firm is wiped out, successful resolution without taxpayer assistance would be most effectively accomplished if a firm has sufficient long-term unsecured debt to absorb additional losses and to recapitalize the business transferred to a bridge operating company. The presence of a substantial tranche of long-term debt that is subject to bail-in during a resolution and is structurally subordinated to the firm's other creditors should reduce run risk by clarifying the position of those other creditors in an orderly liquidation process. ... [L]ongterm debt also should have the benefit of improving market discipline, since the holders of that debt would know they faced the prospect of loss should the firm enter resolution.[174]

In fact, both FDIC Chairman Gruenberg and FRB Governor Tarullo have acknowledged that the agencies are considering imposing a minimum level of long-term, unsecured debt that must be held by covered financial institution parent holding companies.[175]

It should be noted, however, that long-term, unsecured debt generally is more expensive than short-term, secured debt.[176] Additionally, many of the policy justifications for holding long-term, unsecured debt that are discussed above could prove illusory if creditors of the covered financial institution believe that it will receive emergency governmental assistance if it becomes insolvent or in danger of default.[177]

End Notes

[1] P.L. 111-203.

[2] The preamble to the DFA states: "To promote financial stability of the United States by improving accountability and transparency in the financial system, to end 'too big to fail,' to protect the American taxpayer by ending bailouts, to protect consumers from abusive financial services practices, and for other purposes."

[3] TARP was implemented pursuant to the Emergency Economic Stabilization Act of 2008, P.L. 110-343. For more information on TARP, see CRS Report R41427, *Troubled Asset Relief Program (TARP): Implementation and Status*, by Baird Webel.

[4] The voting members of the FSOC are: the Secretary of the Treasury; the Chairman of the Board of Governors of the Federal Reserve System (FRB); the Chairperson of the Federal Deposit Insurance Corporation (FDIC); the Comptroller of the Currency; the Director of the Bureau of Consumer Financial Protection (CFPB); the Chairman of the Securities and Exchange

Commission (SEC); the Chairperson of the Commodity Futures Trading Commission (CFTC); the Director of the Federal Housing Finance Agency (FHFA); the Chairman of the National Credit Union Administrations (NCUA), and a presidential appointee with expertise in insurance. There also are five nonvoting members of FSOC. For more information on the FSOC, see CRS Report R42083, *Financial Stability Oversight Council: A Framework to Mitigate Systemic Risk*, by Edward V. Murphy.

[5] 12 U.S.C. §5322(a).

[6] The DFA provides the FRB the flexibility to establish heightened prudential standards that account for the distinctions between the three classes of covered financial institution, including considerations regarding the prudential standards to which foreign-based covered institutions are subject in their home countries. 12 U.S.C. §5365(b)(2). See also Enhanced Prudential Standards for Bank Holding Companies and Foreign Bank Holding Companies, 79 Fed. Reg. 17,240, 17,263-64 (Mar. 27, 2014) ("In applying section 165 to a foreign-based bank holding company, the [DFA] directs the [FRB] to give due regard to the principle of national treatment and equality of competitive opportunity, and to take into account the extent to which the foreign banking organization is subject, on a consolidated basis, to home country standards that are comparable to those applied to financial companies in the United States. Section 165 also directs the [FRB] to take into account differences among nonbank financial companies, bank holding companies, and foreign banking organizations based on a number of factors.").

[7] U.S. Code, Title 11.

[8] E.g., the FDIC's conservatorship/receivership insolvency regime for FDIC-insured depository institutions; state insolvency regimes for insurance companies; and the insolvency regime established by the Securities Investor Protection Act for broker-dealers.

[9] 12 U.S.C. §§5381-93.

[10] A financial institution does not have to be a covered financial institution subject to heightened regulation by the FRB in order to be placed in this special insolvency regime. 12 U.S.C. §§5381, 5383.

[11] 12 U.S.C. §5383(a)(1)(A).

[12] 12 U.S.C. §5382(d).

[13] 12 U.S.C. §§5384(d), 5390(n)(9), 5390(o), 5394(b). Any assessments charged against surviving covered financial institutions would be risk-based, "with financial companies having greater assets and risk being assessed at a higher rate." 12 U.S.C. §5390(o)(2).

[14] The SEC would be involved in the recommendation for financial firms whose largest domestic subsidiary is a broker or dealer. 12 U.S.C. §5383(a)(1)(B).

[15] The Director of the Federal Insurance Office, in consultation with the FDIC, would be involved in the recommendation for financial firms whose largest domestic subsidiary is an insurance company. 12 U.S.C. §5383(a)(1)(C).

[16] The written recommendation must provide, among other things, assessments of: whether the company is in "default or in danger of default"; why the company could not be effectively resolved under the Bankruptcy Code or through other "private sector alternatives"; and "the effect that the default of the financial company would have on financial stability in the United States." 12 U.S.C. §5383(a)(2).

[17] The terms "default or danger of default" means:

(A) a case has been, or likely will promptly be, commenced with respect to the financial company under the Bankruptcy Code;

(B) the financial company has incurred, or is likely to incur, losses that will deplete all or substantially all of its capital, and there is no reasonable prospect for the company to avoid such depletion;

(C) the assets of the financial company are, or are likely to be, less than its obligations to creditors and others; or

(D) the financial company is, or is likely to be, unable to pay its obligations (other than those subject to a bona fide dispute) in the normal course of business.

12 U.S.C. §5383(c)(4).

[18] 12 U.S.C. §5383(b) (emphasis added). Judicial review of a determination by the Secretary to subject an institution to OLA is limited to whether the company meets the definition of "financial institution" and whether it is in "default or danger of default," on an arbitrary and capricious standard—a high standard of review in which a reviewing court likely will accord significant deference to the Secretary's determination. 12 U.S.C. §5382(a). The courts also could hear challenges based on the Constitution.

[19] *Resolution Plans*, Bd. of Gov. of the Fed. Reserve Sys., available at http://www.federalreserve.gov/bankinforeg/ resolution-plans.htm. This includes the three nonbank financial institutions designated by FSOC for heightened regulation by the FRB—American International Group, Inc. (AIG), General Electric Capital Corporation, Inc. (GE Capital), and Prudential Financial, Inc.

[20] *Wall Street Reform: Assessing and Enhancing the Financial Regulatory System, Hearing Before the Senate Comm. on Banking, Housing, and Urban Affairs*, 113th Cong. (2014) (written statement of the Hon. Martin J. Gruenberg at p. 5).

[21] *The Semiannual Monetary Policy Report to the Congress: Hearing Before the Senate Committee on Banking, Housing and Urban Development*, 113th Cong. (2014) (oral testimony of Janet L. Yellen, Chairman of the Bd. of Gov. of the Fed. Reserve Sys.).

[22] *Agencies Provide Feedback on Second Round Resolution Plans of "First-Wave" Filers*, Joint Press Release, Bd. of Gov. of the Fed. Reserve Sys., Fed. Deposit Ins. Corp., Aug. 5, 2014, available at http://www.federalreserve.gov/ newsevents/press/bcreg/20140805a.htm.

[23] *Id.*

[24] See *infra* the "Increasing Long-Term, Unsecured Debt" section of this report.

[25] More specifically, U.S. bank holding companies, as well as foreign banks, foreign bank holding companies, and other foreign institutions that are treated as bank holding companies pursuant to the International Banking Act of 1978 (12 U.S.C. §3106(a)) with greater than $50 billion in assets.

[26] 12 U.S.C. §5365(d)(1).

[27] 12 U.S.C. §5365(d)(1).

[28] 12 U.S.C. §5365(d)(2).

[29] 12 U.S.C. §5365(d)(3).

[30] *The Semiannual Monetary Policy Report to the Congress: Hearing Before the Senate Committee on Banking, Housing and Urban Development*, 113th Cong. (2014) (oral testimony of Janet L. Yellen, Chairman of the Bd. of Gov. of the Fed. Reserve Sys.). See also Michael McAuliff, *Elizabeth Warren Grills Fed Chair Janet Yellen on Too-Big-ToFail Banks*, Huffington Post, July 15, 2014, available at http://www.huffingtonpost.com/2014/07 /15/too-big-tofail_n_5588558.html.

[31] 12 U.S.C. §5365(d)(4).

[32] 12 U.S.C. §5365(d)(5).

[33] Resolution Plans Required, 76 Fed. Reg. 67,323 (Nov. 1, 2011) (to be codified at 12 C.F.R. Part 243 (FDIC) and 12 C.F.R. Part 381 (FRB)). The regulations at times make distinctions

between domestic covered companies and foreign-based covered companies, i.e., covered companies that are not incorporated in the United States. 12 C.F.R. §___.2(j). This report focuses on domestic covered companies.

34 12 C.F.R. §___.4(a)(4).

35 12 C.F.R. §___.8(c).

36 12 C.F.R. §___.3.

37 12 C.F.R. §___.4.

38 12 C.F.R. §___.5.

39 12 C.F.R. §§___.6 and .9.

40 12 U.S.C. §5365(i)(1)(B). The stress tests are conducted by the financial institutions and overseen by regulators.

41 12 C.F.R. §___.4(a)(4).

42 12 C.F.R. §___.8(c).

43 12 C.F.R. §___.8(c).

44 12 C.F.R. §___.8(d).

45 12 C.F.R. Part 261.

46 12 C.F.R. Part 309.

47 5 U.S.C. §552(b). For more information on FOIA and other federal nondisclosure laws, see CRS Report R41406, *The Freedom of Information Act and Nondisclosure Provisions in Other Federal Laws*, by Gina Stevens.

48 12 C.F.R. §___.8(d).

49 *The Semiannual Monetary Policy Report to the Congress: Hearing Before the Senate Committee on Banking, Housing and Urban Development*, 113th Cong. (2014) (oral testimony of Janet L. Yellen, Chairman of the Bd. of Gov. of the Fed. Reserve Sys.).

50 *Resolution Plans*, Bd. of Gov. of the Fed. Reserve Sys., available at http://www.federalreserve.gov/bankinforeg/ resolution-plans.htm.

51 Under the regulations, covered companies that have at least 85% of total consolidated assets held by federal insured depositories and less than $100 billion in nonbank assets are allowed to include less information in their living wills than other covered companies. 12 C.F.R. §§___.4(a)(3). The FRB and FDIC are authorized to exempt covered companies from including various pieces of generally required information in their resolution plans. 12 C.F.R. §___.4(k).

52 "Material entity" is defined as "a subsidiary or foreign office of the covered company that is significant to the activities of a critical operation or core business line.... " 12 C.F.R. §§___.2(*l*). "Critical operations" are defined as "those operations of the covered company ... the failure or discontinuance of which, in the view of the covered company or as jointly directed by the [FRB and FDIC], would pose a threat to the financial stability of the United States." 12 C.F.R. §___.2(g). "Core business lines" are defined as "those business lines of the covered company ... that, in the view of the covered company, upon failure would result in a material loss of revenue, profit, or franchise value." 12 C.F.R. §___.2(d).

53 12 C.F.R. §___.4(c). These terms are defined in *supra* n. 52.

54 12 C.F.R. §___.4(d)(1).

55 12 C.F.R. §___.4(d)(2).

56 12 C.F.R. §___.4(e)(1).

57 12 C.F.R. §§___.4(e)(2)-(12).

58 12 C.F.R. §___.4(g).

59 12 C.F.R. §___.3(a)(1)(i).

[60] See *Resolution Plans*, Bd. of Gov. of the Fed. Reserve Sys., available at http://www.federalreserve.gov/bankinforeg/ resolution-plans.htm.
[61] 12 C.F.R. §___.3(a)(1)(ii).
[62] 12 C.F.R. §___.3(a)(1)(iii).
[63] 12 C.F.R. §___.3(a)(3).
[64] 12 C.F.R. §___.3(c)(1).
[65] 12 C.F.R. §___.3(a)(4). The regulators must provide at least 180 days' notice.
[66] 12 C.F.R. §___.3(c)(2).
[67] 12 C.F.R. §___.3(b)(1).
[68] 12 C.F.R. §___.3(b)(2).
[69] 12 C.F.R. §___.5(a).
[70] 12 C.F.R. §___.5(a).
[71] 12 C.F.R. §___.5(c).
[72] 12 C.F.R. §___.6(b).
[73] 12 C.F.R. §___.6(c). To the extent that any heightened standard or activity restriction, or compulsory divesture "is likely to have a significant impact on a functionally regulated subsidiary or depository institution subsidiary of the covered company," then the FRB generally must consult with that subsidiary's primary federal regulator. 12 C.F.R. §___.7.
[74] 12 C.F.R. §___.9.
[75] 12 U.S.C. §1818.
[76] See, generally, *Examining the Settlement Practices of U.S. Financial Regulators Before the House Comm. on Fin. Serv.*, 112th Cong. (2012) (written statement of Scott G. Alvarez, Gen. Counsel, FRB p. 2).
[77] 12 U.S.C. §1818(h); 12 C.F.R. §___.9 (FRB)). See also 12 U.S.C. §5362 (subjecting nonbank financial institutions supervised by the FRB to 12 U.S.C. §§1818(b)-(n)).
[78] Guidance for 2013 §165(d) Annual Resolution Plan Submissions by Domestic Covered Companies that Submitted Initial Resolutions Plans in 2012, at I.A., Bd. of Gov. of the Fed. Reserve Sys., Fed. Deposit Ins. Corp., Apr. 15, 2013, available at http://www.federalreserve.gov/newsevents/press/bcreg/bcreg20130415c2.pdf (hereinafter, 2013 Resolution Plan Guidance). The FRB and FDIC actually issued two different guidance documents—one for domestic and the other for foreign first-wave filers. Agencies Provide Additional Instructions for Submission of Some Resolution Plans, Joint Press Release, Bd. of Gov. of the Fed. Reserve Sys., Fed. Deposit Ins. Corp., Apr. 15, 2013, available at http://www.federalreserve.gov/newsevents/press/bcreg/20130415c.htm. The two guidance documents are largely the same, with a few exceptions. The guidance for foreign-based institutions allows institutions to supply a "supplemental analysis" of expected home-governmental support, both ordinary and extraordinary. Guidance for 2013 §165(d) Annual Resolution Plan Submissions Foreign-Based Covered Companies that Submitted Initial Resolution Plans in 2012, II.C.1, Bd. of Gov. of the Fed. Reserve Sys., Fed. Deposit Ins. Corp., Apr. 15, 2013, available at http://www.federalreserve.gov/newsevents /press/bcreg/20130415c.htm (hereinafter, 2013 Foreign-Based Resolution Plan Guidance). It also states that covered foreign-based institutions' living wills should focus on their "Critical Operations ... that are conducted in whole or material part in the United States," as well as the interconnectedness between their Critical Operations (both U.S. and foreign) and U.S.-based branches, subsidiaries, and agencies. 2013 Foreign-Based Guidance at I.D.
[79] *2013 Resolution Plan Guidance* at I.B.
[80] *2013 Resolution Plan Guidance* at I.C.1.
[81] *2013 Resolution Plan Guidance* at I.C.2.

[82] *2013 Resolution Plan Guidance* at I.C.2.

[83] *2013 Resolution Plan Guidance* at II.A.

[84] *2013 Resolution Plan Guidance* at II.C.2.

[85] *The Semiannual Monetary Policy Report to the Congress: Hearing Before the Senate Committee on Banking, Housing and Urban Development*, 113th Cong. (2014) (oral testimony of Janet L. Yellen, Chairman of the Bd. of Gov. of the Fed. Reserve Sys.).

[86] *Agencies Provide Feedback on Second Round Resolution Plans of "First-Wave" Filers*, Bd. of Gov. of the Fed. Reserve Sys., Fed. Deposit Ins. Corp., Joint Press Release, Aug. 5, 2014, available at http://www.federalreserve.gov/ newsevents/press/bcreg/20140805a.htm.

[87] These letters have not been made public.

[88] *Agencies Provide Feedback on Second Round Resolution Plans of "First-Wave" Filers*, Bd. of Gov. of the Fed. Reserve Sys., Fed. Deposit Ins. Corp., Joint Press Release, Aug. 5, 2014, available at http://www.federalreserve.gov/ newsevents/press/bcreg/20140805a.htm.

[89] See the *Amending Default Trigger Provisions in Qualified Financial Contracts* section of this report below. The term "qualified financial contract" is defined in the Federal Deposit Insurance Act (FDI Act). 12 U.S.C. §1821(e)(8)(D) for the purpose of the conservatorship/receivership resolution regime for insured depository institutions and under OLA, 12 U.S.C. 5390(c)(8)(D). The term is not explicitly defined in the Bankruptcy Code; however, certain individual contracts (e.g., securities contract, repurchase agreement, forward contract, swap agreement, commodity contract) that constitute "qualified financial contracts" under the FDI Act and OLA are defined in the Bankruptcy Code, with some differences that are not relevant for the purposes of this report. See, e.g., 11 U.S.C. §§ 101(25), 101(38A), 101(47) 101(53B), 741(7), 761(4). This report refers to the relevant terms under all three legal regimes as "qualified financial contracts" or QFCs.

[90] *Agencies Provide Feedback on Second Round Resolution Plans of "First-Wave" Filers*, Bd. of Gov. of the Fed. Reserve Sys., Fed. Deposit Ins. Corp., Joint Press Release, Aug. 5, 2014, available at http://www.federalreserve.gov/ newsevents/press/bcreg/20140805a.htm.

[91] *Id.*

[92] *Id.*

[93] Section 1818's broad and flexible enforcement powers include the authority to issue cease and desist orders, issue prompt corrective actions, and assess civil money penalties. 12 U.S.C. §1818.

[94] *Agencies Provide Additional Guidance for Certain Resolution Plans*, Joint Press Release, Bd. of Gov. of the Fed. Reserve Sys. and Fed. Deposit Ins., Aug. 15, 2014, available at http://www.federalreserve.gov/newsevents/press/bcreg/ 20140815a.htm.

[95] *Id.*

[96] *2014 Model Template for §165(d) Tailored Resolution Plans*, Bd. of Gov. of the Fed. Reserve Sys. and Fed. Deposit Ins., available at http://www.federalreserve.gov/bankinforeg /resolution

[97] *Agencies Provide Additional Guidance for Certain Resolution Plans*, Joint Press Release, Bd. of Gov. of the Fed. Reserve Sys., Fed. Deposit Ins., Aug. 15, 2014, available at http://www.federalreserve.gov/newsevents/press/bcreg/ 20140815a.htm. It appears that many of these institutions are U.S. branches and agencies of foreign banking organizations. See *id.* and *Resolution Plans*, Bd. of Gov. of the Fed. Reserve Sys., available at http://www.federalreserve.gov/bankinforeg/resolution

[98] See, e.g., Michael McAuliff, *Elizabeth Warren Grills Fed Chair Janet Yellen on Too-Big-To-Fail Banks*, Huffington Post, July 15, 2014, available at http://www.huffingtonpost.com /2014/07/15/too-big-to-fail_n_5588558.html; Simon Johnson, *Break Up the Big Banks*,

N.Y. Times, Jan. 12, 2014, available at http://www.nytimes.com/roomfordebate/ 2014/01/12/are-big-banks-out-of-control/break-up-the-big-banks; Mike Konczal, *Sen. Sherrod Brown explains why he wants to break up the big banks*, Wash. Post, Mar. 9, 2013, available at http://www.washingtonpost.com/blogs wonkblog/wp/2013/03/09/sen-sherrod-brown-explains-why-he-wants-to-break-up-the-big-banks/.

[99] *Financial Stocks Weekly: Living Wills Become a New Pressure Point on Big Banks*, Keefe, Bruyette & Wood (KBW), at 4, Aug. 25, 2014, available at http://op.bna.com/bar.nsf/id/jbar-9nblk8/$File/kbw.pdf.

[100] See *supra* notes 82-83 and surrounding text.

[101] Thomas M. Hoenig, *A Credible Case for Resolving Through Bankruptcy*, Remarks Presented to the George Washington University Law School Conference on Financial Stability After Dodd-Frank: Have We Ended Too Big to Fail?, Nov. 5, 2014, available at https://www.fdic.gov/news/news/speeches/spnov0514.html?source=govdelivery& utm_medium=email&utm_source=govdelivery.

[102] For an understanding of various definitions of the term "ring-fencing," see Steven L. Schwarcz, *Ring-Fencing*, 70 So. Cal. L. Rev. 69 (2013).

[103] This likely would be accomplished through the imposition of a "stay." Stays are discussed in the *infra* "Amending Default Trigger Provisions in Qualified Financial Contracts" section of this report.

[104] Thomas M. Hoenig, FDIC Vice-Chairman, *A Credible Case for Resolving Through Bankruptcy*, Remarks Presented to the George Washington University Law School Conference on Financial Stability After Dodd-Frank: Have We Ended Too Big to Fail?, Nov. 5, 2014, available at https://www.fdic.gov/news/news/speeches/spnov 0514.html? source= govdelivery&utm_medium=email&utm_source=govdelivery; Daniel K. Tarullo, Member of the FRB, *Regulation of Foreign Banking Organizations*, Remarks Presented at the Yale School of Management Leaders Forum, at pp. 8-9, Nov. 28, 2012, available at http://www.federalreserve.gov/newsevents/speech

[105] *Improving Cross Border Resolution to Better Protect Taxpayers and the Economy, Hearing Before the Subcomm. on Nat'l Sec. and Internat'l Trade and Fin. of the S. Comm. on Housing and Urban Dev.*, 113th Cong. (2013) (written testimony of Jim Wigand, Dir. of the Office of Complex Fin. Inst., Fed. Deposit Ins. Corp., at pp. 10-14), available at http://www.banking 485b-b9e9-07c8684a3d36&Witness_ID=6f0037bb-73bb-4278-93ab - f926f0bd7e0d.

[106] It should be noted that by encouraging and in some cases requiring covered financial institutions to take steps to move assets and subsidiaries into the U.S. and to take other steps to improve a multinational covered financial institution's resolvability in the U.S., the FRB and FDIC could be viewed as engaging in U.S.-centric ring fencing, particularly in the eyes of foreign regulators. See Daniel K. Tarullo, Member of the FRB, *Regulation of Foreign Banking Organizations*, Remarks Presented at the Yale School of Management Leaders Forum, at pp. 10-11, Nov. 28, 2012, available at http://www.federalreserve.gov /newsevents/speech (noting the various policies that U.S. and various foreign regulators had begun contemplating "to fortify the resources of internationally active banks within their geographic boundaries.").

[107] *The Financial Crisis Inquiry Report*, Nat'l Com. on the Causes of the Fin. and Econ. Crisis in the U.S., at pp. 50, 132-42, Feb. 25, 2011, available at http://www.gpo.gov/fdsys/pkg/GPO-FCIC/pdf/GPO-FCIC.pdf.

[108] CRS Report R42953, *Government Assistance for AIG: Summary and Cost*, by Baird Webel.

[109] *Wall Street Reform: Assessing and Enhancing the Financial Regulatory System, Hearing Before the Senate Comm. on Banking, Housing, and Urban Affairs*, 113th Cong. (2014) (written statement of the Hon. Martin J. Gruenberg at p. 6), available at http://www.banking b15fc832-df18-47d7-8c7d-1367e5770086.

[110] 12 U.S.C. §1831o-1; 12 C.F.R. §225.4(a)(1). See also *Failure to Act as Source of Strength to Subsidiary Banks*, Bd. of Gov. of the Fed. Reserve Sys. Policy Statement, April 24, 1987, available at http://www.kc.frb.org/publicat/banking membership/bhc/FailuretoActAsSource ofStrengthtoSubsidiaryBanks.pdf.

[111] An exception would have to be made for depository institution subsidiaries for which the parent holding company generally is required by law to serve as a source of strength. *Id.*

[112] See, e.g., JPMorgan Chase & Co., Sec. and Exch. Comm'n Form 10-k, Exhibit 21, filed Feb. 20, 2014, available at https://www.sec.gov/Archives/edgar/data/19617 /00000196171 4000289 /corp10k2013exhibit21.htm; Bank of America, Corp., Sec. and Exch. Comm'n Form 10-k, Exhibit 21, filed Feb. 25, 2014, available at https://www.sec.gov /Archives/edgar/data/70858/000007085814000012/bac-12312013x10kex21.htm.

[113] Steven L. Schwarcz, *Ring-Fencing*, 70 So. Cal. L. Rev. 69, 77 (2013).

[114] *The Financial Crisis Inquiry Report*, Nat'l Com. on the Causes of the Fin. and Econ. Crisis in the U.S., at pp. 139- 40, Feb. 25, 2011, available at http://www.gpo.gov/fdsys/pkg/GPO-FCIC/pdf/GPO-FCIC.pdf.

[115] Enhanced Prudential Standards for Bank Holding Companies and Foreign Banking Organizations, 79 Fed. Reg. 17,240 (Mar. 27, 2014) (to be codified at 12 C.F.R. pt. 252), available at http://www.gpo.gov/fdsys/pkg/FR-2014-03- 27/pdf/2014-05699.pdf.

[116] The regulations apply to foreign banking organizations that have $50 billion or more in consolidated assets and $50 billion or more of total U.S. assets. 79 Fed. Reg. 17,420, 17,324 (Mar. 27, 2014) (to be codified at 12 C.F.R. §252.142).

[117] The regulations make exceptions for U.S.-based subsidiaries or U.S. bank branches established for the purpose of holding debt previously contracted in good faith, as well as companies formed pursuant to Bank Holding Company Act Section 2(h)(2) (12 U.S.C. §1841(h)(2)).

[118] Enhanced Prudential Standards for Bank Holding Companies and Foreign Banking Organizations, 79 Fed. Reg. 17,420, 17,278-79 (Mar. 27, 2014).

[119] Enhanced Prudential Standards for Bank Holding Companies and Foreign Banking Organizations, 79 Fed. Reg. 17,420, 17,275 (Mar. 27, 2014).

[120] *UBS publishes prospectus of its share-for-share exchange offer to establish a group holding company, UBS Group AG*, UBS Press Release, Sept. 29, 2014, available at https://www.ubs.com/global/en/about_ubs/media news_display_media_emea.html/en/2014/09/29/prospectus.html.

[121] *Id.*

[122] Enhanced Prudential Standards for Bank Holding Companies and Foreign Banking Organizations, 79 Fed. Reg. 17,240, 17,270 (Mar. 27, 2014).

[123] *Id.* at 17,279.

[124] *Id.* As an analogy, securities issued by Fannie Mae and Freddie Mac were required by law to explicitly state that they were not backed by the full faith and credit of the United States (12 U.S.C. §1719(d) (Freddie Mac); 12 U.S.C §1455(h)(2) (Fannie Mae)), but when the two mortgage giants were in danger of default, the U.S. government, utilizing statutory authorities enacted as part of the Housing and Economic Recovery Act of 2008 (P.L. 110-289), provided hundreds of billions of dollars of governmental support to avoid defaults on those securities. For additional information on the U.S. government's investments in Fannie

Mae and Freddie Mac, see CRS Report R42760, *Fannie Mae's and Freddie Mac's Financial Status: Frequently Asked Questions*, by N. Eric Weiss.

[125] See CRS Report R42150, *Systemically Important or "Too Big to Fail" Financial Institutions*, by Marc Labonte, p. 12.

[126] *Agencies Provide Feedback on Second Round Resolution Plans of "First-Wave" Filers*, Bd. of Gov. of the Fed. Reserve Sys., Fed. Deposit Ins. Corp., Joint Press Release, Aug. 5, 2014, available at http://www.federalreserve.gov/ newsevents/press/bcreg/20140805a.htm.

[127] 12 U.S.C. §5390(c)(8).

[128] 12 U.S.C. §1821(e)(8). The statutory provisions governing the applicability of qualified financial contracts (QFCs) under OLA were modeled after, and largely follow, those of the FDI Act. Although there are some differences between the two laws as they apply to QFCs, most notable in that conservatorships are not permissible under OLA while conservatorships are permissible under the FDI Act, the laws are equivalent for the purposes of this report, unless noted otherwise.

[129] See, e.g., *Statement of Thomas M. Hoenig, Vice Chairman, FDIC on the Credibility of the 2013 Living Wills Submitted by First Wave Filers*, Aug. 5, 2014, available at https://www.fdic.gov/news/news/speeches/spaug0514a.html; *Financial Stocks Weekly: Living Wills Become a New Pressure Point on Big Banks*, Keefe, Bruyette & Wood (KBW), at 2, Aug. 25, 2014, available at http://op.bna.com/bar.nsf/id/jbar-9nblk8/$File/kbw.pdf.

[130] Robert R. Bliss and George G. Kaufman, *U.S. Corporate and Bank Insolvency: An Economic Comparison and Evaluation*, Fed. Reserve Bank of Chicago (2006), available at https://www.chicagofed.org/digital_assets working_papers/2006/wp2006_01.pdf.

[131] 11 U.S.C. §362(a). See *supra* n. 89 for a discussion of the definitions of "qualified financial contracts" under the Bankruptcy Code, FDI Act, and OLA.

[132] 11 U.S.C. §362(b).

[133] See, e.g., 11 U.S.C. §§546, 547, 555, 556, 559, 560, 561.

[134] 11 U.S.C. §547(b). These conditions are: (1) the transfer was made "to or for the benefit of a creditor"; (2) the transfer was for a debt owed before the transfer; (3) the transfer "was made while the debtor was insolvent"; (4) the transfer occurred "on or within 90 days" of the petition or within one year if the transfer was made to an "insider"; and (5) the creditor received more from the transfer than it would have through bankruptcy proceedings. The term "insider" is defined at 11 U.S.C. §101(31).

[135] Collier on Bankruptcy p. 5-547.01 (16th ed. rev.).

[136] 11 U.S.C. §§546(e)-(j).

[137] GuyLaine Charles, *OTC Derivative Contracts in Bankruptcy: The Lehman Experience*, NY Bus. L.J. Vol. 13, No. 1, p. 14 (Spring 2009) (hereinafter "*OTC Derivative Contracts in Bankruptcy*").

[138] Counterparties typically hold the collateral underlying these contracts, which usually consists of liquid assets such as securities or cash. Robert R. Bliss and George G. Kaufman, *Derivatives and Systemic Risk: Netting, Collateral, and Closeout*, Fed. Reserve Bank of Chicago, p. 7 (2005), available at https://www.chicagofed.org/digital_assets publications /working_papers/2005/wp2005_03.pdf (hereinafter "*Derivatives and Systemic Risk*").

[139] *OTC Derivative Contracts in Bankruptcy* at 15.

[140] *Derivatives and Systemic Risk* at 4.

[141] Kenneth Ayotte and David A. Skeel, *Bankruptcy or Bailouts?*, 35 J. Corp. 469, 495 (2010). But see Kimberly Anne Summe, *Lessons Learned from the Lehman Bankruptcy*, at 77-92 (2010), available at http://media default/files/documents/Ending_ Government_Bailouts_as_We_Know_Them_59.pdf ("The application of the automatic

stay, while appearing to preserve the value of the 'assets' of the failing firm, may be illusory as it relates to derivatives since derivative transactions and the collateral associated with those transactions are not really assets in the traditional sense, and the preservation of value may rapidly change, particularly in a distressed market. Moreover, the legal certainty afforded to the termination of these contracts... should not be discounted. Highly liquid derivative transactions ... were terminated by many of Lehman Brothers' counterparties after the investment bank's failure, allowing those counterparties to reduce potential losses by entering into replacement transactions. The loss of an ability to hedge one's trading book because of the application of a stay would result in significant losses for qualified financial contract counterparties, causing a catastrophic decline in the activities of the financial markets.").

[142] Notice of Debtors' Motion For an Order Pursuant to Sections 105 and 365 of the Bankruptcy Code to Establish Procedures for the Settlement or Assumption and Assignment of Prepetition Derivatives Contracts, U.S. Bankr. Ct. S.D.N.Y. Case No. 08-13555, Docket No. 1498. Counterparties to many of these 700,000+ contracts seem to have at least attempted to terminate the contracts within a few days of Lehman Brother's bankruptcy filing. *Lehman Risk Reduction Trading Session and Protocol Agreement,* Int'l Swaps and Derivatives Assoc., Inc. Press Release, Sept. 14, 2008, available at http://www.isda.org/press/press091408lehman.html. However, problems appear to have arisen in the close-out and netting process, which led the International Swaps and Derivatives Association (ISDA), a major trade association representing derivatives participants, to develop a Lehman derivatives "Protocol Agreement" to help rectify these problems. ISDA 2008 Lehman CDS Protocol, available at http://www.isda.org/2008lehmancdsprot/ 2008lehmancdsprot.html. The disruptions in the settlement process likely alleviated the strain that settling 700,000 contracts within hours of one another could have had on the derivatives market, as dozens of counterparties sought replacement contracts/counterparties, and on the Lehman Brothers bankruptcy estate, as collateral was seized outside of the automatic stay's protection. Nevertheless, the process arguably exacerbated the seismic repercussions of Lehman's failure on U.S. and global markets. *The Financial Crisis Inquiry Report*, Nat'l Com. on the Causes of the Fin. and Econ. Crisis in the U.S., p. 343, Feb. 25, 2011, available at http://www.gpo.gov/fdsys/pkg /GPO-FCIC/pdf/GPOFCIC.pdf.

[143] Kimberly Anne Summe, *Lessons Learned from the Lehman Bankruptcy*, at 78 (2010), available at http://media. In response to a motion by the Lehman Brothers bankruptcy estate, the bankruptcy court ultimately approved the assignment to third parties of the QFCs that were not terminated by Lehman's counterparties, without those counterparties' permissions because "the estate might best realize the value of those transactions through assignment." *Id.*

[144] Ayotte and Skeel at 494-95.

[145] *Id.*

[146] *Too Big to Fail: The Role for Bankruptcy and Antitrust Law in Financial Regulation Reform, Subcommittee on Commercial and Administrative Law of the House Committee on the Judiciary*, 111th Cong. (2009) (statement of Harvey R. Miller, Senior Partner, Weil, Gotshal & Manges LLP at 9), available at http://judiciary hearings/pdf/Miller 091022.pdf.

[147] 12 U.S.C. §1823(c)(4). See also Fed. Deposit Ins. Corp. Resolution Handbook, Ch. 2, p. 16, available at https://www.fdic.gov/bank/historical/reshandbook/ch2procs.pdf; Robert R. Bliss and George G. Kaufman, *U.S. Corporate and Bank Insolvency Regimes: A Comparison and Evaluation*, 2 Va. L. & Bus. Rev. 143, 158-59 (2007).

[148] 12 U.S.C. §5384(a). See also Resolution of Systemically Important Financial Institutions: The Single Point of Entry Strategy, 78 Fed. Reg. 76,614, 76,615 (Dec. 18, 2013), available at https://www.fdic.gov/news/board/2013/2013-12- 10_notice_dis-b_fr.pdf; Martin J. Gruenberg, Acting Chairman of the Fed. Deposit Ins. Corp., Remarks to the Fed. Res. Bank of Chicago Bank Structure Conf.; Chicago, IL, May 10, 2012 (" ... the most promising resolution strategy from our point view will be to place the parent company into receivership and to pass its assets, principally investments in its subsidiaries, to a newly created bridge holding company. This will allow subsidiaries that are equity solvent and contribute to the franchise value of the firm to remain open and avoid the disruption that would likely accompany their closings. Because these subsidiaries will remain open and operating as going-concern counterparties, we expect that qualified financial contracts will continue to function normally as the termination, netting and liquidation will be minimal. In short, we believe that this resolution strategy will preserve the franchise value of the firm and mitigate systemic consequences. This responds to the goal of financial stability.").

[149] The FDIC has a number of tools, referred to as "superpowers," to deal with insolvent depository institutions that stem from long-standing judicial decisions, many of which were later enacted into law through the FDI Act and then OLA. For a fuller description of these "superpowers," see Erin Burrows and F. John Podvin, Jr., Revising the FDIC's "Superpowers": Contract Repudiation and D'Oench Duhme,127 Bank. L. J. 395 (May 2010). The superpowers include the power to reorganize the institution, replace its senior management, sell its assets, as well as transfer, repudiate, and avoid certain claims, with little judicial oversight. These powers, in some respects, exceed the authority provided to bankruptcy administrators. *See, e.g.*, Thomas C. Baxter, Jr., Joyce M. Hansen, and Joseph H. Sommer, *Two Cheers for Territoriality: An Essay on International Bank Insolvency Law*, 78 Am. Bankr. L. J. 57, 72 (2004); Robert W. Norcross, Jr., *The Bank Insolvency Game: FDIC Superpowers, the D'Oench Doctrine, and Federal Common Law*, 103 Banking L. J. 316, 328 (1986); Fred Galves, *Might Does Not Make Right: The Call for Reform of the Federal Government's D'Oench, Duhme and 12 U.S.C. 1823(e) Superpowers in Failed Bank Litigation*, 80 Minn. L. Rev. 1323 (1996); Robert W. Norcross, Jr., *The Bank Insolvency Game: FDIC Superpowers, the D'Oench Doctrine, and Federal Common Law*, 103 Banking L. J. 316, n.137 (1986). The FDIC's "superpowers" tend to be broader when pertaining to non-QFCs. Contrast, for example, the FDIC's general avoidance power, 12 U.S.C. §1821(d)(17) (FDI Act); 12 U.S.C. §5390(a)(11) (OLA) to its avoidance power for QFCs, 12 U.S.C. §1821(e)(8)(C) (FDI Act); 12 U.S.C. §5390(c)(8)(C) (OLA). A "qualified financial contract" in the context of an FDIC administered conservatorship or receivership of an insured depository institution is defined as "any securities contract, commodity contract, forward contract, repurchase agreement, swap agreement, and any similar agreement that the ... [FDIC] determines by regulation, resolution, or order to be a qualified financial contract.... " 12 U.S.C. §§1821(e)(1) and (8)(F); 12 U.S.C. §5390(c)(8)(D). Although there are distinctions between the relevant definitions of financial contracts under the OLA receivership and the FDI Act conservatorship/receivership regimes and the U.S. Bankruptcy Code, those distinctions are not relevant for the purposes of this report. Kimberly Anne Summe, *Lessons Learned from the Lehman Bankruptcy*, at 72 (2010), available at http://media

[150] 12 U.S.C. §1821(e)(10)(B)(i) (FDI Act); 12 U.S.C. §5390(c)(10)(B)(i) (OLA). This means that the FDIC often has approximately three days to make decisions because it frequently is appointed receiver on a Friday. Under the FDI Act, counterparties to QFCs whose rights would be triggered by the appointment of a *conservator* or by the financial condition that

results in the appointment of a conservator, *may not* exercise such rights. 12 U.S.C. §1821(e)(10)(B)(ii). However, counterparties are free to exercise rights under QFCs triggered by the default *of the contracts* (as opposed to the insolvency of the depository institution) when a depository is in *conservatorship*. 12 U.S.C. §1821(e)(8)(E). There are no equivalent provisions in OLA because, as previously mentioned, the OLA does not establish a conservatorship regime.

151 12 U.S.C. §1821(e)(8)(A) (FDI Act); 12 U.S.C. §5390(c)(8)(A) (OLA).

152 12 U.S.C. §§1821(e)(8)(F), (e)(9), and (e)(10) (FDI Act); 12 U.S.C. §5390(c)(8)(F), (c)(9), and (c)(10) (OLA).

153 12 U.S.C. §1821(e)(1) (FDI Act); 12 U.S.C. §5390(c)(1) (OLA).

154 12 U.S.C. §1821(e)(11) (FDI Act); 12 U.S.C. §5390(c)(11) (OLA).

155 For a discussion of the avoidance powers in bankruptcy, see *supra* notes 133-136 and surrounding text.

156 12 U.S.C. §1821(e)(8)(C) (FDI Act); 12 U.S.C. §5390(c)(8)(C) (OLA).

157 It also might reduce the potential chaos of closing out and terminating hundreds of thousands of contracts in a short period of time.

158 Thomas J. Fitzpatrick IV and James B. Thomson, *How Well Does Bankruptcy Work When Large Financial Firms Fail? Some Lesson from Lehman Brothers*, Fed. Reserve Bank of Cleveland Economic Commentary, Oct. 26, 2011, available at http://www.clevelandfed.org /research/commentary/2011/2011-23.cfm. Another potential source of uncertainty could be whether the U.S. or another government would provide some form of emergency assistance to the failed firm, like the U.S. did in 2010 with A.I.G., Citigroup, Fannie Mae and Freddie Mac, among others. *Id.*

159 *Major Banks Agree to Sign ISDA Resolution Stay Protocol*, Int'l Swaps and Derivatives Assoc., Inc. Press Release, Oct. 11, 2014, available at http://www2.isda.org/news/major-banks

160 *Id.*

161 *Id.*

162 *Id.*

163 *Federal Reserve Board and FDIC Welcome ISDA Announcement*, Bd. of Gov. of the Fed. Reserve Sys., Fed. Deposit Ins. Corp., Joint Press Release, Oct. 11, 2014, available at https://www.fdic.gov/news/news/press/2014/ pr14083.html.

164 *Wall Street Reform: Assessing and Enhancing the Financial Regulatory System, Hearing Before the Senate Comm. on Banking, Housing, and Urban Affairs*, 113th Cong. (2014) (written statement of the Hon. Martin J. Gruenberg at p. 8; written statement of the Hon. Daniel K. Tarullo at pp. 9-10), available at http://www.banking index.cfm?FuseAction=Hearings.Hearing&Hearing_ID=b15fc832-df18-47d7-8c7d-1367e5770086.

165 *Global systemically important banks: updated assessment methodology and the higher loss absorbency requirement*, Basel Comm. on Bank. Super., July 2013, available at http://www.bis.org/publ/bcbs255.pdf.

166 *2013 update of group of global systemically important banks (G-SIBs)*, Fin. Stability Bd., Nov. 11, 2013, available at http://www.financialstabilityboard.org/publications /r_131111.pdf.

167 *Wall Street Reform: Assessing and Enhancing the Financial Regulatory System, Hearing Before the Senate Comm. on Banking, Housing, and Urban Affairs*, 113th Cong. (2014) (written statement of the Hon. Daniel K. Tarullo at p. 9), available at http://www.banking df18-47d7-8c7d-1367e5770086.

[168] *Wall Street Reform: Assessing and Enhancing the Financial Regulatory System, Hearing Before the Senate Comm. on Banking, Housing, and Urban Affairs*, 113th Cong. (2014) (written statement of the Hon. Daniel K. Tarullo at pp. 9- 10), available at http://www.banking b15fc832-df18-47d7-8c7d-1367e5770086.

[169] CRS Report R42150, *Systemically Important or "Too Big to Fail" Financial Institutions*, by Marc Labonte, at 5.

[170] *Wall Street Reform: Assessing and Enhancing the Financial Regulatory System, Hearing Before the Senate Comm. on Banking, Housing, and Urban Affairs*, 113th Cong. (2014) (written statement of the Hon. Martin J. Gruenberg at p. 8; written statement of the Hon. Daniel K. Tarullo at pp. 9-10), available at http://www.banking index.cfm?FuseAction=Hearings.Hearing&Hearing_ID=b15fc832-df18-47d7-8c7d-1367e5770086.

[171] *Wall Street Reform: Assessing and Enhancing the Financial Regulatory System, Hearing Before the Senate Comm. on Banking, Housing, and Urban Affairs*, 113th Cong. (2014) (written statement of the Hon. Daniel K. Tarullo at pp. 9- 10), available at http://www.banking b15fc832-df18-47d7-8c7d-1367e5770086.

[172] *Id.*

[173] Relatedly, some at the FDIC and FRB also believe that some financial institutions should reduce their reliance on short-term wholesale funding in order to promote financial stability. See, e.g., *Statement of Thomas M. Hoenig, Vice Chairman, FDIC on the Credibility of the 2013 Living Wills Submitted by First Wave Filers*, Aug. 5, 2014, available at https://www.fdic.gov/news/news/speeches/spaug0514a.html; *Wall Street Reform: Assessing and Enhancing the Financial Regulatory System, Hearing Before the Senate Comm. on Banking, Housing, and Urban Affairs*, 113th Cong. (2014) (written statement of the Hon. Daniel K. Tarullo at p. 7), available at http://www.banking index.cfm?FuseAction=Hearings.Hearing&Hearing_ID=b15fc832-df18-47d7-8c7d-1367e5770086. The FRB, FDIC, and the Office of the Comptroller of the Currency (OCC) are imposing liquidity rules pursuant to authorities distinct from the DFA's living wills regime. See Regulatory Capital Rules: Regulatory Capital, Revisions to the Supplementary Leverage Ratio, 79 Fed. Reg. 57,725 (Sept. 26, 2014) (to be codified at 12 C.F.R. Part 3 (OCC), 12 C.F.R. Part 217 (FRB), and 12 C.F.R. Part 324 (FDIC)).

[174] *Wall Street Reform: Assessing and Enhancing the Financial Regulatory System, Hearing Before the Senate Comm. on Banking, Housing, and Urban Affairs*, 113th Cong. (2014) (written statement of the Hon. Daniel K. Tarullo at pp. 9- 10), available at http://www.banking b15fc832-df18-47d7-8c7d-1367e5770086.

[175] *Wall Street Reform: Assessing and Enhancing the Financial Regulatory System, Hearing Before the Senate Comm. on Banking, Housing, and Urban Affairs*, 113th Cong. (2014) (written statement of the Hon. Martin J. Gruenberg at p. 8; written statement of the Hon. Daniel K. Tarullo at pp. 9-10), available at http://www.banking index.cfm?FuseAction=Hearings.Hearing&Hearing_ID=b15fc832-df18-47d7-8c7d-1367e5770086. Such a standard could be imposed pursuant to statutory authority distinct from DFA Section 165(d). See, e.g., 12 U.S.C. §5365.

[176] CRS Report R43345, *Shadow Banking: Background and Policy Issues*, by Edward V. Murphy, pp. 10-11.

[177] See CRS Report R42150, *Systemically Important or "Too Big to Fail" Financial Institutions*, by Marc Labonte, p. 12.

In: Large Financial Institutions
Editors: Franklin Pierce

ISBN: 978-1-63482-261-9

Chapter 2

A Credible Case for Resolving Through Bankruptcy*

Thomas M. Hoenig

Introduction

The U.S. and global financial systems are the definition of concentrated risk. They are composed of systemically important financial institutions (SIFIs) that are highly leveraged, heavily reliant on wholesale funding, and unduly interconnected. When even one of these institutions fails, its impact on world economies can be devastating.

To mitigate this impact, the Dodd-Frank Act of 2010 requires that each SIFI show itself capable of going through bankruptcy without bringing the economy down with it. This is no simple task, especially when such firms have assets at risk that rival the size of the home country's GDP.

Within this context, I want to take the next few minutes to address the topic of resolution through bankruptcy. I will outline from my perspective why the largest SIFIs' second-round bankruptcy plans were noncredible, and what in my mind might be necessary to change this outcome in the next round.

* This is an edited, reformatted and augmented version of remarks presented by the Vice Chairman of the FDIC to the George Washington University Law School Conference on Financial Stability After Dodd-Frank: Have We Ended Too Big to Fail?, Nov. 5, 2014.

ORIGINS OF TOO BIG TO FAIL

As the accompanying chart[1] illustrates, the United States has witnessed a systematic increase in the concentration of resources and risk within the banking and financial sectors. In 1984, the distribution of balance-sheet assets among the different bank-size groups was nearly proportional, from the largest firms with more than $10 billion of assets to those with less than $1 billion. However, in the ensuing decades, control of assets has become disproportional as the largest group has perpetually increased its control to more than 80 percent of industry assets, an amount equal to approximately 75 percent of U.S. GDP.

As banks have evolved into SIFIs, growing in size, complexity, and influence, the failure of any one can be catastrophic to the broader economy, as we have recently experienced. These outsized effects and fear of their consequences have led governments around the world to prop up these SIFIs when they have teetered on failure, rather than let them enter bankruptcy.

LIVING WILLS

In an effort to end this outcome that inevitably involves taxpayer support, Congress in the Dodd-Frank Act requires that each SIFI show how, in the event of an idiosyncratic failure, it could be resolved in bankruptcy without precipitating a crisis. Bankruptcy has a long history as the resolution vehicle for most U.S. companies. Even so, under the best of circumstances it is no easy solution to failure. This is especially so for firms that have evolved into a tangle of complex structures and opaque operating systems, and whose resolution involves a host of difficult choices and actions.

Recognizing these complexities and challenges, the law requires each SIFI to provide plans, called living wills, to the FDIC and Federal Reserve demonstrating how it could successfully untangle itself and enter bankruptcy should it fail. This process has been ongoing since the enactment of Dodd-Frank, but with limited success. Although the law is clear that bankruptcy is the principle resolution vehicle, there may have been confusion among some firms that failure would be dealt with under Dodd-Frank's Title II Orderly Liquidation provisions, which involve government assistance, rather than liquidation through bankruptcy.[2]

On August 5, 2014 the FDIC sent notices to 11 of the largest SIFIs operating in the U.S., informing them that the second round of living wills they had filed were not credible.[3] Some plans, for example, unrealistically assumed that capital and funding would remain available from existing sources long enough to facilitate an orderly bankruptcy. They often assumed that host and home authorities would take no defensive actions, such as ring fencing local affiliates, should bankruptcy appear imminent. Such actions, which have occurred in past crises, interfere with the flow of funds across borders and impair liquidity and critical operations.

Such shortcomings in the planning process tend to perpetuate uncertainties that arise around a SIFI's failure and, as we learned in past crises, this negatively affects asset values, raises concerns of contagion, and exacerbates crisis. Thus, the FDIC was compelled to judge the second round of living wills for the 11 SIFIs as non-credible.

BUILDING CREDIBILITY

Efforts to remedy these issues are ongoing. The firms at this moment are working with the FDIC and Federal Reserve to rebuild the plans and restore confidence in the financial system's ability to withstand the shock of a SIFI's failure. As the process proceeds, CEOs and directors must be fully engaged and confident in their ability to take their firms through bankruptcy. As part of this effort, therefore, I would like to highlight some of the more important issues that I suggest require attention by the firms. The issues concern adequate capital and liquidity, a manageable structure, and a solution to cross-border impediments to orderly bankruptcy.

CAPITAL

No amount of equity capital can save an individual firm from the consequences of poor management. However, sufficient equity does enable good managers to survive errors in judgment and allows an industry to absorb the effects of a poorly managed firm's failure. One of the difficulties during the crisis of 2008 was that nearly all of the largest firms, and thus the industry, were marginally capitalized and lacked resilience. When a firm like Lehman Brothers failed, both markets and the regulatory authorities were hard pressed to distinguish solvent from insolvent firms. All firms were suspect, a liquidity crisis followed, and governments felt compelled to support the firms. If bankruptcy is to be the resolution mechanism, then both individual firms and the industry as a whole must be made far more resilient than they were in 2008, or are today.

The accompanying table[4], titled the Global Capital Index (GCI), suggests why firm and industry resilience is still sorely lacking. Column 3 of the GCI shows Tier I capital to risk weighted assets (RWA) for the largest global firms. The ratios for all banks, largest to smallest, are above 10 percent and some of the largest have ratios of more than 15 percent. Impressive? Not when you study these measures more closely.

This RWA capital ratio relies on a regulator's ex-ante assignment of risk weights to various assets. Its effect is to permit firms literally to reduce the size of their balance sheets. This process, called the Basel Capital Standards, artificially boosts capital ratios, reducing these firms' apparent leverage. No other industry is allowed to do this, and its results have been disastrous. In 2008 firms reported "strong" risk weighted ratios of 10 percent or higher, but this was of little support when problems surfaced and a crisis ensued.

Recognizing that the RWA capital ratio does not adequately capture a SIFI's balance sheet risk and is misleading, a colleague at the Federal Reserve Bank of Kansas City[5] and I developed the Global Capital Index. This index relies on International Financial Reporting Standards (IFRS) to measure a firm's tangible equity (equity loss-absorbing capital) against on- and off-balance sheet assets, as shown in column 8 of the table. It provides a far more accurate measure of balance sheet assets and risk than the balance sheet reported under either GAAP or Basel.[6]

The GCI shows a capital ratio (known inversely as the leverage ratio) that is less than half that reported under the risk-weighted approach. The average ratio falls to near 5 percent, with some firms closer to 3 percent. The irony of the finding should be lost on no one. The portion of the financial industry with the greatest concentration of assets is the least well prepared to absorb loss. With relatively little capital within individual firms, the industry as a whole also is undercapitalized. The effect is that the probability of a SIFI failing is relatively higher than we currently perceive it to be and should one fail, the probability of the industry being dragged down with it is higher as well. Thus, the industry continues to be vulnerable to contagion and systemic crisis, and the lack of adequate tangible capital remains among the greatest impediments to successful bankruptcy and resolution.[7]

To finish the point, the largest regional and community banks, shown in the last three rows of column 8 of the GCI, have tangible capital ratios that are nearly double those of the largest SIFIs. The market requires these smaller firms, which are not too big to fail, to carry this greater capital.

LIQUIDITY

Liquidity, the ability to access funds or convert assets to cash quickly, is key to a successful bankruptcy. On a global level, SIFIs engage not only in deposit taking and lending, but also in an array of other on- and off-balance sheet leveraged activities. Funding for these operations is most often short term and, moreover, continued funding depends on public confidence in a firm's solvency. When confidence is lost, it often results in a liquidity crisis as the market and public seek safer ground.

In anticipating bankruptcy, each firm should assume its liquidity shock will be severe. It should not assume it has weeks or even days to wind down its funding operations. It should assume the worst: that it is insolvent; that its bank will be sold or taken into a FDIC receivership; and that its broker-dealer will enter bankruptcy. It should outline how in bankruptcy the broker-dealer and other affiliates will access sufficient unencumbered assets to provide debtor-in-possession financing.

Recently, 18 of the largest firms globally agreed to change protocols around bankruptcy that will facilitate the placement of "stays" when closing out derivatives.[8] These stays delay parties from rushing to take collateral and provide time for trustees to resolve creditor positions as bankruptcy unfolds. More of this kind of work is needed to mitigate the liquidity challenges that inevitably follow failure and the loss of confidence in firms and markets. Similar actions, for example, may be needed for those parts of the repo book that use long-term assets to secure short-term funding.

STRUCTURE AND CROSS-BORDER CHALLENGES

A SIFI's corporate structure almost certainly influences whether and how it can be taken through bankruptcy. The complexities of its global reach, operational interdependencies, inter- and intracompany transactions, and cross-border activities only increase in bankruptcy. Countries have their own laws, courts, and regulatory environment. Contracts enforceable in one country might not be so in another. Depositor preference, wholesale funding arrangements, derivatives, and repurchase agreements often are treated differently among countries when a firm enters bankruptcy.

One danger from such circumstances is that a SIFI, its affiliates and branches could be subject to sovereign ring fencing of local funds. This has the unfortunate effect of tying up funds when it is least expected and when access to liquid assets is most needed. This is particularly relevant for broker-dealer activities where volatile wholesale funding is most vulnerable to runs across borders and institutions.

A SIFI cannot assume these challenges away or anticipate that regulators or politicians will solve them. It will need to carefully prepare for the legal and operational demands to sell or unwind branch and corporate affiliates. It should outline how it would disentangle the bank from the parent and broker-dealer affiliates, and how it would support operations and its link to the payments system as it navigates bankruptcy and relationships across borders.

To avoid an idiosyncratic failure becoming a global crisis, these issues and others like them must be dealt with well before a SIFI fails. I would note, for example, that some firms have gone so far as to choose a corporate structure of subsidiarization to manage various cross-border issues.[9] In the end, whatever structure is chosen, it should not impede bankruptcy and should facilitate order over panic.

Conclusion

The U.S. financial system has become increasingly concentrated, as have related financial risks. Following the most recent crisis, an effort is underway globally to address these risks. The purpose is not to take appropriate risk out of the financial system. Rather, it is to address risk levels that have become excessive and that are sustainable only with public support. Our success in achieving this goal depends in large part on how we deal with failing firms. The choice we make – bankruptcy, government-assisted resolution, or bailout -- will determine the financial system's future and whether it remains primarily market driven.

* * *

Thomas M. Hoenig is the Vice Chairman of the FDIC and the former President of the Federal Reserve Bank of Kansas City. His research and other material can be found at http://www.fdic.gov/about/learn/board/hoenig/

CONSOLIDATION OF THE CREDIT CHANNEL

Change in Assets by Bank Size Groups (1984-2012)

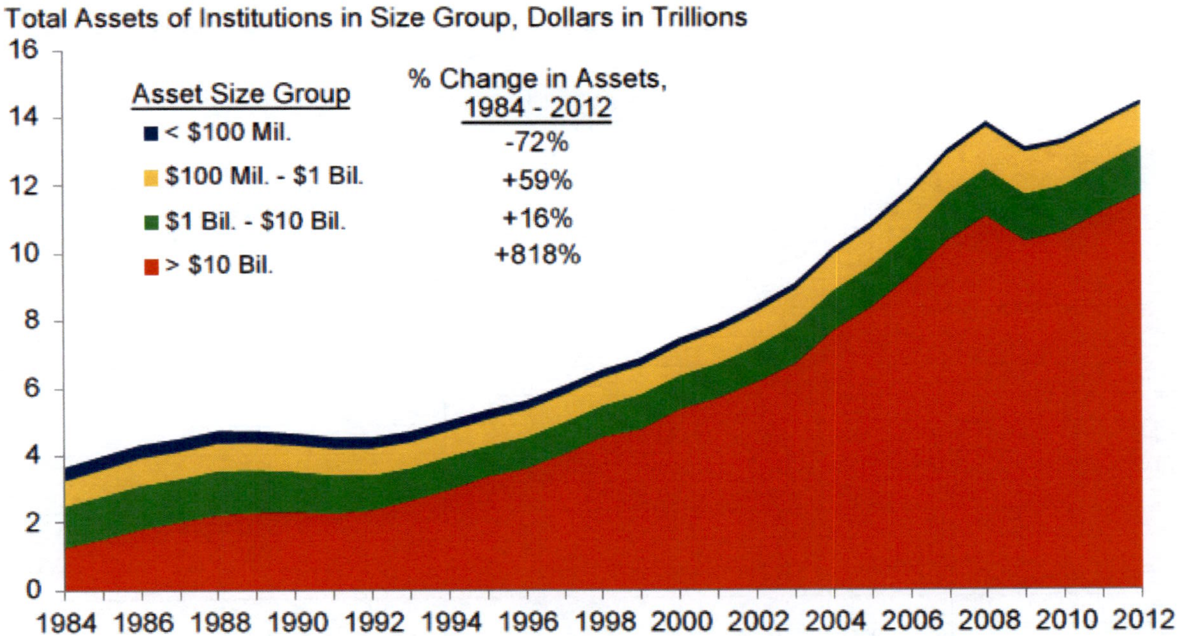

Source: FDIC. Reflects the aggregation of total assets of FDIC-insured institutions by bank holding company and also includes charter-level assets for banks with no holding company.

Global Capital Index

Capitalization Ratios for Global Systemically Important Banks (GSIBs)
Data as of June 30, 2014

Institution[1]	Basel Risk-Based Capital			Self-Reported Basel III Leverage Ratio[4] (Percent)	Tangible Capital				Components of Tangible Capital			Price-to-Book	
					GAAP		IFRS ESTIMATE 5						
	Tier 1 Capital[2] ($Billions)	Risk-Weighted Assets ($Billions)	Tier 1 Capital Ratio[3] (Percent)		Total Assets ($Billions)	Leverage Ratio[5] (Percent)	Total Assets ($Billions)	Leverage Ratio[6] (Percent)	Total Equity[7] ($Billions)	Goodwill and Other Intangibles ($Billions)	Deferred Tax Assets[11] ($Billions)	Price-to-Book Ratio[8] (Percent)	Price-to-Adjusted Tangible Book Ratio[8] (Percent)
	(1)	(2)	(3)	(4)	(5)	(6)	(7)	(8)	(9)	(10)	(11)	(12)	(13)
U.S. G-SIBs													
Bank of America	161	1,285	12.51	5.00	2,172	6.21	2,930	4.54	237	79	30	0.76	1.49
Bank of New York Mellon	21	133	15.54	...	401	4.17	416	4.01	38	23	0	1.20	3.10
Citigroup	164	1,124	14.62	5.70	1,910	7.02	2,549	5.20	211	32	51	0.77	1.31
Goldman Sachs	76	466	16.35	4.50	860	8.55	1,630	4.49	82	4	4	1.08	1.23
JPMorgan Chase	180	1,459	12.33	5.40	2,520	6.80	3,558	4.78	227	58	2	1.07	1.49
Morgan Stanley	65	403	16.02	4.60	827	6.82	1,397	4.01	71	10	6	1.02	1.33
State Street	16	89	17.73	6.10	282	4.81	289	4.70	22	8	0	1.49	2.55
Wells Fargo	152	1,193	12.72	...	1,599	8.69	1,650	8.42	181	46	0	1.66	2.31
U.S. G-SIBs ($ Total, % Average)	834	6,151	13.55	...	10,571	7.00	14,421	5.09	1,069	260	94	1.07	1.49
Foreign G-SIBs													
Banco Santander (Spain)	83	764	10.92	4.50			1,624	3.04	117	40	30	1.19	3.72
Bank of China Limited (China)	155	1,531	10.13	...			2,512	6.29	163	2	3	0.81	0.84

	Basel Risk-Based Capital				Tangible Capital				Components of Tangible Capital			Price-to-Book	
					GAAP		IFRS ESTIMATE 5						
Institution[1]	Tier 1 Capital[2] ($Billions)	Risk-Weighted Assets ($Billions)	Tier 1 Capital Ratio[3] (Percent)	Self-Reported Basel III Leverage Ratio[4] (Percent)	Total Assets ($Billions)	Leverage Ratio[5] (Percent)	Total Assets ($Billions)	Leve-rage Ratio[6] (Percent)	Total Equity[7] ($Billions)	Goodwill and Other Intangibles ($Billions)	Deferred Tax Assets[11] ($Billions)	Price-to-Book Ratio[8] (Percent)	Price-to-Adjusted Tangible Book Ratio[8] (Percent)
	(1)	(2)	(3)	(4)	(5)	(6)	(7)	(8)	(9)	(10)	(11)	(12)	(13)
Barclays (UK)	69	692	9.92	3.40			2,213	3.36	94	13	7	0.63	0.80
BBVA (Spain)	53	460	11.58	5.80			819	5.30	64	9	13	1.21	1.87
BNP Paribas (France)	95	854	11.17	3.50			2,606	3.30	112	17	9	0.82	1.09
BPCE Group (France)	67	552	12.18	4.00			1,575	4.36	84	8	8	...	...
Crédit Agricole Group (France)	84	685	12.29	4.10			2,274	3.92	117	21	8	...	...
Deutsche Bank (Germany)	85	548	15.53	3.40			2,277	2.93	94	19	8	0.52	0.75
HSBC (UK)	154	1,249	12.32	4.30			2,754	5.52	187	30	7	1.10	1.36
ING Bank (Netherlands)	48	401	11.97	...			1,119	3.87	47	2	2	...	...
Nordea bank (Sweden)	34	297	11.39	4.30			870	4.02	39	4	0	1.36	1.54
Royal Bank of Scotland (UK)	80	660	12.05	3.70			1,702	4.06	94	20	5	0.69	0.92
Société Générale (France)	60	479	12.46	3.60			1,808	2.81	64	6	8	0.66	0.84
Standard Chartered (UK)	41	352	11.77	4.80			690	6.11	49	6	1	0.66	0.78
UBS (Switzerland)	47	259	18.21	4.20			1,106	3.64	56	7	9	1.24	1.74
UniCredit (Italy)	62	545	11.29	...			1,146	3.78	71	7	...	0.71	1.25
Foreign IFRS ($ Total, % Average)	1,217	10,328	11.79	...			27,095	4.18	1,452	214	119	0.81	1.25
Other Foreign G-SIBs													
Credit Suisse (Switzerland; CHF, U.S. GAAP)	51	321	15.95	...	1,003	3.22			47	9	6	1.01	1.52

Capitalization Ratios for Global Systemically Important Banks (GSIBs) Data as of June 30, 2014 (Continued)

	Basel Risk-Based Capital				Tangible Capital				Components of Tangible Capital			Price-to-Book	
					GAAP		IFRS ESTIMATE 5						
Institution[1]	Tier 1 Capital[2] ($Billions)	Risk-Weighted Assets ($Billions)	Tier 1 Capital Ratio[3] (Percent)	Self-Reported Basel III Leverage Ratio[4] (Percent)	Total Assets ($Billions)	Leverage Ratio[5] (Percent)	Total Assets ($Billions)	Leverage Ratio[6] (Percent)	Total Equity[7] ($Billions)	Goodwill and Other Intangibles ($Billions)	Deferred Tax Assets[11] ($Billions)	Price-to-Book Ratio[8] (Percent)	Price-to-Adjusted Tangible Book Ratio[8] (Percent)
	(1)	(2)	(3)	(4)	(5)	(6)	(7)	(8)	(9)	(10)	(11)	(12)	(13)
Mitsubishi UFJ FG (Japan; JPY, Local GAAP)	123	992	12.37	...	2,540	3.67			105	12	1	0.70	0.78
Mizuho FG (Japan; JPY, Local GAAP)	69	586	11.76	...	1,780	2.86			56	5	1	0.80	0.89
Sumitomo Mitsui FG (Japan; JPY, Local GAAP)	73	531	13.80	...	1,590	3.47			64	8	2	0.82	0.95
All Foreign G-SIBs ($ Total, % Average)	1,534	12,759	12.02	...	34,008	4.01			1,726	248	128	0.81	0.94
U.S. BHC by Size Group[9]													
U.S. G-SIBs	834	6,151	13.55		10,571	7.00	14,421	5.09	1,069	260	94	1.07	1.49
Ten Largest Non-G-SIBs	194	1,600	12.12		1,987	8.98	1,996	8.94	248	70	6	1.18	1.90
Ten Largest Less Than $50 Billion[10]	27	218	12.53		322	7.69	322	7.69	35	9	2	1.38	2.16
Ten Largest Less Than $1 Billion[10]	1	7	13.86		10	8.57	10	8.57	1	0	0	...	...

Source: Bankscope (Data updated as of August 28, 2014), Bloomberg LP, Federal Reserve Y-9C Reports, International Monetary Fund, and 10-K reports.

Notes:

[1] Global systemically important banks (G-SIBs) are defined by the Financial Stability Board and include eight U.S. bank holding companies (BHC). Foreign G-SIBs report in local currencies, which are converted into U.S. dollars using IMF International Financial Statistics exchange rates.

[2] Tier 1 Capital is equity capital less unrealized gains on available-for-sale debt securities, unrealized losses on available-for-sale equity securities, disallowed preferred stock, disallowed goodwill, disallowed servicing assets, disallowed deferred tax assets, and other tier 1 capital components.

[3] Tier 1 capital ratios and underlying data are calculated and reported under the Capital Rules for Commercial Banks for the Bank of China, under Basel I capital standards for U.S. Banks , under Basel II for Banco Santander, BBVA, ING Bank, Nordea Bank, Standard Chartered, and Unicredit, under Basel 2.5 for Barclays, BNP Paribas, BPCE Group, Credit Agricole, Deutsche Bank, HSBC, Royal Bank of Scotland, and Societe Generale, and under Basel 3 for Credit Suisse, Mitsubishi UFJ, Mizuho FG, Sumitomo Mitsui, and UBS.

[4] Basel III leverage ratios are self-reported by institutions in published financial statements and presentations. They have not been reviewed for accuracy.

[5] Differences in accounting requirements for netting and offsetting of assets and liabilities result in significant differences in banks' total assets. The ability to offset under International Financial Reporting Standards (IFRS) is limited in comparison with Generally Accepted Accounting Principles (GAAP), especially for derivatives traded with the same counterparty under an International Swaps and Derivatives Association (ISDA) Master Netting Agreement. U.S. GAAP permits the netting of derivative receivables and payables, and the related cash collateral received and paid when a legally enforceable master netting agreement exists between a firm and a derivative counterparty. U.S. GAAP discloses gross derivative assets and liabilities and the offset amount applied to derivatives in the notes to the consolidated financial statements rather than in the consolidated balance sheet. To narrow the difference in total assets between IFRS and U.S. GAAP reporting institutions, the U.S. G-SIBs IFRS estimates follow the methodology used by ISDA in its Netting and Offsetting Report (May 2012, http://www2.isda.org/functional-areas/research/studies/) and adds the disclosed offsetting amount applied to derivatives back to total assets in order to calculate total assets. Total assets are as reported in the consolidated balance sheet while the offset applied to derivatives is as reported in the notes to the consolidated financial statements on derivatives in each firm's 10-Q report.

[6] The Leverage Ratio is the ratio of adjusted tangible equity to adjusted tangible assets. Adjusted tangible equity, adjusted tangible assets, and adjusted tangible book subtract goodwill, other intangibles, and deferred tax assets.

[7] Equity Capital is the basic GAAP measure of net worth, defined as total assets minus total liabilities.

[8] Median price-to-book ratios and price-to-adjusted tangible book ratios are used instead of averages for subgroups and for U.S. BHC size groups. Data are not available for six bank holding companies with assets less than $1 billion, as well as for BPCE Group and Credit Agricole Group.

[9] Bank holding companies that are owned by a foreign parent or reported a net loss in fourth quarter 2013, and thrift holding companies that did not file a full FRY-9C report as of fourth quarter 2013 were excluded.

[10] The ten largest U.S. bank holding companies with assets less than $50 billion and the ten largest U.S. bank holding companies with assets less than $1 billion reported de minimis derivative exposures. We assume that total assets and the adjusted tangible equity to adjusted tangible assets ratio are essentially the same under U.S. GAAP and the IFRS estimate.

[11] Deutsche Bank and Societe Generale do not report deferred tax assets separately at mid-year. Deferred tax assets presented for Deutsche Bank and Societe Generale use the ratio of deferred tax assets to income tax assets at the prior year-end applied to the income tax assets reported at mid-year.

End Notes

[1] Consolidation of the Credit Channel https://www.fdic.gov/about/learn/board/ hoenig/credit channel.pdf

[2] Title II of Dodd-Frank, known as Orderly Liquidation Authority, is subordinate to bankruptcy and triggered when the Secretary of Treasury, with the concurrence of the President, declares that a financial firm is in danger of default and that its failure would be systemic and detrimental to financial stability and harmful to the public. The law provides that the FDIC be appointed receiver to carry out the liquidation of not only the commercial bank but also the financial company. In bankruptcy, the cost of the resolution goes against the stockholders and uninsured creditors. In a government resolution, costs go against stockholders, some creditors, and eventually to the financial industry through assessments. The taxpayer also plays a role in providing necessary funding during the transition.

[3] The FDIC on August 5, 2014 determined that the living wills submitted by the 11 largest complex banking organizations were not credible and do not facilitate an orderly resolution under the U.S. Bankruptcy Code. The Federal Reserve Board determined that the 11 banking organizations must take immediate action to improve their resolvability and reflect those improvements in their 2015 plans. The agencies agreed that in the event that the first-wave filers have not, on or before July 1, 2015, submitted plans responsive to the identified shortcomings, the agencies expect to use their authority...to determine that a resolution plan does not meet the requirements of the Dodd-Frank Act. https://www.fdic.gov/news/news/ press/2014/pr14067.html

[4] Global Capital Index https://www.fdic.gov/about/learn/board/hoenig/ capitalizationratios 2q14.pdf

[5] Charles Morris, Vice President and Economist at the Federal Reserve Bank of Kansas City.

[6] Differences in accounting requirements for netting and offsetting of assets and liabilities result in significant differences in banks' total assets. The ability to offset under International Financial Reporting Standards (IFRS) is limited in comparison with Generally Accepted Accounting Principles (GAAP), especially for derivatives traded with the same counterparty under an International Swaps and Derivatives Association (ISDA) Master Netting Agreement. U.S. GAAP permits the netting of derivative receivables and payables, and the related cash collateral received and paid when a legally enforceable master netting agreement exists between a firm and a derivative counterparty. U.S. GAAP discloses gross derivative assets and liabilities and the offset amount applied to derivatives in the notes to the consolidated financial statements rather than in the consolidated balance sheet. To narrow the difference in total assets between IFRS and U.S. GAAP reporting institutions, the U.S. G-SIBs IFRS estimates follow the methodology used by ISDA in its Netting and Offsetting Report (May 2012, http://www2.isda.org/functionalareas/research/studies/) and adds the disclosed offsetting amount applied to derivatives back to total assets in order to calculate total assets. Total assets are as reported in the consolidated balance sheet while the offset applied to derivatives is as reported in the notes to the consolidated financial statements on derivatives in each firm's 10-Q report.

[7] International regulators are working to address Total Loss Absorbency Capacity (TLAC) by developing methods that include both equity and debt to facilitate resolution without public support. It is important that the amount of equity, and the amount of debt and its conversion to equity, will work in bankruptcy and are calibrated to assure confidence in this approach as a means to facilitate an orderly resolution under bankruptcy.

[8] The International Swaps and Derivatives Association announced October 11, 2014 that its Resolution Stay Protocol will impose a stay on cross-default and early termination rights within standard ISDA derivatives contracts between G-18 firms in the event one of them is subject to resolution action in its jurisdiction. The stay is intended to give regulators time to facilitate an orderly resolution of a troubled bank. http://www2.isda.org/newsroom/press-releases/

[9] Under a subsidiarization structure, a banking entity is incorporated and chartered in the country in which it operates and is subject to local capital and liquidity requirements.

In: Large Financial Institutions
Editors: Franklin Pierce

ISBN: 978-1-63482-261-9

Chapter 3

STATEMENT OF DANIEL K. TARULLO, MEMBER, BOARD OF GOVERNORS OF THE FEDERAL RESERVE SYSTEM. HEARING ON "WALL STREET REFORM: ASSESSING AND ENHANCING THE FINANCIAL REGULATORY SYSTEM"*

Chairman Johnson, Ranking Member Crapo, and other members of the committee, thank you for the opportunity to testify on the Federal Reserve's activities in mitigating systemic risk and implementing the Dodd-Frank Wall Street Reform and Consumer Protection Act (Dodd-Frank Act). In testifying before this committee in February, I noted my hope and expectation that this year would be the beginning of the end of our implementation of the major provisions of the Dodd-Frank Act. Seven months later, we are on track to fulfill that expectation. The Federal Reserve and other banking supervisors have continued to make progress in implementing the congressional mandates in the Dodd-Frank Act, promoting a stable financial system, and strengthening the resilience of banking organizations. In today's testimony, I will provide an update on the Federal Reserve's implementation of the Dodd-Frank Act and describe key upcoming regulatory and supervisory priorities to address the problems of "too big to fail" and systemic risk. The Federal Reserve is committed to continuing to work with our fellow banking agencies and with

* This is an edited, reformatted and augmented version of a statement presented September 9, 2014 before the Senate Committee on Banking, Housing, and Urban Affairs.

the market regulators to help ensure that the organizations we supervise operate in a safe and sound manner and are able to support activity in other sectors of the economy.

As we complete our revisions to the financial regulatory architecture, we are cognizant that regulatory compliance can impose a disproportionate burden on smaller financial institutions. In addition to overseeing large banking firms, the Federal Reserve supervises approximately 800 state-chartered community banks that are members of the Federal Reserve System, as well as several thousand small bank holding companies. In my testimony, I also will describe how the Federal Reserve is seeking to ensure that its regulations and supervisory framework are not unnecessarily burdensome for community banking organizations so they can continue their important function of safe and sound lending to local communities.

RECENT DODD-FRANK ACT IMPLEMENTATION MILESTONES

Since the passage of the Dodd-Frank Act more than four years ago, the Federal Reserve and the other agencies represented at this hearing have completed wide-ranging financial regulatory reforms that have remade the regulatory landscape for financial firms and markets. Internationally, at the Basel Committee on Banking Supervision (BCBS), we have helped develop new standards for global banks on risk-based capital, leverage, liquidity, singlecounterparty credit limits, and margin requirements for over-the-counter derivatives. We have also worked with the Financial Stability Board (FSB) to reach global agreements on resolution regimes for systemic financial firms and on a set of shadow banking regulatory reforms.

Domestically, we have completed many important measures. We approved final rules implementing the Basel III capital framework, which help ensure that U.S. banking organizations maintain strong capital positions and are able to continue lending to creditworthy households and businesses even during economic downturns. We implemented the Dodd-Frank Act's stress testing requirements, which are complemented by the Federal Reserve's annual Comprehensive Capital Analysis and Review. Together, these supervisory exercises provide a forward-looking assessment of the capital adequacy of the largest U.S. banking firms. Pursuant to section 165 of the Dodd-Frank Act, we established a set of enhanced standards for large U.S.

banking organizations to help increase the resiliency of their operations and thus promote financial stability. In addition, the Federal Reserve implemented a rule requiring foreign banking organizations with a significant U.S. presence to establish U.S. intermediate holding companies over their U.S. subsidiaries and subjecting such companies to substantially the same prudential standards applicable to U.S. bank holding companies. We finalized the Volcker rule to implement section 619 of the Dodd-Frank Act and prohibit banking organizations from engaging in short-term proprietary trading of certain securities and derivatives. These and other measures have already created a financial regulatory architecture that is much stronger and much more focused on financial stability than the framework in existence at the advent of the financial crisis.

More recently, the Federal Reserve, often in tandem with some or all of the other agencies represented at this hearing, has made progress on a number of other important regulatory reforms. I will discuss those steps in more detail.

Liquidity Rules for Large Banking Firms

Last week, the Federal Reserve and the other U.S. banking agencies approved a final rule, consistent with the enhanced prudential standards requirements in section 165 of the Dodd-Frank Act, which implements the first broadly applicable quantitative liquidity requirement for U.S. banking firms. Liquidity standards for large U.S. banking firms are a key contributor to financial stability, as they work in concert with capital standards, stress testing, and other enhanced prudential standards to help ensure that large banking firms manage liquidity in a manner that mitigates the risk of creditor and counterparty runs.

The rule's liquidity coverage ratio, or LCR, requires covered banking firms to hold minimum amounts of high-quality liquid assets--such as central bank reserves and high-quality government and corporate debt--that can be converted quickly and easily into cash sufficient to meet expected net cash outflows over a short-term stress period. The LCR applies to bank holding companies and savings and loan holding companies with $250 billion or more in total consolidated assets or $10 billion or more in on-balance-sheet foreign exposures. The rule also applies a less stringent, modified LCR to bank holding companies and savings and loan holding companies that are below these thresholds but with more than $50 billion in total assets. The rule does not apply to bank holding companies or savings and loan holding companies with less than $50 billion in total assets, nor to nonbank financial companies designated by the Financial Stability Oversight Council (FSOC). The Federal Reserve will apply enhanced liquidity standards to designated nonbank financial companies through a subsequently issued order or rule following an evaluation of each of their business models, capital structures, and risk profiles.

The rule's LCR is based on a liquidity standard agreed to by the BCBS but is more stringent than the BCBS standard in several areas, including the range of assets that qualify as high-quality liquid assets and the assumed rate of outflows for certain kinds of funding. In addition, the rule's transition period is shorter than that in the BCBS standard. The accelerated phase-in of the U.S. LCR reflects our objective that large U.S. banking firms maintain the improved liquidity positions they have already built following the financial crisis, in part because of our supervisory oversight. We believe the LCR will help ensure that these improved liquidity positions will not weaken as memories of the financial crisis fade.

The final rule is largely identical to the proposed rule, with a few key adjustments made in response to comments from the public. Those adjustments include changing the scope of corporate debt securities and publicly traded equities qualifying as high-quality liquid assets, phasing in reporting requirements, and modifying the stress period and reporting frequency for firms subject to the modified LCR.

Swap Margin Reproposal

Sections 731 and 764 of the Dodd-Frank Act require the establishment of initial and variation margin requirements for swap dealers and major swap participants (swap entities) on swaps that are not centrally cleared. These requirements are intended to ensure that the counterparty risks inherent in swaps are prudently limited and not allowed to build to unsustainable levels that could pose risks to the financial system. In addition, requiring all uncleared swaps to be subject to robust margin requirements will remove economic incentives for market participants to shift activity away from contracts that are centrally cleared.

The Federal Reserve and four other U.S. agencies originally issued a proposed rule to implement these provisions of the Dodd-Frank Act in April 2011. Following the release of the original proposal, the BCBS and the International Organization of Securities Commissions began working to establish a consistent global framework for imposing margin requirements on uncleared swaps. This global framework was finalized last September. After considering the comments that were received on the April 2011 U.S. proposal and the recently established global standards, the agencies issued a reproposal last week. Under the reproposal, swap entities would be required to collect and post initial and variation margin on uncleared swaps with another swap entity and other financial end user counterparties. The requirements are intended to result in higher initial margin requirements than would be required for cleared swaps, which is meant to reflect the more complex and less liquid nature of uncleared swaps.

In accordance with the statutory requirement to establish margin requirements regardless of counterparty type, the reproposal would require swap entities to collect and post margin in connection with any uncleared swaps they have with nonfinancial end users. These requirements, however, are quantitatively and qualitatively different from the margin requirements for swaps with financial end users. Specifically, swaps with nonfinancial end users would not be subject to specific, numerical margin requirements but would only be subject to initial and variation margin requirements at such times, in such forms, and in such amounts, if any, that the swap entity determines is necessary to address the credit risk posed by the counterparty and the transaction. There are currently cases where a swap entity does not collect initial or variation margin from nonfinancial end users because it has determined that margin is not needed to address the credit risk posed by the counterparty or the transaction. In such cases, the reproposal would not require a change in current practice. The agencies believe that these requirements are consistent with the Dodd-Frank Act and appropriately reflect the low level of risk presented by most nonfinancial end users.

The agencies in the reproposal have taken several steps to help mitigate any impact to the liquidity of the financial system that could result from the swap margin requirements. These steps include incorporating an initial margin requirement threshold below which exchanges of initial margin are not required, allowing for a wider range of assets to serve as eligible collateral, and providing smaller swap entities with an extended timeline to come into compliance. We look forward to receiving comments on the reproposal.

Modifications to the Supplementary Leverage Ratio and Adoption of the Enhanced Supplementary Leverage Ratio

Also last week, the Federal Reserve and the other U.S. banking agencies approved a final rule that modifies the denominator calculation of the supplementary leverage ratio in a manner consistent with the changes agreed to earlier this year by the BCBS. The revised supplementary leverage ratio will apply to all banking organizations subject to the advanced approaches risk-based capital rule starting in 2018. These modifications to the supplementary leverage ratio will result in a more appropriately measured set of leverage capital requirements and, in the aggregate, are expected to modestly increase the stringency of these requirements across the covered banking organizations.

This rule complements the agencies' adoption in April of a rule that strengthens the internationally agreed-upon Basel III leverage ratio as applied to U.S.-based global systemically important banks (GSIBs). This enhanced supplementary leverage ratio, which will be effective in January 2018, requires U.S. GSIBs to maintain a tier 1 capital buffer of at least 2 percent above the minimum Basel III supplementary leverage ratio of 3 percent, for a total of 5 percent, to avoid restrictions on capital distributions and discretionary bonus payments. In light of the significantly higher risk-based capital rules for GSIBs under Basel III, imposing a stricter leverage requirement on these firms is appropriate to help ensure that the leverage ratio remains a relevant backstop for these firms.

KEY REGULATORY PRIORITIES

As we near the completion of the implementation of the major provisions of the Dodd-Frank Act, some key regulatory reforms remain unfinished. To that end, the Federal Reserve contemplates near- to medium-term measures to enhance the resiliency and resolvability of U.S. GSIBs and address the risks posed to financial stability from reliance by financial firms on short-term wholesale funding.

The financial crisis made clear that policymakers must devote significant attention to the potential threat to financial stability posed by our most systemic financial firms. Accordingly, the Federal Reserve has been working to develop regulations that are designed to reduce the probability of failure of a GSIB to levels that are meaningfully below those for less systemically important firms and to materially reduce the potential adverse impact on the broader financial system and economy in the event of a failure of a GSIB.

GSIB Risk-Based Capital Surcharges

An important remaining Federal Reserve initiative to improve GSIB resiliency is our forthcoming proposal to impose graduated common equity risk-based capital surcharges on U.S. GSIBs. The proposal will be consistent with the standard in section 165 of the Dodd-Frank Act that capital requirements be progressively more stringent as the systemic importance of a firm increases. It will build on the GSIB capital surcharge framework developed by the BCBS, under which the size of the surcharge for an individual GSIB is a function of the firm's systemic importance. By further increasing the amount of the most loss-absorbing form of capital that is required to be held by firms that potentially pose the greatest risk to financial stability, we intend to improve the resiliency of these firms. This measure might also create incentives for them to reduce their systemic footprint and risk profile.

While our proposal will use the GSIB risk-based capital surcharge framework developed by the BCBS as a starting point, it will strengthen the BCBS framework in two important respects. First, the surcharge levels for U.S. GSIBs will be higher than the levels required by the BCBS, noticeably so for some firms. Second, the surcharge formula will directly take into account each U.S. GSIB's reliance on short-term wholesale funding. We believe the case for including short-term wholesale funding in the surcharge calculation is compelling, given that reliance on this type of funding can leave firms vulnerable to runs that threaten the firm's solvency and impose externalities on the broader financial system.

Resolvability of GSIBs

Our enhanced regulation of GSIBs also includes efforts to improve their resolvability. Most recently, in August, the Federal Reserve and the Federal Deposit Insurance Corporation (FDIC) completed reviews of the second round of resolution plans submitted to the agencies in October 2013 by 11 U.S. bank holding companies and foreign banks. Section 165(d) of the Dodd-Frank Act requires banking organizations with total consolidated assets of $50 billion or more and nonbank financial companies designated by the FSOC to submit resolution plans to the Federal Reserve and the FDIC. Each plan must describe the organization's strategy for rapid and orderly resolution in the event of material financial distress or failure. In completing the second round reviews of these banking organizations' resolution plans, the FDIC and the Federal Reserve noted certain shortcomings in the resolution plans that the firms must address to improve their resolvability in bankruptcy. Both agencies also indicated the expectation that the firms make significant progress in addressing these issues in their 2015 resolution plans.

In addition, the Federal Reserve has been working with the FDIC to develop a proposal that would require the U.S. GSIBs to maintain a minimum amount of long-term unsecured debt at the parent holding company level. While minimum capital requirements are designed to cover losses up to a certain statistical probability, in the even less likely event that the equity of a financial firm is wiped out, successful resolution without taxpayer assistance would be most effectively accomplished if a firm has sufficient long-term unsecured debt to absorb additional losses and to recapitalize the business transferred to a bridge operating company. The presence of a substantial tranche of long-term unsecured debt that is subject to bail-in during a resolution and is structurally subordinated to the firm's other creditors should reduce run risk by clarifying the position of those other creditors in an orderly liquidation process. A requirement for longterm debt also should have the benefit of improving market discipline, since the holders of that debt would know they faced the prospect of loss should the firm enter resolution.

The Federal Reserve is working with global regulators, under the auspices of the FSB, to develop a proposal that would require the largest, most complex global banking firms to maintain a minimum amount of loss absorbency capacity beyond the levels mandated in the Basel III capital requirements.

Another element of our efforts to promote resolvability of large banking organizations involves the early termination rights of derivative counterparties to GSIBs. Some of the material operating subsidiaries of GSIBs are counterparties to large volumes of over-the-counter derivatives and other qualifying financial contracts that provide for an event of default based solely on the insolvency or receivership of the parent holding company. Although the Dodd-Frank Act created an orderly liquidation authority (OLA) to better enable the government to resolve a failed systemically important financial firm--and the OLA's stay and transfer provisions can prevent exercise of such contractual rights by counterparties to contracts under U.S. law--the OLA provisions may not apply to contracts under foreign law. Accordingly, counterparties of the foreign subsidiaries and branches of GSIBs may have contractual rights and substantial economic incentives to accelerate or terminate those contracts as soon as the U.S. parent GSIB enters OLA. This could render a resolution unworkable by resulting in the disorderly unwind of an otherwise viable foreign subsidiary and the disruption of critical intra-affiliate activities that rely on the failing subsidiary. The challenge would be compounded in a bankruptcy resolution because derivatives and other qualifying financial contracts are exempt from the automatic stay under bankruptcy law, regardless of whether the contracts are governed by U.S. or foreign law.

The international regulatory community is working to mitigate this risk as well. The Federal Reserve is working with the FDIC and global regulators, financial firms, and other financial market actors to develop a protocol to the International Swaps and Derivatives Association (ISDA) Master Agreement to address the impediments to resolvability generated by these early termination rights. The FSB will be reporting progress on this effort in the fall.

Short-Term Wholesale Funding

As I have noted in prior testimony before this committee, short-term wholesale funding plays a critical role in the financial system. During normal times, it helps to satisfy investor demand for safe and liquid investments, lowers funding costs for borrowers, and supports the functioning of important markets, including those in which monetary policy is executed. During periods of stress, however, runs by providers of short-term wholesale funding and associated asset liquidations can result in large fire sale externalities and otherwise undermine financial stability. A dynamic of this type engulfed the financial system in 2008.

Since the crisis, the Federal Reserve has taken several steps to address short-term wholesale funding risks. The Basel III capital framework and the Federal Reserve's stress testing regime have significantly increased the quantity and quality of required capital in the banking system, particularly for those banking organizations that are the most active participants in short-term wholesale funding markets. Similarly, the implementation of liquidity regulations such as the LCR, together with related efforts by bank supervisors, will help to limit the amount of liquidity risk in the banking system.

We have also taken steps to reduce risks posed by the use of short-term wholesale funding by actors outside the banking system. These include leading an effort to reduce reliance by borrowers in the tri-party repo market on intraday credit from clearing banks and increasing the regulatory charges on key forms of credit and liquidity support that banks provide to shadow banks. In part because of these actions and in part because of market adjustments, there is less risk embedded in short-term wholesale funding markets today than in the period immediately preceding the financial crisis. The short-term wholesale funding markets are generally smaller, the average maturity of short-term funding arrangements is moderately greater, and collateral haircuts are more conservative. In addition, the banking organizations that are the major intermediaries in short-term wholesale funding markets are much more resilient based on the measures I discussed earlier.

Nevertheless, we believe that more needs to be done to guard against short-term wholesale funding risks. While the total amount of short-term wholesale funding is lower today than immediately before the crisis, volumes are still large relative to the size of the financial system. Furthermore, some of the factors that account for the reduction in short-term wholesale funding volumes, such as the unusually flat yield curve environment and lingering risk aversion from the crisis, are likely to prove transitory.

Federal Reserve staff is currently working on three sets of initiatives to address residual short-term wholesale funding risks. As discussed above, the first is a proposal to incorporate the use of short-term wholesale funding into the risk-based capital surcharge applicable to U.S. GSIBs. The second involves proposed modifications to the BCBS's net stable funding ratio (NSFR) standard to strengthen liquidity requirements that apply when a bank acts as a provider of short-term funding to other market participants. The third is numerical floors for collateral haircuts in securities financing transactions (SFTs)--including repos and reverse repos, securities lending and borrowing, and securities margin lending.

Modifications to the NSFR could be designed to help address the types of concerns described in my previous testimony regarding SFT matched book activity. In the classic fact pattern, a matched book dealer uses SFTs to borrow on a short-term basis from a cash investor, such as a money market mutual fund, to finance a short-term SFT loan to a client, such as a leveraged investment fund. The regulatory requirements on SFT matched books are generally low despite the fact that matched books can pose significant microprudential and macroprudential risks. Neither the BCBS LCR nor the NSFR originally finalized by the Basel Committee would have imposed a material charge on matched book activity.

In January, the BCBS proposed a revised NSFR that would require banks to hold a material amount of stable funding against short-term SFT loans, as well as other short-term credit extensions, to nonbank financial entities. By requiring banks that make short-term loans to hold stable funding, such a charge would help limit the liquidity risk that a dealer would face if it experiences a run on its SFT liabilities but is unable to liquidate corresponding SFT assets. In addition, by making it more expensive for the dealer to provide short-term credit, the charge could help lean against excessive short-term borrowing by the dealer's clients.

Turning to numerical floors for SFT haircuts, the appeal of this policy measure is that it would help address the risk that post-crisis reforms targeted at banking organizations will drive systemically risky activity toward places in the financial system where prudential standards do not apply. In its universal form, a system of numerical haircut floors for SFTs would require any entity that wants to borrow against a security to post a minimum amount of excess margin to its lender that would vary depending on the asset class of the collateral. Like minimum margin requirements for derivatives, numerical floors for SFT haircuts would serve as a mechanism for limiting the build-up of leverage at the transaction level and could mitigate the risk of procyclical margin calls.

Last August, the FSB issued a consultative document that represented an initial step toward the development of a framework of numerical floors. However, the FSB's proposal contained some significant limitations, including that its scope was limited to transactions in which a bank or broker-dealer extends credit to an unregulated entity and that the calibration of the numerical floor levels was relatively low. Since then, the FSB has been actively considering whether to strengthen the proposal along both of these dimensions.

Financial Sector Concentration Limits

In May, the Federal Reserve proposed a rule to implement section 622 of the Dodd-Frank Act, which prohibits a financial company from combining with another company if the resulting financial company's liabilities exceed 10 percent of the aggregate consolidated liabilities of all financial companies. Under the proposal, financial companies subject to the concentration limit would include insured depository institutions, bank holding companies, savings and loan holding companies, foreign banking organizations, companies that control insured depository institutions, and nonbank financial companies designated by the FSOC for Federal Reserve supervision. Consistent with section 622, the proposal generally defines liabilities of a financial company as the difference between its risk-weighted assets, as adjusted to reflect exposures deducted from regulatory capital, and its total regulatory capital. Firms not subject to consolidated risk-based capital rules would measure liabilities using generally accepted accounting standards. We anticipate finalizing this rule in the near term.

Credit Risk Retention

Section 941 of the Dodd-Frank Act requires firms generally to retain credit risk in securitization transactions they sponsor. Retaining credit risk creates incentives for securitizers to monitor closely the quality of the assets underlying a securitization transaction and discourages unsafe and unsound underwriting practices by originators. In August 2013, the Federal Reserve, along with several other agencies, revised a proposal from 2011 to implement section 941. The Federal Reserve is working with the other agencies charged by the Dodd-Frank Act with implementing this rule to complete it in the coming months.

RATIONALIZING THE REGULATORY FRAMEWORK FOR COMMUNITY BANKS

Before closing, I would like to discuss the Federal Reserve's ongoing efforts to minimize regulatory burden consistent with the effective implementation of our statutory responsibilities for community banks, given the important role they play within our communities. Over the past few decades, community banks have substantially reduced their presence in lines of businesses such as consumer lending in the face of competition from larger banks benefiting from economies of scale. Today, as a group, their most important forms of lending are to small- and medium-sized businesses. Smaller community banks--those with less than $1 billion in assets-- account for nearly one-fourth of commercial and industrial lending, and nearly 40 percent of commercial real estate lending, to small- and medium-sized businesses, despite their having less than 10 percent of total commercial banking assets. These figures reveal the importance of community banks to local economies and the damage that could result if these banks were unable to continue operating within their communities.

Banking regulators have taken many steps to try to avoid unnecessary regulatory costs for community banks, such as fashioning more basic supervisory expectations for smaller, less complex banks and identifying which provisions of new regulations are relevant to smaller banks. In this regard, the Federal Reserve has worked to communicate clearly the extent to which new rules and policies apply to smaller banks and to tailor them as appropriate. We also work closely with our colleagues at the federal and state banking regulatory agencies to ensure that supervisory approaches and methodologies are consistently applied to community banks.

But several new statutory provisions apply explicitly to some smaller banks or, by failing to exclude any bank from coverage, apply to all banks. The Federal Reserve is supportive of considering areas where the exclusion of community banks from statutory provisions that are less relevant to community bank practice may be appropriate. For example, we believe it would be worthwhile to consider whether community banks should be excluded from the scope of the Volcker rule and from the incentive compensation requirements of section 956 of the Dodd-Frank Act. The concerns addressed by statutory provisions like these are substantially greater at larger institutions and, even where a practice at a smaller bank might raise concerns, the supervisory process remains available to address what would likely be unusual circumstances.

Another area in which the Federal Reserve has made efforts to right-size our supervisory approach with regard to community banks is to improve our off-site monitoring processes so that we can better target higher risk institutions and activities. Research conducted for a 2013 conference sponsored by the Federal Reserve System and the Conference of State Bank Supervisors addressed the resilience of the community bank model and showed how some banks performed better than others during the recent crisis. Building on this research, we are updating our off-site monitoring screens to reflect experience gained during the crisis and recalibrating our examination scoping process for community banks to focus our testing on higher-risk banks and activities, and whenever possible reduce procedures for banks of lower risk.

Recognizing the burden that the on-site presence of many examiners can place on the day-to-day business of a community bank, we are also working to increase our level of off-site supervisory activities. Responding to on-site examinations and inspections is of course a cost for community banks, but this cost must be weighed against the supervisory benefit of face-to-face interactions with bank examiners to explore and resolve institution-specific concerns. The Federal Reserve aims to strike the appropriate balance of off-site and on-site supervisory activities to ensure that the quality of community bank supervision is maintained without creating an overly burdensome process. To that end, last year we completed a pilot on conducting parts of the labor-intensive loan review off-site using electronic records from banks. Based on good results with the pilot, we are planning to continue using this approach in future reviews at banks where bank management is supportive of the process and where electronic records are available. We are also exploring whether other examination procedures can be conducted off-site without compromising the ability of examiners to accurately assess the safety and soundness of supervised banks.

CONCLUSION

The Federal Reserve has made significant progress in implementing the Dodd-Frank Act and other measures designed to improve the resiliency of banking organizations and reduce systemic risk. We are committed to working with the other U.S. financial regulatory agencies to promote a stable financial system in a manner that does not impose a disproportionate burden on smaller institutions. To help us achieve these goals, we will continue to seek the views of the institutions we supervise and the public as we further develop regulatory and supervisory programs to preserve financial stability at the least cost to credit availability and economic growth.

Thank you for your attention. I would be pleased to answer any questions you might have.

In: Large Financial Institutions
Editors: Franklin Pierce
ISBN: 978-1-63482-261-9

Chapter 4

STATEMENT OF MARTIN J. GRUENBERG, CHAIRMAN, FEDERAL DEPOSIT INSURANCE CORPORATION. HEARING ON "WALL STREET REFORM: ASSESSING AND ENHANCING THE FINANCIAL REGULATORY SYSTEM"*

Chairman Johnson, Ranking Member Crapo and members of the Committee, thank you for the opportunity to testify today on the Federal Deposit Insurance Corporation's (FDIC) actions to implement the Dodd-Frank Wall Street Reform and Consumer Protection Act (Dodd-Frank Act).

My written testimony will address several key topics. First, I will discuss capital and liquidity rules that the bank regulatory agencies recently finalized, as well as a recently proposed margin rule on derivatives. Second, I will provide an update on our progress in implementing the authorities provided the FDIC relating to the resolution of systemically important financial institutions (SIFIs). I will then discuss an updated proposed risk retention rule for securitizations and implementation of the Volcker Rule. Finally, I will discuss our supervision of community banks, including the FDIC's efforts to address emerging cybersecurity and technology issues.

* This is an edited, reformatted and augmented version of a statement presented September 9, 2014 before the Senate Committee on Banking, Housing, and Urban Affairs.

Capital, Liquidity and Derivative Margin Requirements

The new regulatory framework established under the Dodd-Frank Act augments and complements the banking agencies' existing authorities to require banking organizations to maintain capital and liquidity well above the minimum requirements for safety and soundness purposes, as well as to establish margin requirements on derivatives. The recent actions by the agencies to adopt a final rule on the leverage capital ratio, a final rule on the liquidity coverage ratio, and a proposed rule on margin requirements for derivatives address three key areas of systemic risk and, taken together, are an important step forward in addressing the risks posed particularly by the largest, most systemically important financial institutions.

Supplementary Leverage Ratio

In April 2014, the FDIC published a final rule that, in part, revises minimum capital requirements and, for advanced approaches banks,[1] introduces the supplementary leverage ratio requirement. The Office of the Comptroller of the Currency (OCC) and the Federal Reserve adopted a final rule in October 2013 that is substantially identical to the FDIC's final rule. Collectively, these rules are referred to as the Basel III capital rules.

The Basel III rulemaking includes a new supplementary leverage ratio requirement – an important enhancement to the international capital framework. Prior to this rule, there was no international leverage ratio requirement. For the first time, the Basel III accord included an international minimum leverage ratio, and consistent with the agreement, the Basel III rulemaking includes a three percent minimum supplementary leverage ratio. This ratio, which takes effect in 2018, applies to large, internationally active banking organizations, and requires them to maintain a minimum supplementary leverage ratio of three percent (in addition to meeting other capital ratio requirements, including the agencies' long-standing Tier 1 leverage ratio).

In April 2014, the FDIC, the OCC and the Federal Reserve also finalized an Enhanced Supplementary Leverage Ratio final rule for the largest and most systemically important bank holding companies (BHCs) and their insured banks. This rule strengthens the supplementary leverage capital requirements beyond the levels required in the Basel III accord. Eight banking organizations are covered by these Enhanced Supplementary Leverage standards based on the thresholds in the final rule.

The agencies' analysis suggests that the three percent minimum supplementary leverage ratio contained in the international Basel III accord would not have appreciably mitigated the growth in leverage among SIFIs in the years leading up to the crisis. Accordingly, the Enhanced Supplementary Leverage standards that the agencies finalized in April will help achieve one of the most important objectives of the capital reforms: addressing the buildup of excessive leverage that contributes to systemic risk.

Under the Enhanced Supplementary Leverage standards, covered insured depository institutions (IDIs) will need to satisfy a six percent supplementary leverage ratio to be considered well capitalized for prompt corrective action (PCA) purposes. The supplementary leverage ratio includes off-balance sheet exposures in its denominator, unlike the longstanding U.S. leverage ratio which requires capital only for balance sheet assets. This means that more capital is needed to satisfy the supplementary leverage ratio than to satisfy the U.S. leverage ratio if both ratios were set at the same level. For example, based on recent supervisory estimates of the off-balance sheet exposures of these banks, a six percent supplementary leverage ratio would correspond to roughly an 8.6 percent U.S. leverage requirement. Covered BHCs will need to maintain a supplementary leverage ratio of at least five percent (a three percent minimum plus a two percent buffer) to avoid restrictions on capital distributions and executive compensation. This corresponds to roughly a 7.2 percent U.S. leverage ratio.

An important consideration in calibrating the Enhanced Supplementary Leverage ratio was the idea that the increase in stringency of the leverage requirements and the risk-based requirements should be balanced. Leverage capital requirements and risk-based capital requirements are complementary, with each type of requirement offsetting potential weaknesses of the other. In this regard, the Basel III rules strengthened risk-based capital requirements to a much greater extent than they strengthened leverage requirements. The Enhanced Supplementary Leverage ratio standard will ensure that the leverage requirement continues to serve as an effective complement to the risk-based capital requirements of the largest, most systemically important banking organizations, thereby strengthening the capital base and the stability of the U.S. banking system.

Maintaining a strong capital base at the largest, most systemically important financial institutions (SIFIs) is particularly important because capital shortfalls at these institutions can contribute to systemic distress and lead to material adverse economic effects. These higher capital requirements will also put additional private capital at risk before the Deposit Insurance Fund (DIF) and the federal government's resolution mechanisms would be called upon. The final Enhanced Supplementary Leverage ratio rule is one of the most important steps the banking agencies have taken to strengthen the safety and soundness of the U.S. banking and financial systems.

On September 3, 2014, the FDIC Board also finalized a rule originally proposed in April 2014 that revises the denominator measure for the supplementary leverage ratio and introduced related public disclosure requirements. The changes in this rule apply to all advanced approaches banking organizations, including the eight covered companies that would be subject to the Enhanced Supplementary Leverage standards. The denominator changes are consistent with those agreed upon by the Basel Committee on Banking Supervision and would, in the aggregate, result in a modest further strengthening of the supplementary leverage ratio requirement as compared to the capital rules finalized in April.

Liquidity Coverage Ratio

On September 3, 2014, the FDIC issued a joint interagency final rule with the Federal Reserve Board and the OCC implementing a liquidity coverage ratio (LCR). During the recent financial crisis, many banks had insufficient liquid assets and could not borrow to meet their liquidity needs. The LCR final rule is designed to strengthen the liquidity positon of our largest financial institutions, thereby promoting safety and soundness and the stability of the U.S. financial system.

This final rule applies to the largest, internationally active banking organizations: U.S. banking organizations with $250 billion or more in total consolidated assets or $10 billion or more in on-balance sheet foreign exposure and their subsidiary depository institutions with $10 billion or more in total assets. The Federal Reserve also finalized a separate rule that would apply a modified LCR requirement to BHCs with between $50 billion and $250 billion in total consolidated assets. Other insured banks are not subject to the rule.

The LCR final rule establishes a quantitative minimum liquidity coverage ratio that builds upon approaches already used by a number of large banking organizations to manage liquidity risk. It requires a covered company to maintain an amount of unencumbered high-quality liquid assets (HQLA) sufficient to meet the total stressed net cash outflows over a prospective 30 calendar-day period. A covered company's total net cash outflow amount is determined by applying outflow and inflow rates described in the rule, which reflect certain stressed assumptions, against the balances of a covered company's funding sources, obligations, and assets over a 30 calendar-day period.

A number of commenters have expressed concern about the exclusion of municipal securities from HQLA in the final rule. It is our understanding that banks do not generally hold municipal securities for liquidity purposes, but rather for longer term investment and other objectives. We will monitor closely the impact of the rule on municipal securities and consider adjustments if necessary.

Margin Rule for Derivatives

Before the passage of the Dodd-Frank Act, the derivatives activities of financial institutions were largely unregulated. One of the issues observed in the crisis was that some financial institutions had entered into large over-the-counter (OTC) derivatives positions with other institutions without the prudent initial exchange of collateral — a basic safety-andsoundness practice known as margin — in support of the positions. Title VII addressed this situation in part by requiring the use of central clearinghouses for certain standardized derivatives contracts, and by requiring the exchange of collateral, i.e., margin, for derivatives that are not centrally cleared.

Central clearinghouses for derivatives routinely manage their risks by requiring counterparties to post collateral at the inception of a trade. This practice is known as initial margin, in effect a type of security deposit or performance bond. Moreover, central clearinghouses routinely require a counterparty to post additional collateral if the market value of the position moves against that counterparty, greatly reducing the likelihood the clearinghouse will be unable to collect amounts due from counterparties. This type of collateral is known as variation margin.

Sections 731 and 764 of the Dodd Frank Act requires the large dealers in swaps to adopt certain prudent margining practices for their OTC derivatives activities that clearinghouses use, namely the posting and collecting of initial and variation margin. The exchange of margin between parties to a trade on OTC derivatives is an important check on the buildup of counterparty risk that can occur with OTC derivatives without margin. More generally, the appropriate exchange of margin promotes financial stability by reducing systemic leverage in the derivatives marketplace and promotes the safety and soundness of banks by discouraging the excessive growth of risky OTC derivatives positions.

The FDIC recently approved an interagency proposed rule to establish minimum margin requirements for the swaps of an insured depository institution or other entity that: (1) is supervised by the FDIC, Federal Reserve, OCC, Federal Housing Finance Administration (FHFA), or Farm Credit Administration (FCA); and (2) is also registered with the Commodity Futures Trading Commission (CFTC) or the Securities and Exchange Commission (SEC) as a dealer or major participant in swaps. The proposed rule will be published in the Federal Register with a 60-day public comment period.

In developing this proposal, the FDIC, along with the other banking agencies, worked closely with the Basel Committee on Banking Supervision (BCBS) and the International Organization of Securities Commissions (IOSCO) to develop a proposed framework for margin requirements on non-cleared swaps (the "international margin framework") with the goal of creating an international standard for margin requirements on non-cleared swaps. After considering numerous comments, BCBS and IOSCO issued a final international margin framework in September 2013. The agencies' 2014 proposed rule is closely aligned with the principles and standards from the 2013 international framework. The E.U. and other jurisdictions also have issued similar proposals.

The proposed rule would require a covered swap entity (a swap dealer, major swap participant, security-based swap dealer, or major security-based swap participant) to exchange initial margin with counterparties that are: (1) registered with the CFTC or SEC as swap entities; or (2) financial end users with material swaps exposure -- that is, with more than $3 billion in notional exposure of OTC derivatives that are not cleared. The rule would not require a covered swap entity to collect initial margin from commercial end users. The agencies intend to maintain the status quo with respect to the way that banks interact with commercial end users.

The proposed rule would also require a covered swap entity to exchange variation margin on swaps with all counterparties that are: (1) swap entities; or (2) financial end users (regardless of whether the financial end user has a material swaps exposure). There is no requirement that a covered swap entity must collect or post variation margin with commercial end users.

Because community banks typically do not have more than $3 billion in notional exposure of OTC derivatives that are not cleared, the agencies expect that the proposed rule will not result in community banks being required to post initial margin. Community banks that do engage in OTC derivatives that are not cleared are likely already posting variation margin in the normal course of business, or in amounts too small to fall within the scope of the rule. As a result, the margin rule likely will have little, if any, impact on the vast majority of community banks.

RESOLUTION OF SYSTEMICALLY IMPORTANT FINANCIAL INSTITUTIONS

Resolution Plans – "Living Wills"

Under the framework of the Dodd-Frank Act, bankruptcy is the preferred option in the event of a SIFI's failure. To make this objective achievable, Title I of the Dodd-Frank Act requires that all BHCs with total consolidated assets of $50 billion or more, and nonbank financial companies that the Financial Stability Oversight Council (FSOC) determines could pose a threat to the financial stability of the United States, prepare resolution plans, or "living wills," to demonstrate how the company could be resolved in a rapid and orderly manner under the Bankruptcy Code in the event of the company's financial distress or failure. The living will process is an important new tool to enhance the resolvability of large financial institutions through the bankruptcy process.

In 2011, the FDIC and the FRB jointly issued a final rule (the 165(d) rule) implementing the resolution plan requirements of Section 165(d) of the Dodd-Frank Act. The 165(d) rule provided for staggered annual submission deadlines for resolution plans based on the size and complexity of the companies. Eleven of the largest, most complex institutions (collectively referred to as "first wave filers") submitted initial plans in 2012 and revised plans in 2013.

During 2013, the remaining 120 institutions submitted their initial resolution plans under the 165(d) rule. The FSOC also designated three nonbank financial institutions for Federal Reserve supervision that year. In July 2014, 13 firms that previously had submitted at least one resolution plan submitted revised resolution plans, and the 3 nonbank financial companies designated by the FSOC submitted their initial resolution plans. The Federal Reserve and the FDIC granted requests for extensions to two firms whose second resolution plan submissions would have been due July 1. Those plans are now due to the agencies by October 1, 2014. The remaining 116 firms are expected to submit their second submission revised resolution plans in December 2014.

Following the review of the initial resolution plans submitted in 2012, the Federal Reserve and the FDIC issued joint guidance in April 2013 to provide clarification and direction for developing 2013 resolution plan submissions. The Federal Reserve and the FDIC identified an initial set of obstacles to a rapid and orderly resolution that covered companies were expected to address in the plans. The five obstacles identified in the guidance—multiple competing insolvencies, potential lack of global cooperation, operational interconnectedness, counterparty actions, and funding and liquidity—represent the key impediments to an orderly resolution. The 2013 plans should have included the actions or steps the companies have taken or propose to take to remediate or otherwise mitigate each obstacle and a timeline for any proposed actions. The agencies also extended the deadline for submitting revised plans from July 1, 2013, to October 1, 2013, to give the firms additional time to develop resolution plan submissions that addressed the agencies' instructions.

Section 165(d) of the Dodd-Frank Act and the jointly issued implementing regulation[2] require the FDIC and the Federal Reserve to review the 165(d) plans. If the agencies jointly determine that a plan is not credible or would not facilitate an orderly resolution under the U. S. Bankruptcy Code, the FDIC and the Federal Reserve must notify the filer of the areas in which the plan is deficient. The filer must resubmit a revised plan that addresses the deficiencies within 90 days (or other specified timeframe).

The FDIC and the Federal Reserve have completed their reviews of the 2013 resolution plans submitted to the agencies by the eleven bank holding companies that submitted their revised resolution plans in October 2013. On August 5, 2014, the agencies issued letters to each of these first wave filers detailing the specific shortcomings of each firm's plan and the requirements for the 2015 submission.

While the shortcomings of the plans varied across the first wave firms, the agencies have identified several common features of the plans' shortcomings, including: (1) assumptions that the agencies regard as unrealistic or inadequately supported, such as assumptions about the likely behavior of customers, counterparties, investors, central clearing facilities, and regulators; and (2) the failure to make, or even to identify, the kinds of changes in firm structure and practices that would be necessary to enhance the prospects for orderly resolution. The agencies will require that the annual plans submitted by the first wave filers on July 1, 2015, demonstrate that those firms are making significant progress to address all the shortcomings identified in the letters, and are taking actions to improve their resolvability under the U.S. Bankruptcy Code. These actions include:

- establishing a rational and less complex legal structure which would take into account the best alignment of legal entities and business lines to improve the firm's resolvability;
- developing a holding company structure that supports resolvability, including maintaining sufficient longer term debt;
- amending, on an industry-wide and firm-specific basis, financial contracts to provide for a stay of certain early termination rights of counterparties triggered by insolvency proceedings;
- ensuring the continuity of shared services that support critical operations and core business lines throughout the resolution process; and
- demonstrating operational capabilities for resolution preparedness, such as the ability to produce reliable information in a timely manner.

Agency staff will work with each of the first wave filers to discuss required improvements in its resolution plan and the efforts, both proposed and in progress, to facilitate each firm's preferred resolution strategy. The agencies are also committed to finding an appropriate balance between transparency and confidentiality of proprietary and supervisory information in the resolution plans. As such, the agencies will be working with these firms to explore ways to enhance public transparency of future plan submissions.

Based upon its review of submissions by first wave filers, the FDIC Board of Directors determined, pursuant to section 165(d) of the Dodd-Frank Act, that the plans submitted by the first wave filers are not credible and do not facilitate an orderly resolution under the U.S. Bankruptcy Code. The FDIC and the Federal Reserve agreed that in the event that a first wave filer has not, by July 1, 2015, submitted a plan responsive to the shortcomings identified in the letter sent to that firm, the agencies expect to use their authority under section 165(d) to determine that a resolution plan does not meet the requirements of the Dodd-Frank Act.

Improvements to Bankruptcy

At the December 2013 meeting of the FDIC's Systemic Resolution Advisory Committee, the FDIC heard how the existing bankruptcy process could be improved to better apply to SIFIs. The current provisions of the U.S. Bankruptcy Code do not expressly take into account certain features of SIFIs that distinguish these firms from other entities that are typically resolvable under bankruptcy without posing risk to the U.S. financial system. Issues such as the authority to impose a stay on qualified financial contracts and the ability to move part of a bankrupt firm into a bridge entity in an expeditious and efficient fashion are left unaddressed in current law. It also is unclear whether traditional debtor-in-possession financing, which is available under bankruptcy, would be sufficient to address the significant liquidity needs arising from the failure of a SIFI. A further challenge in a U.S. bankruptcy proceeding would be how it could foster global cooperation with foreign authorities, courts, creditors, or other pertinent parties, including U.S. financial regulatory officials, to ensure that their interests will be protected.

Additionally, a number of scholars, policy analysts, and public officials have made helpful proposals for changes to the U.S. Bankruptcy Code that would facilitate the resolution of a SIFI in bankruptcy. The FDIC has been reaching out to those in the bankruptcy community to discuss ways to enhance the U.S. Bankruptcy Code to facilitate an orderly failure of a SIFI. In addition, the FDIC has been working with foreign authorities to encourage the International Swaps and Derivatives Association (ISDA) to modify its standard-form contracts to facilitate resolution in bankruptcy. The FDIC supports these efforts and is prepared to work with Congress on modifications to the U.S. Bankruptcy Code for the treatment of SIFIs in bankruptcy.

Implementation of Title II

Congress also recognized that there may be circumstances in which the resolution of a SIFI under the U.S. Bankruptcy Code would have serious adverse effects on financial stability in the U.S. Accordingly, in Title II of the Dodd-Frank Act, Congress provided the FDIC with orderly liquidation authority to resolve a failing SIFI as a last resort in the event that resolution under the U.S. Bankruptcy Code would result in systemic disruption of the financial system. This Orderly Liquidation Authority serves as a backstop to protect against the risk of systemic disruption to the U.S. financial system and allows for resolution in a manner that results in shareholders losing their investment, creditors taking a loss and management responsible for the failure being replaced, resulting in an orderly unwinding of the firm without cost to U.S. taxpayers.

In my February testimony before this Committee, I described how the FDIC is developing a strategic approach, referred to as Single Point of Entry (SPOE) strategy, to carry out its Orderly Liquidation Authority for resolving a SIFI in the event it is determined that a firm cannot be resolved under bankruptcy without posing a risk to the U.S. financial system. Under the SPOE strategy, the FDIC would be appointed receiver of the top-tier parent holding company of the financial group following the company's failure and the completion of the recommendation, determination, and expedited judicial review process set forth in Title II of the Act. For the SPOE strategy to be successful, it is critical that the top-tier holding company maintain a sufficient amount of unsecured debt that would be available to provide capital to manage the orderly unwinding of the failed firm. In a resolution, the holding company's debt would be used to absorb losses and keep the operating subsidiaries open and operating until an orderly wind-down could be achieved.

In support of the SPOE strategy, the Federal Reserve, in consultation with the FDIC, is considering the merits of a regulatory requirement that the largest, most complex U.S. banking firms maintain a minimum amount of unsecured debt at the holding company level, in addition to the regulatory capital those companies already are required to maintain. Such a requirement would ensure that there is sufficient debt at the holding company level to absorb losses at the failed firm.

Cross-border Issues

Advance planning and cross-border coordination for the resolution of globally active SIFIs (G-SIFIs) will be essential to minimizing disruptions to global financial markets. Recognizing that G-SIFIs create complex international legal and operational concerns, the FDIC continues to reach out to foreign regulators to establish frameworks for effective cross-border cooperation.

As part of our bilateral efforts, the FDIC and the Bank of England, in conjunction with the prudential regulators in our respective jurisdictions, have been developing contingency plans for the failure of a G-SIFI that has operations in the United States and the United Kingdom. Of the 28 G-SIFIs identified by the Financial Stability Board (FSB) in the G-20 countries, four are headquartered in the United Kingdom, and eight in the United States. Moreover, more than 70 percent of the reported foreign activities of the eight U.S. G-SIFIs originate in the United Kingdom. The magnitude of the cross-border financial relationships and local activity of GSIFIs in the United States and the United Kingdom makes the U.S.-U.K. bilateral relationship by far the most significant with regard to the resolution of G-SIFIs. Therefore, our two countries have a strong mutual interest in ensuring that the failure of such an institution could be resolved at no cost to taxpayers and without placing the financial system at risk.

The FDIC and U.K. authorities are continuing to work together to address the cross-border issues raised in the December 2012 joint paper on resolution strategies and the December 2013 tabletop exercise between staffs at the FDIC, the Bank of England (including the Prudential Regulation Authority), the Federal Reserve, and the Federal Reserve Bank of New York. This work is intended to identify actions that could be taken by each regulator to implement the SPOE resolution strategy in the event of a resolution.

The FDIC also has continued to coordinate with representatives from other European authorities to discuss issues of mutual interest, including the resolution of European G-SIFIs and ways in which we can harmonize receivership actions. The FDIC and the European Commission (E.C.) continue to work collaboratively through a joint Working Group composed of senior executives from the FDIC and the E.C., focusing on both resolution and deposit insurance issues. The Working Group meets twice a year, in addition to less formal meetings and exchanges of detailees. In 2014, the Working Group convened in May, and there has been ongoing collaboration at the staff level. The FDIC and the E.C. have had in-depth discussions regarding the FDIC's experience with resolution as well as the FDIC's SPOE strategy.

The E.U. recently adopted important legislation related to the resolution of global SIFIs, such as the E.U.-wide Credit Institution and Investment Firm Recovery and Resolution Directive, amendments that further harmonize deposit guarantee schemes E.U.-wide, and a Single Resolution Mechanism for Euro-area Member States and others that opt-in. The E.U. is now working to implement that legislation through secondary legislation, in the form of guidelines and standards, and by establishing the organizational capacity necessary to support the work of the Single Resolution Board under the Single Resolution Mechanism. FDIC and E.C. staffs continue to collaborate in exchanging information related to this implementation work. In June 2014, at the request of the E.C., the FDIC conducted a two-day seminar on resolutions for resolution authorities and a broad audience of E.C. staff involved in resolutions-related matters.

The FDIC continues to foster relationships with other jurisdictions that regulate G-SIFIs, including Switzerland, Germany, France and Japan. So far in 2014, the FDIC has had significant principal and staff-level engagements with these countries to discuss cross-border issues and potential impediments that would affect the resolution of a G-SIFI. We will continue this work during the remainder of 2014 and in 2015 and plan to host tabletop exercises with staff from these authorities. We also held preliminary discussions on developing joint resolution strategy papers, similar to the one with the United Kingdom, as well as possible exchanges of detailees.

In a significant demonstration of cross-border cooperation on resolution issues, the FDIC signed a November 2013 joint letter with the Bank of England, the Swiss Financial Market Supervisory Authority and the German Federal Financial Supervisory Authority to ISDA. This letter encouraged ISDA to develop provisions in derivatives contracts that would provide for short-term suspension of early termination rights and other remedies in the event of a G-SIFI resolution. The authorities are now providing comments on proposed draft ISDA protocols that would contractually implement these provisions during a resolution under bankruptcy or under a special resolution regime. The adoption of the provisions would allow derivatives contracts to remain in effect throughout the resolution process under a number of potential resolution strategies. The FDIC believes that the development of a contractual solution has the potential to remove a key impediment to cross-border resolution.

We anticipate continuation of our international coordination and outreach and will continue to work to resolve impediments to an orderly resolution of a G-SIFI.

RISK RETENTION

On August 28, 2013, the FDIC approved an NPR issued jointly with five other federal agencies to implement the credit risk retention requirement in Section 941 of the Dodd-Frank Act. The proposed rule seeks to ensure that securitization sponsors have appropriate incentives to monitor and ensure the underwriting and quality of assets being securitized. The proposed rule generally requires that the sponsor of any asset-backed security (ABS) retain an economic interest equal to at least five percent of the aggregate credit risk of the collateral. This was the second proposal under Section 941; the first was issued in April 2011.

The FDIC reviewed approximately 240 comments on the August 2013 NPR. Many comments addressed the proposed definition of a "qualified residential mortgage" (QRM), which is a mortgage that is statutorily exempt from risk retention requirements under the Dodd-Frank Act. The NPR proposed to align the definition of QRM with the definition of "qualified mortgage" (QM) adopted by the Consumer Financial Protection Bureau (CFPB) in 2013. The NPR also included a request for public comment on an alternative QRM definition that would add certain underwriting standards to the existing QM definition. The August 2013 proposal also sets forth criteria for securitizations of commercial real estate loans, commercial loans, and automobile loans that meet specific conservative credit quality standards to be exempt from risk retention requirements.

The issuing agencies have reviewed the comments, met with interested groups to discuss their concerns and have given careful consideration to all the issues raised. The agencies have made significant progress toward finalizing the rule and expect to complete the rule in the near term.

VOLCKER RULE IMPLEMENTATION

In adopting the Volcker Rule, the agencies recognized that clear and consistent application of the final rule across all banking entities would be extremely important. To help ensure this consistency, the five agencies formed an interagency Volcker Rule Implementation Working Group. The Working Group has been meeting on a weekly basis and has been able to make meaningful progress on coordinating implementation. The Working Group has been able to agree on a number of interpretive issues and has published several Frequently Asked Questions. In addition, the Working Group has been able to successfully develop a standardized metrics reporting template, which has been provided to and tested by the industry. In addition, the Working Group is developing a collaborative supervisory approach by the agencies.

COMMUNITY BANKS

Focus of Research

Since 2011, the FDIC has been engaged in a sustained research effort to better understand the issues related to community banks – those institutions that provide traditional, relationship-based banking services in their local communities. Our initial findings were presented in a comprehensive study published in December 2012. The study covered topics such as structural change, geography, financial performance, lending strategies and capital formation, and it highlighted the critical importance of community banks to our economy and our banking system. While the study found that community banks account for about 14 percent of the banking assets in the U.S, they also account for around 45 percent of all the small loans to businesses and farms made by all banks in the U.S. In addition, the study found that, of the more than 3,100 U.S. counties, nearly 20 percent (more than 600 counties) – including small towns, rural communities and urban neighborhoods – would have no physical banking presence if not for the community banks operating there.

The study also showed that community banks' core business model – defined around careful relationship lending, funded by stable core deposits, and focused on the local geographic community that the bank knows well – performed comparatively well during the recent banking crisis. Among the more than 500 banks that have failed since 2007, the highest rates of failure were observed among non-community banks and among community banks that departed from the traditional model and tried to grow with risky assets often funded by volatile brokered deposits.

Our community bank research agenda remains active. Since the beginning of the year, FDIC analysts have published new papers dealing with consolidation among community banks, the effects of long-term rural depopulation on community banks, and the efforts of Minority Depository Institutions to provide essential banking services in the communities they serve.

We have also instituted a new section in the FDIC *Quarterly Banking Profile*, or QBP, that focuses specifically on community banks. Although some 93 percent of FDIC-insured institutions met our community bank definition in the first quarter, they hold a relatively small portion of industry assets; as a result, larger bank trends tend to obscure community bank trends. This new quarterly report on the structure, activities and performance of community banks should help smaller institutions compare their results with those of other community banks as well as those of larger institutions. Introducing this regular quarterly report is one example of the FDICs commitment to maintain an active program of research and analysis on community banking issues in the years to come.

Subchapter S

The Basel III capital rules introduce a capital conservation buffer for all banks (separate from the supplementary leverage ratio buffer applicable to the largest and most systemically important BHCs and their insured banks). If a bank's risk-based capital ratios fall below specified thresholds, dividends and discretionary bonus payments become subject to limits. The buffer is meant to conserve capital in banks whose capital ratios are close to the minimums and encourage banks to remain well-capitalized.

In July 2014, the FDIC issued guidance clarifying how it will evaluate requests by S corporation banks to make dividend payments that would otherwise be prohibited under the capital conservation buffer. S corporation banks have expressed concern about the capital conservation buffer because of a unique tax issue their shareholders face. Federal income taxes of S corporation banks are paid by their investors. If an S corporation bank has income, but is limited or prohibited from paying dividends, its shareholders may have to pay taxes on their pass-through share of the S-corporation's income from their own resources. Relatively few S corporation banks are likely to be affected by this issue, and in any case not for several years. The buffer is phased-in starting in 2016 and is not fully in place until 2019.

As described in the guidance, if an S corporation bank faces this tax issue, the Basel III capital rules allow it (like any other bank) to request an exception from the dividend restriction that the buffer would otherwise impose. The primary regulator can approve such a request if consistent with safety and soundness. Absent significant safety and soundness concerns about the requesting bank, the FDIC expects to approve on a timely basis exception requests by well-rated S corporations to pay dividends of up to 40 percent of net income to shareholders to cover taxes on their pass-through share of the bank's earnings.

Cybersecurity

In its role as supervisor of state-chartered financial institutions that are not members of the Federal Reserve System, the FDIC works with other bank regulators to analyze emerging cyber threats, bank security breaches, and other technology incidents. An important initiative of the FFIEC is a project to assess the level of cybersecurity readiness at banks, technology service providers and our own supervisory policies. The agencies plan to review any identified gaps to enhance supervisory policies to address cyber threats.

Recognizing that addressing cyber risks can be especially challenging for community banks, the FDIC has taken a number of actions in addition to those taken by the FFIEC to further improve awareness of cyber risks and encourage practices to protect against threats. In April, the FDIC issued a press release urging financial institutions to utilize available cyber resources to identify and help mitigate potential threats. During the first quarter of 2014, the FDIC distributed a package to all FDIC supervised banks that included a variety of tools to assist them in developing cyber readiness. As part of this kit, the FDIC developed a "Cyber Challenge" resource for community banks to use in assessing their preparedness for a cyber-related incident, and videos and simulation exercises were made available on www.FDIC.gov and mailed to all FDIC-supervised banks. The Cyber Challenge is intended to assist banks in beginning a discussion of the potential impact of IT disruptions on important banking functions. In April, the FDIC also re-issued three documents on technology outsourcing that contain practical ideas for community banks to consider when they engage in technology outsourcing. The documents are: *Effective Practices for Selecting a Service Provider*; *Tools to Manage Technology Providers' Performance Risk: Service Level Agreements*; and *Techniques for Managing Multiple Service Providers*.

In addition to the FDIC's operations and technology examination program, the FDIC monitors cyber-security issues in the banking industry on a regular basis through on-site examinations, regulatory reports, and intelligence reports. The FDIC also works with a number of groups, including the Finance and Banking Information Infrastructure Committee, the Financial Services Sector Coordinating Council for Critical Infrastructure Protection and Homeland Security, the Financial Services Information Sharing and Analysis Center, other regulatory agencies and law enforcement to share information on emerging issues.

CONCLUSION

Thank you for the opportunity to share with the Committee the work that the FDIC has been doing to address systemic risk in the aftermath of the financial crisis. I would be glad to respond to your questions.

STATUS OF FDIC DODD-FRANK ACT RULEMAKINGS AUGUST 2014

Completed FDIC-only Rulemakings

FDIC has met all applicable deadlines in issuing those required regulations in the Dodd-Frank Wall Street Reform and Consumer Protection Act for which it is solely responsible. These include:

- Orderly Liquidation Authority (OLA) Regulations
  - Inflation adjustment for wage claims against financial company in receivership;
  - Executive compensation clawbacks and definition of compensation;
  - Definition of 'predominantly engaged in activities financial in nature' for title II purposes; and
  - Rules governing asset purchaser eligibility.
- Deposit Insurance Fund Management Regulations
  - Regulations establishing an asset-based assessment base;
  - Regulations implementing permanent $250,000 coverage;
  - Elimination of pro-cyclical assessments; dividend regulations;
  - Restoration plan to increase the minimum reserve ratio from 1.15 to 1.35% by Sept. 30, 2020; and
  - Regulations implementing temporary full Deposit Insurance coverage for non-interest bearing transaction accounts (Program expired 12/31/12).

The FDIC has also issued several optional rules, including the following OLA rules:

- Rules governing payment of post-insolvency interest to creditors;

- Rules establishing the proper measure of actual, direct, compensatory damages caused by repudiation of contingent claims;
- Rules governing the priority of creditors and the treatment of secured creditors;
- Rules governing the administrative claims process;
- Rules governing the treatment of mutual insurance holding companies; and
- Rules providing for enforcement of contracts of subsidiaries or affiliates of a covered financial company.

Completed Interagency Rules

FDIC and its fellow agencies have issued a number of joint or interagency regulations. These include:

- Title I resolution plan requirements;
- Regulations implementing self-administered stress tests for financial companies;
- Minimum leverage capital requirements for IDIs (Collins §171(b)(1));
- Minimum risk-based capital requirements (Collins §171(b)(2));
- Capital requirements for activities that pose risks to the financial system (Collins §171(b)(7)) (as of July 9, 2013);
- Rules providing for calculation of the "maximum obligation limitation";
- Regulations on foreign currency futures;
- Removing regulatory references to credit ratings;
- Property appraisal requirements for higher cost mortgages;
- Appraisals for higher priced mortgages supplemental rule;
- Appraisal independence requirements;
- Volcker Rule Prohibition on Proprietary Trading and Investments in Covered Funds; and
- Interim final rule authorizing Retention of Interests in CDOs backed by Bank-Issued Trust Preferred Securities

Rulemakings in process—FDIC-only

- Annual Stress Test – revisions to "as-of" dates for financial data;
- Integration and Streamlining of adopted OTS regulations.

Interagency Rulemakings in process

- Additional OLA Rules:
    - Orderly liquidation of covered brokers and dealers;
    - Regulations regarding treatment of officers and directors of companies resolved under Title II; and
    - QFC recordkeeping rules;
- Regulations implementing the credit exposure reporting requirement for large BHCs and nonbank financial companies supervised by the FRB;
- Regulations implementing the "source of strength" requirement for BHCs, S&LHCs, and other companies that control IDIs;
- Capital and margin requirements for derivatives that are not cleared OTC;
- Regulations governing credit risk retention in asset-backed securitizations, including ABS backed by residential mortgages;
- Regulations governing enhanced compensation structure reporting and prohibiting inappropriate incentive-based payment arrangements;
- Rulemaking prohibiting retaliation against an IDI or other covered person that institutes an appeal of conflicting supervisory determinations by the CFPB and the appropriate prudential regulator; and
- Additional appraisals and related regulations:
    - Minimum requirements for registration of appraisal management companies and for the reporting of the activities of appraisal management companies to Appraisal Subcommittee;
    - Regulations to implement quality controls standards for automated valuation models; and
    - Regulations providing for appropriate appraisal review.

Other DFA Regulations and Guidance

- OMWI – Proposed Standards for Assessing Diversity in Regulated Entities;
- Stress Testing Guidance, including:
    - Economic Scenarios for 2014 Stress Testing;
    - Policy Statement on the Principles for Development and Distribution of Annual Stress Test Scenarios (FDIC-supervised institutions); and
    - Interagency Supervisory Guidance on Implementing Dodd-Frank Act Company-Run Stress Tests for Banking Organizations With Total Consolidated Assets of More Than $10 Billion But Less Than $50 Billion; and
- Interagency Statement on Supervisory Approach for Qualified and Non-Qualified Mortgage Loans

End Notes

[1] An advanced approaches bank is an insured depository institution (IDI) that is an advanced approaches national bank or Federal savings association under 12 CFR 3.100(b)(1), an advanced approaches Board-regulated institution under 12 CFR 217.100(b)(1), or an advanced approaches FDIC-supervised institution under 12 CFR 324.100(b)(1). In general, an IDI is an advanced approaches bank if it has total consolidated assets of $250 billion or more, has total consolidated on-balance sheet foreign exposures of $10 billion or more, or elects to use or is a subsidiary of an IDI, bank holding company, or savings and loan holding company that uses the advanced approaches to calculate risk-weighted assets.

[2] 12 CFR Part 243 and 12 CFR Part 381.

In: Large Financial Institutions
Editors: Franklin Pierce

ISBN: 978-1-63482-261-9

Chapter 5

SYSTEMICALLY IMPORTANT OR "TOO BIG TO FAIL" FINANCIAL INSTITUTIONS*

Marc Labonte

SUMMARY

Although "too big to fail" (TBTF) has been a perennial policy issue, it was highlighted by the near-collapse of several large financial firms in 2008. Financial firms are said to be TBTF when policy makers judge that their failure would cause unacceptable disruptions to the overall financial system, and they can be TBTF because of their size or interconnectedness. In addition to fairness issues, economic theory suggests that expectations that a firm will not be allowed to fail create moral hazard—if the creditors and counterparties of a TBTF firm believe that the government will protect them from losses, they have less incentive to monitor the firm's riskiness because they are shielded from the negative consequences of those risks. If so, they could have a funding advantage compared with other banks, which some call an implicit subsidy. S.Con.Res. 8, passed by the Senate on March 22, 2013, and H.Con.Res. 25, as amended and passed by the Senate on October 16, 2013, create a non-binding budget reserve fund that allows for future legislation to address the TBTF funding advantage.

There are a number of policy approaches—some complementary, some conflicting—to coping with the TBTF problem, including providing

* This is an edited, reformatted and augmented version of a Congressional Research Service publication, No. R42150, dated September 19, 2014.

government assistance to prevent TBTF firms from failing or systemic risk from spreading; enforcing "market discipline" to ensure that investors, creditors, and counterparties curb excessive risk-taking at TBTF firms; enhancing regulation to hold TBTF firms to stricter prudential standards than other financial firms; curbing firms' size and scope, by preventing mergers or compelling firms to divest assets, for example; minimizing spillover effects by limiting counterparty exposure; and instituting a special resolution regime for failing systemically important firms. A comprehensive policy is likely to incorporate more than one approach, as some approaches are aimed at preventing failures and some at containing fallout when a failure occurs.

Parts of the Wall Street Reform and Consumer Protection Act (Dodd-Frank Act; P.L. 111-203) address all of these policy approaches. For example, it created an enhanced prudential regulatory regime administered by the Federal Reserve for non-bank financial firms designated as "systemically important" by the Financial Stability Oversight Council (FSOC) and banks with more than $50 billion in assets. About 30 U.S. bank holding companies and a larger number of foreign banks have more than $50 billion in assets, and the FSOC has designated two insurers (AIG and Prudential) and GE Capital as systemically important. According to the insurer MetLife, FSOC has proposed to designate it as well. In addition, eight banks headquartered in the United States will be assessed capital surcharges under Basel III. H.R. 4881, ordered to be reported by the House Financial Services Committee on June 20, 2014, would place a one-year moratorium on FSOC designations. H.R. 5016, which passed the House on July 16, 2014, would not allow any funds to be used to designate a non-bank as systemically important or as posing a systemic threat to financial stability. S. 2270, as passed by the Senate, and H.R. 5461, as passed by the House, would allow regulators to exempt insurers from bank capital requirements (the "Collins Amendment" to the Dodd-Frank Act).

The Dodd-Frank Act also created a special resolution regime administered by the Federal Deposit Insurance Corporation to take into receivership failing firms that pose a threat to financial stability. This regime has not been used to date, and has some similarities to how the FDIC resolves failing banks. Statutory authority used to prevent financial firms from failing during the crisis has either expired or been narrowed by the Dodd-Frank Act.

INTRODUCTION

Although "too big to fail" (TBTF) has been a perennial policy issue, it was highlighted by the near-collapse of several large financial firms in 2008. Large financial firms that failed or required extraordinary government assistance in the recent crisis included depositories (Citigroup and Washington Mutual), government-sponsored enterprises (Fannie Mae and Freddie Mac), insurance companies (AIG), and investment banks (Bear Stearns and Lehman Brothers).[1] In many of these cases, policy makers justified the use of government resources on the grounds that the firms were "systemically important" or "too big to fail." TBTF is the concept that a firm's disorderly failure would cause widespread disruptions in financial markets that could not easily be contained. While the government had no explicit policy to rescue TBTF firms, several were rescued on those grounds once the crisis struck. TBTF subsequently became one of the systemic risk issues that policy makers grappled with in the wake of the recent crisis.

Systemic risk mitigation, including eliminating the TBTF problem, was a major goal of the Dodd-Frank Wall Street Reform and Consumer Protection Act (P.L. 111-203), comprehensive financial regulatory reform enacted in 2010.[2] Different parts of this legislation jointly address the "too big to fail" problem through requirements for enhanced regulation for safety and soundness for "systemically important" (also called "systemically significant") financial institutions (SIFIs), limits on size and the types of activities a firm can engage in (including proprietary trading and hedge fund sponsorship), and the creation of a new receivership regime for resolving failing non-banks that pose systemic risk.

About 30 U.S. bank holding companies and a larger number of foreign banks will automatically be subject to enhanced regulation because they have at least $50 billion in assets. In addition, the Financial Stability Oversight Council (FSOC), a council of U.S. regulators headed by the Treasury Secretary,[3] has designated two insurers (AIG and Prudential) and one other non-bank (GE Capital) as "systemically important," and therefore subject to heightened prudential regulation.[4] According to the insurer MetLife, FSOC has proposed to designate it as well.[5] H.R. 4881, ordered to be reported by the House Financial Services Committee on June 20, 2014, would place a one-year moratorium on FSOC designations of non-banks as systemically important upon enactment. The Financial Services and General Government Appropriations Act of 2014 (H.R. 5016), which passed the House on July 16, 2014, would not allow any funds to be used to designate a non-bank as systemically important or as posing a systemic threat to financial stability. S. 2270, which passed the Senate on June 5, 2014, would allow the regulators to exempt insurers from the "Collins Amendment" to the Dodd-Frank Act—bank capital requirements that would otherwise apply because the insurers are bank holding companies or have been designated as systemically important. Title I of H.R. 5461, which passed the House on September 16, 2014, contains the same language as S. 2270.

In addition, the Financial Stability Board, an international forum, has identified 29 banks, 8 of which are headquartered in the United States, as "globally systemically important banks" (GSIBs) and 9 insurers as "globally systemically important insurers," 3 of which are headquartered in the United States.[6] Under the Basel III Accord, banks identified by the Financial Stability Board as systemically important are subject to higher capital standards, including a higher supplementary leverage ratio.

Ultimately, the failure of a large firm is the only test of whether the TBTF problem still exists. In the meantime, studies have found mixed evidence as to whether large financial firms can still borrow at advantageous rates compared with other firms because investors—rightly or wrongly— perceive that they enjoy TBTF status.[7] S.Con.Res. 8, passed by the Senate on March 22, 2013, and H.Con.Res. 25, as amended and passed by the Senate on October 16, 2013, create a nonbinding budget reserve fund that allows for future legislation to address the TBTF funding advantage. Some critics argue that this legislation does not go far enough to solve the TBTF problem, and others argue it will have the perverse effect of exacerbating the TBTF problem. There has not yet been legislation enacted to reform Fannie Mae and Freddie Mac, which remain in government receivership.

This report discusses the economic issues raised by TBTF, broad policy options, and policy changes made by the relevant Dodd-Frank provisions. This report also discusses recent legislation addressing the TBTF issue in the 113th Congress. The report ends with an **Appendix** reviewing the historical experience with TBTF before and during the recent crisis.

ECONOMIC ISSUES

Context

Evidence on the size of financial firms can be viewed in absolute and relative terms—relative to other industries and within the industry (i.e., concentration). In the first quarter of 2014, there were 39 U.S. banks with more than $50 billion in assets, of which 4 had more than $1.5 trillion in assets. Ten years earlier, there was only one U.S. bank with more than $1 trillion in assets.[8]

In recent decades, the U.S. banking industry has become more concentrated, meaning that a greater percentage of total industry assets is held by large banks. Assets of the five largest bank holding companies (BHCs) totaled 52% of total BHC assets at the end of 2013.[9] According to one study, the three largest banks held 5% to 15% of total commercial banking depository assets from the 1930s until the 1990s. The share of the top three then rose until it had reached about 40% by 2008.[10] By international standards, U.S. banks are not that large, however. Relative to GDP, the combined assets of the top three U.S. banks were the lowest of any major OECD economy in 2009.[11]

The four largest BHCs each held a majority of their assets in commercial bank subsidiaries. Not all very large financial institutions are commercial banks, however. Companies with more than $100 billion in assets include insurers, broker-dealers, investment funds, specialized lenders, and government-sponsored enterprises (Fannie Mae and Freddie Mac are among the largest firms overall by assets). Over the long run, large non-banks have emerged, in part because of the growth in "shadow banking."[12] Shadow banking refers to bank-like activities, such as lending, in the non-bank financial sector.[13] According to one estimate, assets of broker-dealers grew from 3% of commercial bank assets in 1980 to nearly 30% in 2007. Over the same period, hedge fund capital increased from less than 1% of bank capital to more than 100%.[14] While non-banks have been engaging in more bank-like activities, banks have also moved into non-banking businesses. Today, a bank can incorporate as a financial holding company that has depository subsidiaries, insurance subsidiaries, and broker-dealer subsidiaries, for example.

A few large firms make up a large fraction of revenues in each major segment of the financial industry. **Table 1** shows the 4 largest and 20 largest firms' respective shares of total industry revenue for the major industry NAICS (North American Industrial Classification System) classifications. According to the latest available Census data, securities firms are the most concentrated when measured by revenue, and the industry grew more concentrated between 1997 and 2007, whether measured by the top 4 or top 20 firms. Credit intermediation, which includes banking, grew significantly more concentrated between 1997 and 2002, but became slightly less concentrated between 2002 and 2007. Insurance firms became slightly more concentrated between 1997 and 2007.

Table 1. Large Financial Firms' Share of Total Industry Revenue, 1997-2007 (percentage)

	Top 4 Firms			Top 20 Firms		
	1997	2002	2007	1997	2002	2007
Credit Intermediation (NAICS 522)	12.6	21.5	20.6	33.4	46.4	45.0
Securities (NAICS 523)	19.3	23.6	24.6	47.7	50.0	51.8
Insurance (NAICS 524)	13.7	12.6	14.6	37.9	36.9	40.6
Funds and Trusts (NAICS 525)	19.0	24.4	n/a	48.9	57.0	n/a

Source: U.S. Census Bureau, *Economic Census*, various years.
Notes: Data are reported by NAICS code.

It remains to be seen how concentration, as measured by the Census, was affected by the financial crisis. The financial crisis reduced the number of large financial firms, but also led to an increase in the size of the remaining large firms, through a series of mergers and acquisitions.[15]

Compared with other industries, financial firms are large in dollar terms when measured by assets and liabilities but not by measures such as revenue because of the nature of financial intermediation. For example, there are only two firms (Berkshire Hathaway and General Electric) with revenues from financial businesses—and both have substantial non-financial revenues—and no bank holding companies among the 10 largest Fortune 500 firms in 2013 when measured by revenue, but financial companies are the only Fortune 500 firms with more than $1 trillion in assets.[16] Financial firms are also not as concentrated as some other industries.[17] In layman's terms, there is no "Pepsi/Coke" dominance in the financial sector. These comparisons may help to illustrate why traditional policy tools such as antitrust have not been used against large financial firms recently and suggest that the TBTF phenomenon in finance lies in the nature of financial intermediation, which is the topic of the next section.

Economic Effects of Too Big to Fail

Contagion can be transmitted from small or large financial institutions (see the following text box), but large firms pose unique problems. Firms are likely to have more counterparty exposure to large firms, and the losses or disruptions caused by counterparty exposure when a large firm fails could be severe enough to lead to failure of third parties. Problems at large firms could also lead to "fire sales" in specific securities markets that depress market prices, thereby imposing losses on other holders of similar securities.[18] Some economists argue that the real problem is some firms are "too interconnected to fail." That is, it is not the sheer size of certain firms that causes contagion, but the fact that most activity in certain key market segments flows through those firms.[19] According to the International Monetary Fund (IMF), a few large firms "dominate key market segments ranging from private securitization and derivatives dealing to triparty repo and leveraged investor financing."[20] Were the interconnected firm to fail, other firms would have difficulty absorbing the failed firm's business, and there would be disruptions to the flow of credit. If problems in one market segment undermine an interconnected firm, problems can spread to the other market segments in which the firm operates.

Why Are Financial Firms Vulnerable to Instability?

Economists consider financial firms to be uniquely vulnerable to instability because a fundamental feature of financial intermediation is the use of short-term liabilities (debt or deposits) to finance long-term assets (e.g., loans). As a result, assets cannot be liquidated fast enough or at a sufficient price to fund redemptions in a panic. The use of liabilities, rather than equity, to finance most assets (referred to as "leverage") can result in losses exceeding equity, which results in insolvency, or an inability to meet obligations to all creditors in full. These features make financial intermediaries inherently vulnerable to runs—since those who redeem funds first are thought more likely to access their funds, there is an incentive for creditors to rush to redeem, whether the firm is suffering from a liquidity problem or a solvency problem. Panics can be self-fulfilling: whether or not the institution originally had financial problems, a panic can lead to its failure. Panics are also prone to contagion—the observation of a run at one institution can lead creditors to run on other institutions, because of perceived connections or similarities to the original firm.

The classic run involves depositors at banks, but the recent crisis demonstrated that other debt markets can also be susceptible to runs for banks and non-bank financial firms. Non-bank financial firms were highly reliant on short-term borrowing, through financial instruments such as repurchase agreements and commercial paper. They favor short-term borrowing because in normal conditions these short-term funds are inexpensive and readily available.

The short maturity of these instruments meant that loans needed to be rolled over frequently. The proximate cause of most of these firms' failure was the inability to roll over maturing debt. When these firms experienced financial difficulties, counterparties became reluctant (or were not in a position) to transact and maintain business relationships with them. For example, major investment banks are "market-makers" (ready buyers and sellers) for securities markets; provide prime brokerage services for hedge funds; are major participants in over-the-counter markets for securities such as derivatives; play important roles in payment, clearing, and settlement activities; and so on. If counterparties in any of these areas are no longer willing to transact with the firm because of fears of a run, the firm's financial difficulties can quickly compound.

Although some policy makers have dismissed the claim that any firm could be too big to fail, many analysts believe the failure of Lehman Brothers, occurring in the context of difficulties at several large financial firms, was the proximate cause of the worsening of the crisis in September 2008.[21] One can debate whether policy actions in the months leading up to Lehman Brothers' failure made its failure more or less disruptive, but it is fair to say that it is unlikely that the panic that followed could have been avoided since the nature of the disruptions its failure caused (notably, its effect on money markets) was not widely foreseen.[22] "Bailing out" TBTF firms may not be an intended policy objective, but may become the second-best crisis containment measure when the failure of a TBTF firm is imminent to prevent fallout to the broader financial system and the economy as a whole.

While many people object to rescuing TBTF firms on moral or philosophical grounds, there are also economic reasons why having firms that are TBTF is inefficient. In general, for market forces to lead to an efficient allocation of resources, finding a good use of resources must be financially rewarded and a bad use must be financially punished. Firms generally run into financial problems when they have persistently allocated capital to inefficient uses. To save such a firm would be expected to retard efforts to shift that capital to more efficient uses, and may allow the firm to continue making more bad decisions in the future. The TBTF problem results in too much financial intermediation taking place at large firms and too little at other firms from the perspective of economic efficiency, although not necessarily from the perspective of noneconomic policy rationales.[23] Because large and small financial firms do not serve exactly the same customers or operate in exactly the same lines of business, too much capital will flow to the customers and in the lines of business of large firms and too little to those of small firms in the presence of TBTF.

Preventing TBTF firms from failing is argued to be necessary for maintaining the stability of the financial system in the short run. But rescuing TBTF firms is predicted to lead to a less stable financial system in the long run because of moral hazard that weakens market discipline. Moral hazard refers to the theory that if TBTF firms expect that failure will be prevented, they have an incentive to take greater risks than they otherwise would because they are shielded from at least some negative consequences of those risks.[24] In general, riskier investments have a higher rate of return to compensate for the greater risk of failure. If TBTF firms believe that they will not be allowed to fail, then private firms capture any additional profits that result from high-risk activities, while the government bears any extreme losses. Thus, if TBTF firms believe that they will be rescued, they have an incentive to behave in a way that makes it more likely they will fail.

To see how the moral hazard problem is transmitted, it is helpful to examine who gets directly "rescued" when the government intervenes to prevent the fallout to the overall financial system and broader economy. The direct beneficiaries of a rescue will include some combination of the firm's management, owners (e.g., shareholders), creditors (including depositors), account holders, and counterparties. Under bankruptcy, these groups would bear losses to differing degrees depending on the legal priority of their claims. Government assistance, depending on its terms, can protect some or all of these groups from losses. In some recent government rescues, management has been replaced; in others, it has not. Even if management believes that losses will lead to removal, managers may prefer excessive risk taking (with higher expected profits) because they are not personally liable for the firms' losses.[25] In some cases, shareholders have borne some losses through stock dilution, although their losses may have been smaller than they would have been in a bankruptcy. Creditors, account holders, and counterparties have generally been shielded from any losses. Thus, government rescues have not mitigated the moral hazard problem for creditors and counterparties. Because the government will only intervene in the case of extreme losses, moral hazard may manifest itself primarily in areas affected only by systemic events (referred to as "tail risk"). For example, extreme losses from counterparty risk may be ignored by counterparties to TBTF firms if they believe that government will always intervene to prevent failure; if so, costs (such as the amount of margin a counterparty will require) will be lower for TBTF firms than competitors in these markets.

Do TBTF Firms Enjoy a Funding Advantage or Implicit Subsidy?

Economic theory predicts that in the presence of moral hazard, creditors and counterparties of TBTF firms provide credit at an inefficiently low cost. Some studies have provided evidence that the funding advantage exists, although many of these studies cover time periods that end before the enactment of the Dodd-Frank Act.[26] Identifying a lower funding cost for large banks alone is not enough to prove a moral hazard effect because lower cost could also be due to other factors, such as greater liquidity or lower risk (e.g., greater diversity).[27] A GAO review of the empirical literature found that a funding advantage for large firms during the financial crisis had declined by 2011. Its own econometric analysis found evidence of a funding advantage during the crisis, but mixed evidence on the existence of a funding advantage in 2012 and 2013—indeed, more versions of their model found higher funding costs for large banks rather than the expected lower costs, holding other factors equal.[28]

Some view the decision by certain credit rating agencies to rate the largest financial firms more highly because they assume the firms would receive government support as evidence of the funding advantage, although two of the three major rating agencies have reduced the magnitude of this "ratings uplift" in recent years.[29] (It should be noted that credit ratings do not directly determine funding costs.)

This funding advantage is sometimes referred to as the TBTF subsidy, although a subsidy typically implies a government willingness to provide the recipient with a benefit. Note also that a subsidy typically takes the form of an explicit direct payment, financial support, or guarantee, whereas in this case, if the funding advantage exists, it would derive from the expectation of future support that has not been pledged.

POLICY OPTIONS

Policy before and during the Crisis

TBTF policy before the crisis could be described as purposeful ambiguity—policy was not explicit about what would happen in the event that large financial firms become insolvent, or which firms were considered TBTF.[30] (Certain statutory benefits conferred to Fannie Mae and Freddie Mac came closer to an explicit TBTF status, and markets treated them as such.) Conventional wisdom before the crisis was that this ambiguity would help contain the moral hazard problem—if investors and creditors did not know if a firm was TBTF, they would err on the side of caution and treat it as if it were not TBTF.[31] Problems with large firms in the recent crisis suggest that this approach was not effective.

Theoretically, moral hazard can be mitigated through prudential regulation for safety and soundness. Generally, the regulatory regime before the crisis was not based on firm size, but rather on charter type. Depository institutions were regulated for safety and soundness to minimize the costs of, and the moral hazard that results from, deposit insurance and access to the Fed's discount window. Because some non-bank financial firms did not receive analogous government protection before the crisis, there was not seen to be a moral hazard problem that justified regulating them for safety and soundness. Pre-crisis safety and soundness regulation did not explicitly address the additional moral hazard that results from TBTF, in part because TBTF firms were not explicitly identified.

Before the crisis, large financial firms were subject to Federal Reserve prudential oversight at the holding company level if they were organized as bank holding companies or financial holding companies.[32] Prudential regulation entailed supervision and examination for safety and soundness. In 1997, the Fed and the Office of the Comptroller of the Currency (OCC) set up an internal team to supervise large complex banking organizations.[33] Regulation at the holding company level did not mean that all subsidiaries were regulated for safety and soundness by the Fed. Bank holding companies (BHCs) could operate non-banking subsidiaries, but banking regulators could only regulate banking subsidiaries for safety and soundness. "Firewalls" were meant to protect the depository subsidiary from losses at other types of subsidiaries. The holding company had to demonstrate that it was a source of strength for the depository subsidiary.[34] Government-sponsored enterprises, such as Fannie Mae, Freddie Mac, and the Federal Home Loan Banks, were also subject to prudential regulation by their own regulators. Prudential regulation did not prevent all large banks or the GSEs from experiencing financial difficulties during the crisis.

Some of the large firms that experienced financial difficulties in the recent crisis, however, were not bank holding companies, under Fed regulation, at that time. Types of large firms that were not BHCs included some government sponsored enterprises, insurance companies, investment banks (or broker-dealers), and hedge funds. Insurance subsidiaries were regulated for safety and soundness at the state level. Investment banks complied with an SEC net capital rule. Some large financial firms, including AIG and Lehman Brothers, were thrift holding companies supervised by the Office of Thrift Supervision before the crisis. The Office of Thrift Supervision was mainly concerned with the health of AIG's and Lehman Brothers' thrift subsidiaries, although those were a minor part of their businesses.

Some large financial firms voluntarily became BHCs during the crisis. Specifically, the five largest investment banks either merged with BHCs (Bear Stearns, Merrill Lynch), became BHCs (Goldman Sachs, Morgan Stanley), or declared bankruptcy (Lehman Brothers) in 2008.

If a bank is heading toward insolvency, the FDIC normally takes it into receivership and resolves it. Statutory requirements of least cost resolution of failing depositories by the FDIC may also help to minimize moral hazard, because bailing out firms (i.e., making creditors whole) is often more costly than shutting a firm down. But least cost resolution could be waived by the Treasury Secretary, upon the recommendation of the FDIC and Federal Reserve, if a systemic risk exception were invoked.[35] Market participants may have expected that the systemic risk exception would be invoked for large firms. The presumption before the crisis was that a failed non-bank would be subject to the standard corporate bankruptcy process; there was no standing policy of government involvement in the failure of a non-bank, with the exception of conservatorship authority for Fannie Mae and Freddie Mac.[36]

The Federal Reserve was authorized to provide liquidity to banks through collateralized loans at the discount window, with limitations for banks that are not well capitalized. In previous episodes of financial turmoil such as 1987 and 1998, the Fed's decision to flood markets with liquidity had proven sufficient to restore confidence.[37] There was no standing policy to provide liquidity to non-bank financial firms to guard against runs before the recent crisis. Such a policy did not prove necessary to maintain stability before the recent crisis, perhaps because there was less historical experience with non-bank runs, and perhaps because non-bank financial firms have become a more important part of the financial system over time. The Fed had broad existing emergency authority under Section 13(3) of the Federal Reserve Act to lend to non-banks, but prior to the crisis had not done so since the 1930s.

Policy during the recent crisis could be described as reactive, developing ad hoc in fits and starts in reaction to events. Ultimately, banks received federal assistance, and a lack of an explicit safety net and federal prudential regulation did not prevent some non-banks from receiving federal assistance as well. In the absence of explicit authority to rescue a TBTF firm, as the crisis unfolded, the broad standing authority was used: Section 13(3) was used to prevent the failures of Bear Stearns and AIG. Section 13(3) and the FDIC's systemic risk authority[38] was used to offer asset guarantees to Bank of America and Citigroup. These authorities were also used to create broadly based emergency programs. Other programs were created after the crisis began under authority granted by Congress in 2008. Assistance was given under the Housing and Economic Recovery Act (HERA; P.L. 110-289) to prevent Fannie Mae and Freddie Mac from becoming insolvent. In October 2008, Congress passed the Emergency Economic Stabilization Act (EESA; P.L. 110-343), creating the Troubled Asset Relief Program (TARP), which was used, among other things, to inject capital into several large financial firms.[39] The Fed and FDIC authorities are permanent; as discussed below, both authorities were modified by the Dodd-Frank Act. The HERA and EESA authority expired in 2010, although funds continued to be available after expiration under several outstanding contracts.

Policy Options and the Policy Response after the Crisis

Policy options for TBTF can be categorized as preventive (how to prevent TBTF firms from either emerging or posing systemic risk) or reactive (how to contain the fallout when a TBTF firm experiences a crisis). A comprehensive policy is likely to incorporate more than one approach because different approaches are aimed at different parts of the problem. A policy approach that would not solve the TBTF problem in isolation could be successful in conjunction with others. Some policy approaches are complementary—others could counteract each other.

Although there are costs to having large financial firms because of the moral hazard problems, these costs must be weighed against potential benefits to determine the economically optimal policy response. These benefits are discussed in the section below entitled "Limiting the Size of Financial Firms."

When considering each policy option discussed in this section, an alternative perspective to consider is that problems at large firms during the crisis—such as overleveraging, a sudden loss of liquidity, concentrated or undiversified losses, investor uncertainty caused by opacity—were not TBTF problems per se. If, in fact, they were representative of problems that firms of all sizes were experiencing, policy should directly treat these problems in a systematic and uniform way for all firms, and not just for TBTF firms, in this view. In other words, prudential regulation, a special resolution regime, and policies limiting spillover effects could be applied to all firms operating in a given area rather than just large firms, so arguments for and against these policy options do not apply only to their application to large firms. If the causes of systemic risk are not tied to firm size or interconnectedness, then policies based on differential treatment of TBTF firms could result in systemic risk migrating to non-TBTF firms rather than being eliminated.

End or Continue ' ' Bailouts' ' ?

Options

"Bailouts" are defined differently by different people. For the purposes of this report, they are defined as government assistance to a single firm to prevent it from failing (i.e., allow it to meet all ongoing obligations in full), in contrast to widely available emergency government programs to provide liquidity to solvent firms. TBTF bailouts could be delivered through assistance unique to the firm or through existing government programs on a preferential, subsidized basis.[40] They could come in the form of federal loans, insurance, guarantees, capital injections, or other firm-specific commitments.

Three broad policy approaches to government "bailouts" of failing TBTF firms are available: (1) institutionalize the availability of assistance in standing programs with standards and procedures for access enumerated beforehand; (2) offer assistance on an ad hoc basis using broad, discretionary authority, adding authority as necessary; or (3) eliminate any source of broad authority that could potentially make assistance available (often referred to as a "market discipline" policy).

The policy approach pursued before and during the crisis was essentially the second, as discussed in the previous section. The crisis left many policy makers and observers criticizing this approach as arbitrary, unfair, lacking in transparency, and too costly (although, in most cases, funds were eventually repaid in full).[41] Many economists would also credit it with eventually restoring financial stability, however, by restoring healthy and unhealthy financial firms' access to liquidity and capital.[42]

One problem with a "bailouts" approach is that one can only learn whether a firm's failure would be disruptive if it is allowed to fail. Once a firm has been rescued, there is no way of knowing how disruptive its failure would have been. As a result, policy makers may decide to err on the side of caution and rescue any firm that they believe poses risk of contagion since the short-term costs of disruption to financial markets may be high. In this sense, the number of firms that are politically TBTF, particularly at times of market stress, may be larger than the number that are economically TBTF (i.e., pose systemic risk).

Under the market discipline approach, policy makers would pledge to provide no federal assistance to any failing firm going forward. In theory, if creditors believed that a firm would not receive government support, they would not enable firms to take what they perceived to be excessive risks, and risky actions would be priced more efficiently.[43] Unfortunately, accomplishing this goal is not as simple as proclaiming a "no bailouts" policy. If the moral hazard problem is to be avoided, market participants must be convinced that when faced with a failure that could potentially be highly damaging to the broader economy—and just how damaging cannot be fully known until after the fact—policy makers will not deviate from the stated policy and provide bailouts. But current policy makers cannot prevent future policy makers from offering assistance to a failing TBTF firm. Although it is in the long-term interest of policy makers to withhold assistance to prevent moral hazard, it is in the short-term interest of policy makers to provide assistance to prevent systemic risk. This makes it difficult to craft a "market discipline" policy that is credible to market participants.[44] Even if policy makers did intend to maintain a market discipline policy, as long as creditors disbelieved such a policy would be maintained in the event of a crisis, the moral hazard problem would remain.

Events in the crisis rewarded size and interconnectedness and arguably made any future "market discipline" policy approach less credible. As discussed in the **Appendix**, widespread financial assistance was provided in 2007-2009 to large institutions, although official policy prior to the crisis could have been construed as a "no bailouts" policy. Creditors may view the 2007-2009 policy response as the most likely outcome in future systemic risk episodes. According to the Congressional Oversight Panel, "In light of these events, it is not surprising that markets have incorporated the notion that 'too big to fail' banks are safer than their 'small enough to fail' counterparts."[45] An alternative perspective is that market participants may view public dissatisfaction with the 2007-2009 policy response as making a repeat unlikely.

Although it is impossible to prevent future policy makers from making statutory changes to current policy, current policy makers can make it more difficult for future policy makers to "bail out" firms by repealing or limiting the existing standing authority that policy makers used to provide assistance in the crisis. Enacting new authority is likely to be a higher hurdle than invoking existing authority. Examples of standing authority include the Fed's 13(3) emergency authority and the FDIC's systemic risk exception to least cost resolution. The advantage to maintaining broad discretionary emergency authority is that it allows policy makers to react quickly to unforeseen contingencies, and the authority may be used for other purposes than bailouts, as defined in this report. If assistance became necessary in a fast-moving crisis, new authority might take too long to enact. By then, the damage to the economy could be worse. In other words, eliminating broad authority could still result in a TBTF rescue, but after more financial disruption had occurred. TARP is an example of authority that was enacted relatively quickly during a crisis; nevertheless, its enactment took weeks, whereas contagion can spread in days.

If one believes that assistance is inevitable because of short-term incentives, there are two advantages to institutionalizing the terms of assistance. First, making the terms and conditions explicit reduces the likelihood that assistance could be provided arbitrarily or on the basis of favoritism, and provides an opportunity to create a funding mechanism so that funding is not shifted to the taxpayer. Second, an explicit policy avoids policy uncertainty, which can heighten systemic risk. Arguably, lack of explicit policy added to the panic after Lehman Brothers failed, because market participants may have incorrectly based decisions on the expectation that Lehman Brothers would receive the same type of government assistance that Bear Stearns received.[46] A drawback is that setting forth standards for coping with problems at large firms before the fact could make the moral hazard problem worse by leaving no ambiguity about which firms will receive assistance.

A related approach would be to allow TBTF firms to fail, but stop contagion by creating standing credit facilities ahead of time to aid solvent counterparties. This would reduce moral hazard on the firm's part (because its managers would have a greater incentive to avoid failure), but would not eliminate it because counterparties would have less reason to monitor the firm's riskiness. An example of this approach is the decision to let Lehman Brothers fail, then subsequently offer a blanket guarantee for money market mutual funds (MMFs) to prevent a run triggered by one such fund's financial difficulties related to its holdings of Lehman debt.[47] As the MMF example illustrates, sometimes this approach could require assistance to be extended much more broadly than to just direct counterparties. Further, if standing facilities are too easily accessed, they could crowd out private inter-firm lending.

The optimal approach to bailouts from an economic perspective is arguably the one that is least costly to the economy in the short and long run. The cost of TBTF to the economy includes the direct expenditures by the government and the costs of a less stable financial system due to moral hazard. It can be argued that a failure to bail out TBTF firms would make the system less stable, because it would potentially allow systemic risk to spread. Alternatively, if bailouts increase moral hazard, it can be argued that greater moral hazard causes the system to be less stable by encouraging TBTF firms to act less prudently. However, even without moral hazard, firms would sometimes fail, as finance is inherently risky.

The 2008 experience lacks a counterfactual to definitively answer the question of which approach is least costly in the short run. The crisis worsened after Lehman Brothers was allowed to fail and ended after TARP and other broadly based emergency programs were created. Ad hoc rescues of failing TBTF firms had not succeeded in stabilizing financial markets to that point, but it is unknown whether financial conditions would have eventually normalized had that ad hoc policy been pursued consistently and continually. There is also no counterfactual as to what would have happened if there had been a consistent policy of allowing firms to fail in the crisis dating back to Bear Stearns, but the outcome that policy makers believed would occur if Bear Stearns had not been rescued is similar to events following the Lehman Brothers bankruptcy.

During the crisis, it appeared that the ultimate cost to the government of TBTF "bailouts" could run into the hundreds of billions, collectively.[48] In hindsight, all of the special assistance to large financial firms (Bear Stearns, the GSEs, Ally Financial, Chrysler Financial, AIG, Citigroup, and Bank of America), as well as the broadly based emergency programs that large and small financial firms accessed, turned out to be cash-flow positive for the government (i.e., income and principal repayments exceeded outlays).[49] Cash-flow measures, however, do not reflect the economic cost of assistance, which would factor in the rate of return a private investor would have required to make a similar investment, incorporating risk and the time value of money. On an economic basis, CBO has estimated that special assistance through TARP to Citigroup, Bank of America and broadly based programs have generated positive profits for the government, while the TARP assistance to AIG and the auto finance firms was subsidized.[50] Although there were ultimately no net losses in these cases, these government interventions exposed the government to large potential losses.

Estimates of the cost to the government of "bailouts" do not include the broader costs of a systemic disruption to the economy, which would have feedback effects on the federal budget. In this sense, the question of whether it is more costly to bail out TBTF firms or allow them to fail cannot be definitively settled. Arguably, it was the government's interventions following Lehman Brothers' collapse that ultimately ended the panic, as measured by standard measures of financial stress such as the spread between Treasury rates and the London Inter-bank Offering Rate (LIBOR), which did not begin to fall until legislation creating TARP was enacted.[51]

Policy Response

Maintaining broad discretionary authority, but attempting to limit its scope to prevent bailing out insolvent firms could be seen as the approach taken by Title XI of the Dodd-Frank Act. It limits the Fed to providing emergency assistance only through widely available facilities, requires the Fed to issue rules and regulations on how such assistance will be provided, and prohibits the Fed from lending to failing firms. It also created new statutory authority for the FDIC to set up emergency liquidity programs in the future with restrictions and limitations, including that the recipient must be solvent, rather than allowing the FDIC to again rely on an open-ended systemic risk exception. Critics would argue that emergency authority remains broad enough under the Dodd-Frank Act that regulators would be likely to use it to save TBTF firms in the future. The Dodd-Frank Act did not institutionalize a broadly based capital injection program similar to TARP's Capital Purchase Program, which expired in 2010.

Limiting the Size of Financial Firms

Options

One approach to eliminating TBTF is to alter the characteristics of firms that make them TBTF. If TBTF is primarily a function of size, policy makers could require TBTF firms to sell businesses, divest assets, or break up to the point that they are no longer TBTF. Size can be measured in different ways, and regulators would likely need to use discretion to weigh a number of measures.[52] It is also not obvious at what size a firm becomes a source of systemic risk—should the line be drawn at, say, $1 trillion, $100 billion, or $50 billion of assets?—and could not be confirmed until firms failed. A firm could be TBTF because of its overall size or because of its size or importance in a particular segment of the financial market, suggesting that overall size alone may not be a sufficient determinant of systemic importance. It is also possible that if all institutions were smaller because of a size cap, the largest institutions would still be systemically important, even though their size would not be large by today's standards. A parallel might be the decision to rescue

Continental Illinois in 1984—it was the seventh-largest bank, but had assets of only $45 billion at its peak, as geographic restrictions meant that the average size of all banks was smaller.[53]

The benefits of reducing the size of firms are that, if successful, it could eliminate the moral hazard and the need for future "bailouts" stemming from TBTF. Other potential costs and benefits are more ambiguous. Size restrictions may raise the cost or reduce the quality of financial products currently provided by TBTF firms to consumers and investors; whether this is good or bad from an economic perspective depends on the cause. If low costs currently stem primarily from the TBTF "subsidy," then economic efficiency would improve if large firms are eliminated even if costs rose as a result.[54] Alternatively, if low costs currently stem primarily from economies of scale, then economic efficiency would be reduced by size restrictions.[55] Beyond cost, large firms may make markets more liquid and enhance customer convenience (such as a nationwide physical presence). Large non-financial firms may also have financial needs (such as the underwriting of securities) that would overwhelm small financial firms.[56] Similarly, if the success of the largest firms comes primarily through their ability to innovate and provide more sophisticated or superior products, then size restrictions could reduce economic efficiency.[57]

Alternatively, if success of large firms comes primarily through the ability to extract monopoly rents, size restrictions could improve economic efficiency.[58] While reducing size should reduce systemic risk, there is mixed evidence on whether large firms are more or less likely to fail than small firms.[59] They could be less likely to fail because of greater diversification or more sophisticated risk management. Canada's unique experience in avoiding the recent financial crisis is attributed by some to its highly concentrated banking system.[60]

Unless rules to limit the size of financial firms are global, size restrictions could place U.S. firms at a disadvantage at home and abroad in their competition with foreign financial firms. (Some types of financial activities can be performed abroad more easily than others, so the relevance of this factor depends on the activity in question.) If business were to shift to large foreign firms, the overall level of systemic risk in the financial system (which already involves large international capital flows) may not decline, or could even increase if prudential regulation in the foreign firm's home country were inferior to U.S. regulation.

An alternative to restricting size would be to penalize size through a tax or assessment on assets or liabilities above a stated threshold. In theory, the tax could be set at the rate that would neutralize any funding advantage that a bank enjoys because of its TBTF status. Given that it is uncertain at what size a financial firm becomes TBTF, a tax could be viewed as less harmful than a cap if set at the wrong threshold and perhaps more easily adjusted over time. Other policy options that raise funding costs for large firms, such as higher capital requirements, can be viewed as having a similar effect to a tax.[61]

If policy makers decided to reduce the size of firms, a phase-in or transition period might be desirable to avoid significant short-term disruptions to the overall financial system. Likewise, when designing a policy that applies only to firms above a size threshold, one consideration is whether to make the threshold graduated to avoid cliff effects. Otherwise, firms might take actions to remain just below the threshold.

Policy Response

Section 121 of the Dodd-Frank Act allows the Federal Reserve to prevent mergers and acquisitions, restrict the products a firm is allowed to offer, terminate activities, and sell assets if the Federal Reserve and at least two-thirds of the Financial Stability Oversight Council believes that a firm that has more than $50 billion in assets poses a "grave threat to the financial stability of the United States." It does not allow the Fed to undertake these actions simply because a firm is large. Before the crisis, a BHC was limited to holding no more than 10% of national deposits and 30% of any state's deposits.

Section 622 of the Dodd-Frank Act prevents mergers or consolidations that would result in a firm with more than 10% of total liabilities of certain financial firms or, in the case of a bank, 10% of the total amount of deposits of insured depository institutions in the United States. This limit can be waived in the case of the acquisition of a failing firm. The limit does not prevent firms from increasing their market share "organically." The FSOC has determined that Section 622 will limit the acquisitions of only the four largest bank holding companies at this time.[62] A proposed rule implementing the limit was released in May 2014.[63]

The Dodd-Frank Act allowed fees to be assessed on banks with more than $50 billion in assets and non-banks designated as systemically important. The fees were intended to finance the costs of supervision and resolution, as well as the budget of the Office of Financial Research, as opposed to being punitive, however.

Limiting the Scope of Financial Firms

Options

The activities in which bank subsidiaries may engage are restricted by statute, but bank holding companies may own non-bank subsidiaries.[64] The subsidiaries of, and off-balance sheet entities associated with, the largest BHCs are active participants, to varying degrees, in multiple lines of business outside of traditional bank lending, including asset-backed securitization, trust services, insurance, money market mutual funds, and broker-dealers.[65] A large firm's presence throughout the financial system is one source of its "interconnectedness."

Imposing a size restriction on firms is relatively straightforward—it requires establishing a measure of size, identifying the threshold size that makes a firm TBTF, and preventing firms from exceeding that threshold. Altering firms so that they are not too interconnected to fail is more complicated because there is less consensus on what characteristics make a firm "too interconnected."[66] If interconnectedness is taken to mean that the firm is an important participant in several different segments of financial markets, then policy makers could take what has popularly been described as the "reinstate Glass-Steagall" approach.[67] The essence of this proposal is to prevent a single financial holding company from operating in multiple lines of financial business, echoing Glass-Steagall's separation of banking and investing.[68] Reintroducing the separation of lines of business alone would not necessarily prevent the existence of very large or interconnected firms within a market segment, however, in which case the TBTF problem would not be eliminated.

The benefits of reducing the scope of firms are that, if successful, it could reduce the riskiest activities of large firms and thus the need for future "bailouts" stemming from TBTF. It could also reduce the complexity of large firms, making it easier for regulators and creditors to monitor them. Weighed against those benefits would be a number of costs.

First, there may be economies of scope that make the financial system more efficient and complete if firms are large, diversified, and interconnected. Customers may benefit from the convenience, sophistication, and savings of "one-stop shopping" and expertise in multiple market segments.

Second, large firms that operate in multiple lines of business may be better able to reduce risk through diversification, making them less prone to instability in that sense. Traditional banking is not inherently safe, so forbidding banks from engaging in other activities is no panacea to avoid bank failures. Fannie Mae and Freddie Mac are examples of firms that were deemed "too big to fail" and rescued on those grounds although their business was narrowly focused in the mortgage market.

Third, reintroducing Glass-Steagall separations of businesses without other changes to the regulatory system would reinforce a system in which banking is subject to close federal prudential regulation and other financial firms are not. This system would only mitigate systemic risk if non-banking activities and institutions could not be a source of systemic risk—the recent crisis experience casts doubt on that assumption. Further, the growth in "shadow banking" makes it more difficult to segregate activities and their regulation by charter—financial innovation has blurred the distinction between different lines of business in finance to the point where the distinction may not be meaningful. In other words, some activities of non-banks are not fundamentally different from core banking activities from an economic perspective. Thus, the activities that banks could undertake would be limited, but it would be difficult to prevent non-banks from engaging in bank-like activities with the same implications for systemic risk, but less or no prudential regulation. Similar arguments apply to the potential for activities to migrate abroad, where "universal banking" is common.

Another policy approach would be to limit or ban TBTF firms' participation in activities that are deemed inherently too risky—particularly those likely to generate large losses at times of financial stress—and not central to the business model of the firm. This approach usually focuses on banks because of their access to the "federal safety net" (deposit insurance and Fed lending), and hence justified in terms of limiting risk to taxpayers. For example, many policy makers have argued that banks should not participate in proprietary trading of private securities with the bank's own funds.[69] Although all financial activities are risky, some risks can be more easily managed through techniques such as hedging and supervised by regulators. Whether proprietary trading is an inherently riskier activity than other banking functions, such as lending, is subject to debate. In addition to proprietary trading, Thomas Hoenig and Charles Morris have proposed to also ban banks from acting as broker-dealers and market-makers in securities and derivatives.[70]

Another variation of this proposal, made by the Vickers Commission in the United Kingdom[71] and the Liikanen Group in the European Union,[72] is to "ring fence" banking activities from these other types of activities into legally, financially, and operationally separate entities within a holding company structure.[73] This type of approach can be seen in U.S. policies to move swap dealer activities outside of the depository subsidiary and into a separately capitalized subsidiary (referred to as "the swap push out rule").[74] Similarly to proprietary trading, a challenge to this approach is to differentiate between derivatives activities that regulators want depository subsidiaries to engage in, such as risk-mitigating hedging, and the targeted activities, such as swap dealing.

Although proposals limiting scope would apply to both large and small banks, some are likely to have a greater impact on large firms. For example, Bloomberg Government estimates that over 99% of trading assets and liabilities are held by 25 banks.[75]

A drawback to limiting permissible activities is that there is unlikely to be any sharp distinction between the risky activity and similar activities that are central to the firm's core activities. As a result, regulators may have to make arbitrary distinctions between which activities fall under the ban, and firms would have an incentive to skirt the ban by designing transactions that resemble allowed activities but accomplish the same goals as the banned activity. For example, proprietary trading ("playing the market" with a firm's own assets) may be hard to distinguish from market-making (providing clients with a ready buyer and seller of securities) or hedging (buying and selling securities such as derivatives to reduce risk), and there may be economies of scale to market-making that concentrate those activities at large firms.[76] Finally, risky activities may still be a source of systemic risk even if banks or TBTFs are banned from conducting them.

Policy Response

Section 619 of the Dodd-Frank Act, popularly referred to as the "Volcker Rule," prohibits banks from engaging in proprietary trading and owning hedge funds and private equity funds in the United States, and requires additional capital to be held by systemically important non-banks that engage in proprietary trading or own hedge funds and private equity funds in the United States.[77] Insurance companies are excluded from the Volcker Rule. Exemptions from the Volcker Rule include the purchase and sale of assets for purposes of underwriting, market making, hedging, and on behalf of clients. Securities issued by federal, state, or local governments and government-sponsored enterprises (GSEs) are exempted, as are investments in small business investment companies. A final rule implementing the Volcker Rule was adopted in December 2013, with conformance required by June 2015.[78]

Section 716 of the Dodd-Frank Act requires banks to "push out" certain swap dealer activities into separately capitalized affiliates.[79] The stated goal of the provision is to prevent swap dealers and major swap participants from accessing deposit insurance or the Fed's discount window. The rule implementing Section 716 was effective July 2013, with a two-year transition period.[80]

Regulating TBTF

Options

Another approach to addressing the TBTF problem takes as its starting point that no policy can prevent TBTF firms from emerging. In this view, the dominant role of a few firms in key segments of the financial system is unavoidable. Breaking them up or eliminating all spillover effects is unlikely to be practical or feasible, for reasons discussed elsewhere. If so, regulation could be used to try to counteract the moral hazard problem and reduce the likelihood of their failure. Prudential regulation, such as capital requirements, could be set to hold TBTF firms to higher standards than other financial firms, whether or not those firms are already subject to prudential regulation.

A framework for prudential regulation is well established in depository banking regulation, featuring the setting of safety and soundness standards and regulatory supervision to ensure adherence to those standards. Historically, banks have been subject to a closer and more intense federal prudential regulatory regime than non-banks because of the systemic risk and moral hazard problems they posed. Some argue that banks generate unique sources of systemic risk (such as deposit taking) that have no analogue in other types of financial firms.[81] If the recent crisis leads to the conclusion that TBTF non-bank financial firms can also be sources of systemic risk and contagion, the same arguments made for regulating banks for systemic risk also apply to TBTF non-banks, however.[82]

There are a wide variety of types of large non-banks, with diverse features. Some non-banks have some of the features that have been viewed as a source of systemic risk, such as leverage and vulnerability to runs, while others do not. There are a few large insurers, which are already regulated for safety and soundness at the state level. On the other hand, state regulators may not be equipped to regulate non-insurance subsidiaries or the overall firm for systemic risk. A study by the Office of Financial Research (OFR) identified several channels through which "asset managers"—a diverse group that includes hedge funds, pension funds, and mutual funds—could pose systemic risks. Others have argued that only activities, not firms, in this industry pose systemic risk. The OFR report identified 10 asset managers each with more than $1 trillion in assets under management.[83]

A "one size fits all" model for regulating firms in different businesses for safety and soundness is unlikely to be practical. Bringing non-banks under the purview of bank regulators raises questions about whether rules designed for banks can be applied to non-banks, and whether the federal bank regulators have the expertise to do so effectively. For example, insurers have argued that bank regulations are not suitable for them and the Fed does not have any specialized expertise in the area of insurance. Another issue is whether to regulate all of the activities of holding companies operating across several lines of business for safety and soundness, or regulate only certain activities that are deemed systemically important, perhaps with legal and financial "firewalls" that isolate the risks of non-regulated activities to the overall holding company.

Regulation cannot prevent all failures from occurring—large, regulated depository institutions failed during the crisis. Nor is a system without any failures necessarily a desirable one, since risk is inherent in all financial activities. Regulation could aim to prevent large financial firms from taking greater risks than their smaller counterparts because of moral hazard. If successful, fewer failures or episodes involving disruptive losses would occur. If effective, monitoring by regulators might be more economically efficient than monitoring by creditors and counterparties, where a free rider problem reduces the incentive to monitor. In addition, regulators potentially have greater access to relevant information on risk than creditors and counterparties if opacity is a problem with large, complex firms.

This proposal relies on effective regulation by the same regulators who were arguably unable or unwilling to prevent excessive risk taking before and during the crisis by at least a few of the firms that they regulated.[84] Although regulation is intended to limit risky behavior, regulators may inadvertently cause greater correlation of losses across firms by encouraging all firms to engage in similar behavior. Some have argued that large firms are "too complex to regulate," meaning regulators are incapable of identifying or understanding the risks inherent in complicated transactions and corporate structures. For example, the six largest BHCs had more than 1,000 subsidiaries and the two largest had more than 3,000 each in 2012. Further, their complexity has increased over time—only one BHC had more than 500 subsidiaries in 1990, and the share of assets held outside of depository subsidiaries has grown over time for the largest BHCs.[85] One response to addressing this complexity is by making the regulatory regime more sophisticated, but some critics argue that this approach is likely to backfire.[86] One challenge for the effective regulation of non-banks that are TBTF is that regulators have less experience with business lines other than banking, and thus may initially lack the expertise to regulate them effectively. Others have argued that large firms are "too big to jail," meaning regulators cannot take effective supervisory actions against firms if those actions would undermine the firm's financial health, and thus financial stability.[87]

One way that a regulatory approach could potentially backfire is if a special regulatory regime for TBTF firms is not strict enough, in which case it would exacerbate the moral hazard problem. Critics fear that such a regime would be particularly vulnerable to "regulatory capture," the phenomenon in which the regulated exercise influence over their regulators to ease the burden of regulation. If so, a special regulatory regime could wind up exacerbating the moral hazard problem by, in effect, making TBTF status explicit, signaling to market participants that firms in the special regime enjoyed a protected status and would not be allowed to fail.[88] Instead of increasing the cost of being TBTF, firms in the special regulatory regime could end up borrowing at a lower cost than other firms (since, in effect, these firms would enjoy a lower risk of default).

Many would point to the experience with the GSEs, Fannie Mae and Freddie Mac, before conservatorship as a historical example of how a special regulatory regime could backfire. The GSEs could borrow at a lower cost than other firms because markets believed that the government would not let them fail—they enjoyed even lower borrowing costs than firms that markets might believe were implicitly TBTF but not chartered by the government like the GSEs.[89] Institutional shortcomings, critics argue, led to regulatory capture.[90] The GSEs were subject to their own unique capital requirements, set by statute, under which they were found well capitalized by their regulator at the time, OFHEO, two months before being taken into conservatorship.[91] Yet compared with depositories, GSEs held little capital, were not well diversified, and experienced large losses during the crisis. The worst-case scenario of opponents of a separate regulatory regime for TBTF firms is that such a regime would provide a competitive advantage that would enable more risk taking than before. An example of this scenario was the GSEs' ability to borrow at lower cost than other firms.

Adopting these measures may increase overall costs in the financial system, but in the presence of TBTF, market costs may otherwise be too low from a societal perspective, since risk-taking is too high. For example, requiring loans to be backed with more capital may make lending more expensive and less available, but make the firm less likely to fail. If more capital succeeded in creating a more stable financial system, then the availability of credit could be less volatile over time. At least partly offsetting the higher costs of capital for firms designated as systemically important would be relatively lower costs of capital for other firms.[92]

Even if a heightened prudential regime worked as planned, it could still partly backfire from a systemic risk perspective. To the extent that it causes financial intermediation to migrate away from TBTF firms to firms that are not regulated for safety and soundness, the result could be a less regulated financial system.

Policy Response

Title I of the Dodd-Frank Act grants the Financial Stability Oversight Council (FSOC) the authority to identify "systemically important" non-bank financial firms (SIFI) by a two-thirds vote, which must be supported by the Treasury Secretary. Such a firm would be deemed systemically important on the basis of a council determination that "material financial distress at the [firm] or the nature, scope, size, scale, concentration, interconnectedness, or mix of the activities of the [firm] could pose a threat to the financial stability of the United States." Foreign financial firms operating in the United States could be identified by the council as systemically important. Firms with consolidated assets of less than $50 billion are exempted. Besides the $50 billion threshold, FSOC stated in its final rule that it would consider designating only firms with at least $30 billion in gross notional credit default swaps outstanding in which it was the reference entity, $3.5 billion of derivatives liabilities, $20 billion in debt outstanding, a 15 to 1 leverage ratio (a capital-asset ratio that is not risk-weighted), or a 10% short-term debt ratio.[93]

To date, FSOC has designated two insurers (AIG and Prudential) and another non-bank (GE Capital) as SIFIs.[94] According to the insurer MetLife, FSOC has proposed to designate it as well.[95] FSOC has investigated whether any "asset managers" (a diverse group that includes mutual funds, hedge funds, and private equity funds) are systemically important, but has not made any designations to date.

Under Subtitle C of Title I, the Fed is the prudential regulator for firms that the FSOC has designated as a SIFI and any BHC with total consolidated assets of $50 billion. (The FSOC and Fed may raise the asset threshold above $50 billion.) There are currently about 30 U.S. BHCs with more than $50 billion in consolidated assets.[96] BHCs that participated in the Capital Purchase

Program (part of the Troubled Asset Relief Program) would not be able to change their charter to avoid this regulatory regime. A large number of foreign banks operating in the United States are also subject to the enhanced prudential regime.[97] Foreign banks operating with more than $50 billion in assets in the United States are required to set up intermediate bank holding companies that will be subject to heightened standards comparable to those applied to U.S. banks. Less stringent requirements apply to large foreign banks with less than $50 billion in assets in the United States. The Fed, with the FSOC's advice, is required to set safety and soundness standards that are more stringent than those applicable to other nonbank financial firms and BHCs that do not pose a systemic risk. At the recommendation of the council or on its own initiative, the Fed may set different standards for different systemically important firms or categories of firms based on various risk-related factors. Fees are assessed on banks and non-banks regulated under this regime to finance the costs of supervision, as well as the budget of the Office of Financial Research.

The final rule implementing Subtitle C was adopted in February 2014, and banks must be in compliance by January 1, 2015.[98] The final rule includes requirements for stress tests, capital planning, and risk management. The final rule also requires any bank with more than $50 billion in assets to comply with a 15 to 1 debt to equity limit in the event that the FSOC has determined that it poses a "grave threat" to financial stability. Exposure limits of 25% of a company's capital per single counterparty were included in the proposed rule, but the Fed has indicated that it plans to finalize them at a later date. Capital and liquidity standards for the largest banks have been set separately through the Basel III rules, discussed below; enhanced capital requirements have not been required of all BHCs with $50 billion or more in assets. Other prudential standards may be applied at the Fed's discretion.

In addition, Section 171 of the Dodd-Frank Act (the "Collins Amendment") requires the Fed to set capital requirements at the holding company level for non-bank SIFIs and all bank or savings and loan holding companies that are no lower than those applied to banking subsidiaries. For companies with small or no banking subsidiaries, most of the required capital may be based on the activities of and provided by the non-bank subsidiaries. Previously, capital requirements (if there were any) were determined at the subsidiary level by that subsidiary's primary regulator. There are various exceptions to and phase-in periods for this requirement, including an exemption for small holding companies. As BHC regulator, the Fed has not yet determined how to apply the Collins Amendment to insurers, who use different methods to measure capital requirements from banks, or other non-banks.

In conjunction with the Dodd-Frank Act, Basel III, a non-binding international agreement on bank regulation that the United States is in the process of implementing,[99] required that

> global systemically important financial institutions (SIFIs) must have higher loss absorbency capacity to reflect the greater risks that they pose to the financial system. The Committee has developed a methodology that includes both quantitative indicators and qualitative elements to identify global systemically important banks (G-SIBs). The additional loss absorbency requirements are to be met with a progressive Common Equity Tier 1 (CET1) capital requirement ranging from 1% to 2.5%, depending on a bank's systemic importance. For banks facing the highest SIB surcharge, an additional loss absorbency of 1% could be applied as a disincentive to increase materially their global systemic importance in the future.[100]

In addition, Basel III creates a counter-cyclical capital buffer that can be modified over the business cycle and a supplementary leverage ratio incorporating off-balance sheet assets, both of which will be applied to only the largest banks (specifically, those subject to the "Advanced Approaches" Rule). In September 2014, the banking regulators finalized a rule implementing Basel's liquidity coverage ratio, applying it to banks with $250 billion or more in assets or $10 billion or more in on-balance sheet exposure, and a less stringent version of the rule to banks with $50 billion or more in assets. The rule does not apply to non-bank SIFIs, but regulators indicated that non-bank SIFIs would face their own liquidity requirements. The liquidity coverage ratio would require firms to hold enough liquid assets to meet cash flow needs during a stress period.[101]

Since 2011, the Financial Stability Board (FSB), an international forum that coordinates the work of national financial authorities and international standard setting bodies, has annually designated G-SIBs, based on the banks' cross-jurisdictional activity, size, interconnectedness, substitutability, and complexity.[102] The FSB has currently designated 29 banks as G-SIBs. **Table 2** lists the eight G-SIBs that are headquartered in the United States, and the capital surcharge under Basel III recommended by the FSB. In addition, several of the foreign G-SIBs have U.S. subsidiaries. The identified firms are required to meet resolution planning requirements.[103] The FSB has proposed that firms identified as G-SIBs in 2014 meet the capital surcharge requirements beginning in 2016, fully phasing them in by January 2019. The G20, including the U.S. government, endorsed the FSB's non-binding proposal.

Table 2. U.S. Banks Identified as G-SIBs and Capital Surcharge Recommended by the FSB (surcharge as a % of risk-weighted assets)

U.S. Financial Firm	Capital Surcharge as a % of Risk-Weighted Assets
Citigroup	2.5%
JP Morgan Chase	2.5%
Bank of America	1.5%
Bank of New York Mellon	1.5%
Goldman Sachs	1.5%
Morgan Stanley	1.5%
State Street	1.0%
Wells Fargo	1.0%

Source: Financial Stability Board.

In April 2014, the U.S. bank regulators adopted a joint rule that would require these eight banks to meet a supplementary leverage ratio of 5% in order to pay all discretionary bonuses and capital distributions and 6% in order to be considered well capitalized as of 2018.[104] The supplementary leverage ratio includes off-balance sheet exposures.

In addition, the Financial Stability Board has identified nine insurers as "globally systemically important insurers," three of whom (AIG, Prudential, and MetLife) are headquartered in the United States.[105] Designated insurers will be required to develop recovery and resolution plans and hold more capital than other insurers by 2019. The FSB has released a methodology for identifying global systemically important firms that are not banks or insurers, but has not designated any to date.[106] Some Members of Congress have been concerned that the FSB designation process is superseding the national designation process established by the Dodd-Frank Act.[107]

Minimize Spillover Effects

Options

A criticism of regulation before the crisis was that regulators did not focus enough on how a firm's failure would affect its counterparties or broader financial conditions, or conversely, whether a firm could withstand a crisis situation. Another approach holds that if firms are TBTF because their failure would cause spillover effects that would impair the overall financial system, then instead of altering the TBTF firm, regulators should try to neutralize spillover effects to the point where the failure of a firm would not impair the broader financial system. According to this view, once creditors believed that a firm could now safely be allowed to fail regardless of its size or interconnectedness, the moral hazard problem associated with TBTF would vanish.

One way spillover effects occur is through counterparty risk (the risk of losses because a counterparty in a transaction cannot fulfill its obligations). Examples of how counterparty risk can be reduced include moving transactions to clearinghouses and exchanges, requiring capital/margins for transactions, requiring risk exposures to be hedged, and placing limits on exposure to specific counterparties (transactions, debt, equity holdings, etc.).[108] Adopting these measures may increase overall costs in the financial system. For example, counterparty limits could reduce liquidity and raise costs for transactions that are not standardized enough to be traded on exchanges. In the presence of TBTF, however, market costs may otherwise be too low from a society-wide perspective, because firms lack the proper incentives to monitor or price in counterparty risk.

A drawback to this approach is that spillover effects cannot always be identified beforehand. If counterparty exposure were transparent, in theory all market participants could hedge themselves against failure ahead of time and the failure would not have contagion effects, or at least the government could manage the exposure to prevent contagion. In practice, linkages have proven complex and opaque, and the sources of contagion have proven hard to predict. For example, in September 2008, policy makers reasoned that market participants and policy makers had had several months after the rescue of Bear Stearns to prepare for the failure of Lehman Brothers (indicators such as credit default swaps had signaled an elevated risk of default for months), so allowing it to enter bankruptcy should not be disruptive.[109] Nevertheless, few anticipated that Lehman Brothers' failure would lead to a run on money markets, which proved highly disruptive to commercial paper markets, causing financing problems for many financial and non-financial issuers.

Identifying spillover effects is likely to be more difficult if a firm is not already regulated for safety and soundness. Without a prudential regulator closely monitoring the firm's activities and examining its counterparties, it is less likely that policy makers could quickly and accurately identify who would be exposed to a firm's failure. Much of the necessary information to make that judgment is unlikely to be publicly available.

Another problem is that some solutions shift, rather than eliminate, counterparty risk. For example, moving certain activities onto an exchange or clearinghouse may cause that entity to become "too interconnected to fail."

Policy Response

The Federal Reserve's Regulation F (12 C.F.R., Part 206)—in place before the crisis—limits counterparty exposure for depository institutions. Title I of the Dodd-Frank Act allows the Fed to set exposure limits of 25% of a company's capital per counterparty for firms designated as systemically important by the Financial Stability Oversight Council.[110] To date, a rule implementing this exposure limit has been proposed but not finalized. To reduce counterparty risk, Title VII of the Dodd-Frank Act requires certain swaps, particularly those that involve large financial institutions, to be moved onto clearinghouses or exchanges.[111] Title VIII of the Dodd-Frank Act allows the Financial Stability Oversight Council to identify certain payment, clearing, and settlement systems and activities as systemically important "financial market utilities," and allows the Federal Reserve, Securities and Exchange Commission, or Commodity and Futures Trading Commission to regulate those systems and activities for enhanced prudential supervision. It also allows systemically important systems to borrow from the Fed in "unusual or exigent circumstances." In 2012, regulators issued a final rule implementing Title VIII and designated eight financial market utilities as systemically important.[112]

Resolving a Large, Interconnected Failing Firm

Options

Prior to the financial crisis, failing banks were resolved through the FDIC's resolution regime, while certain other financial firms, such as broker-dealers, were resolved through the corporate bankruptcy system.[113] Bankruptcy is a judicial process initiated by creditors in order to recover debts and other liabilities, while the FDIC's resolution regime is an administrative process initiated by the FDIC. Examples of the types of powers that the FDIC can exercise to resolve a depository include transferring and freezing assets, paying obligations, repudiating contracts, and obtaining judicial stays.[114]

The FDIC typically resolves failed banks through the "purchase and assumption" method, under which the bank is closed and some or all of the assets and deposits of the failed bank are sold to healthy banks.[115] If losses are too large to be absorbed by creditors, they are absorbed by the FDIC's deposit insurance fund, which is pre-funded through assessments on depositories. The purchase and assumption method avoids open-ended government assistance and keeps the FDIC out of the business of running banks, but an unintended consequence is that it encourages greater concentration, since the only entity capable of absorbing a large failed bank is likely to be an even larger institution.

One rationale behind a resolution regime for banks is that the need to safeguard federally insured deposits (which can be withdrawn rapidly) requires a swift resolution and gives the FDIC, which insures the deposits, priority over other creditors. Prompt corrective action and least cost resolution requirements are intended to minimize losses to the FDIC. The FDIC may initiate a resolution before failure has occurred—thereby limiting losses to the FDIC and other creditors— whereas a bankruptcy process cannot be initiated by creditors until default has occurred.

Another example of a resolution regime is the one applied to Fannie Mae and Freddie Mac. Their regulator, the Federal Housing Finance Agency (FHFA), assumed control of Fannie Mae and Freddie Mac in September 2008 when FHFA determined that they were critically undercapitalized. Since then, Fannie Mae and Freddie Mac have operated under government conservatorship and received quarterly financial transfers from the Treasury to remain solvent until 2012.[116]

Part of what makes some financial firms too big to fail is the nature of the bankruptcy process, according to some analysts. A firm that dominates important financial market segments cannot be liquidated without disrupting the availability of credit, it is argued. They argue that the deliberate pace of the bankruptcy process is not equipped to avoid the runs and contagion inherent in the failure of a financial firm, and that the effects on systemic risk are not taken into account when decisions are made in the bankruptcy process. The bankruptcy experience of Lehman Brothers is viewed as evidence of why the current bankruptcy process cannot be successful for a TBTF firm.

Proponents argue that a resolution regime for all TBTF financial firms, regardless of whether the firm is a depository, offers an alternative to propping up failing firms with government assistance (as was the case with Bear Stearns and AIG in 2008) or suffering the systemic consequences of a protracted and messy bankruptcy (as was the case with Lehman Brothers).[117] In principle, a TBTF resolution regime could include a receivership process (where the government seizes control of the firm in order to wind it down), a conservatorship process (where the government seizes control in order to continue operations), or both. The FDIC's typical treatment of a failed bank is an example of a receivership process; FHFA's treatment of Fannie Mae and Freddie Mac since 2008 is an example of the conservatorship process.[118] Often, banks in receivership are resolved through acquisitions by healthy firms. In the case of a large firm, acquisitions would result in the acquiring firm becoming even larger. Were one of the nation's very largest firms to fail, it is not clear what firm would have the capacity to acquire it, in which case some other method of resolution would be necessary.

Supporting the argument for a special resolution regime, the failures of large depositories during the crisis that were subject to the FDIC's resolution regime, such as Wachovia and Washington Mutual, were less disruptive to the financial system than the failure of Lehman Brothers, even though Wachovia and Lehman Brothers were sequential (46th and 47th largest, respectively) on *Fortune*'s list of the 500 largest companies of 2007.[119] (Wells Fargo acquired Wachovia before the FDIC formally became receiver.) Whether the resolution of a non-bank could be handled as smoothly as these two banks is an open question.[120]

Critics argue that a resolution regime, depending on its design, could give policy makers too much discretionary power, which could result in higher costs to the government and preferential treatment of favored creditors during the resolution. In other words, it could enable "backdoor bailouts" that could allow government assistance to be funneled to the firm or its creditors beyond what would be available in bankruptcy, perpetuating the moral hazard problem.[121] The normal FDIC resolution regime minimizes the potential for these problems through its statutory requirements of least cost resolution and prompt corrective action. It would be expected that a resolution regime for TBTF firms, by contrast, would at times be required to subordinate a least cost principle to systemic risk considerations, which the FDIC regime permits. Therefore, a resolution could be more costly to the government than the bankruptcy process. (On the other hand, an administrative resolution process could potentially avoid some of the costs of bankruptcy, such as some legal fees and runs by creditors that further undermine the firm's finances.) Critics also point to the conservatorship of Fannie Mae and Freddie Mac—who have received government support on an ongoing basis since 2008—as evidence that a resolution regime could turn out to be too open ended and be used to prop up TBTF firms as ongoing entities, competing with private sector rivals on an advantageous basis because of direct government subsidies. The Housing and Economic Recovery Act (P.L. 110-289) required mandatory receivership for the GSEs if they became insolvent, but quarterly transfers from Treasury prevented insolvency. As noted above, uncertainty before the fact about which firms are TBTF may lead policy makers to err on the side of taking more failing firms than necessary into the special resolution process instead of allowing them to enter bankruptcy.

If policy makers, wary of the turmoil caused by Lehman Brothers' failure, were unwilling to pursue the bankruptcy option in the future, opposing a resolution regime may be tantamount to tacitly accepting future "bailouts," unless some other policy change is made that future policy makers view as a workable alternative. As an alternative to a special resolution regime, some critics call for amending the bankruptcy code to create a special chapter for complex financial firms to address problems that have been identified, such as a speedier process and the ability to reorganize.[122] To some extent, these concerns are already addressed in the bankruptcy code. For example, the bankruptcy process already allows qualified financial contracts to be netted out. In the case of Lehman Brothers, healthy business units were sold to competitors relatively quickly through the bankruptcy process, and remain in operation today.

Until a TBTF firm fails, it is open to debate whether a special resolution regime could successfully achieve what it is intended to do—shut down a failing firm without triggering systemic disruption. One key challenge that has been identified is the resolution of foreign subsidiaries.[123] Given the size of the firms involved and the unanticipated transmission of systemic risk, it remains to be seen whether the government could impose losses on any creditors without triggering contagion—or would be willing to try. A receiver would face the same short-term incentives to limit losses to creditors to limit systemic risk that caused policy makers to rescue firms in the recent crisis in order to restore stability. If the receiver is guided by those short-term incentives, the only difference between a resolution regime and a "bailout" might turn out to be that shareholder equity is wiped out, at presumably relatively little savings to the government.

Policy Response

In July 2008, Congress passed the Housing and Economic Recovery Act (HERA; P.L. 110-289), which included provisions creating a new regulator (the Federal Housing Finance Agency or FHFA) for the housing GSEs (the Federal Home Loan Banks, Fannie Mae, and Freddie Mac). The FHFA was given augmented powers to resolve the GSEs.[124] Under these powers, FHFA can manage assets, sign contracts, terminate claims, collect obligations, and perform management functions. In September 2008, Fannie Mae and Freddie

Mac entered FHFA conservatorship, upon which FHFA took control of their operations while maintaining them as ongoing enterprises.[125] HERA also gave the Treasury Secretary unlimited authority to lend or invest in the GSEs through the end of 2009. This authority has been used to cover the GSEs' losses and prevent insolvency during conservatorship, and funds from Treasury continued to be transferred until 2012.[126] While existing shareholders saw their equity value plummet at the time of conservatorship, creditors and other counterparties have continued to be paid in full.

Title I of the Dodd-Frank Act (P.L. 111-203) requires systemically important firms (SIFIs) and BHCs with at least $50 billion in consolidated assets to periodically prepare resolution plans, also called "living wills," explaining how they could be resolved in a rapid and orderly manner. Failure to submit a credible resolution plan would trigger regulatory action. Title I also creates early remediation requirements for non-bank SIFIs that are in financial distress (banks already had early remediation requirements under existing statute).

Title II of the Dodd-Frank Act creates a resolution regime for financial firms whose failure would have "serious adverse effects on financial stability."[127] However, subsidiaries that are insurance companies would be resolved under state law, certain broker-dealers would be resolved by the Securities Investor Protection Corporation, and insured depository subsidiaries would be resolved under the FDIC's traditional resolution regime. The process for taking a firm into resolution has multiple steps and actors. First, a group of regulators (the group varies depending on the type of firm, but must always include the approval of two-thirds of the Federal Reserve's Board of Governors) must make a written recommendation to the Treasury Secretary that a firm should be resolved, explaining why bankruptcy would be inappropriate. Second, the Treasury Secretary must determine that resolution is necessary to avoid a default that would pose systemic risk to the financial system, and default cannot be prevented through a private sector alternative. Prior identification by the FSOC could be used as evidence that the firm's failure poses systemic risk, but it is not a necessary condition. Third, if the company disputes the Treasury Secretary's findings, it has limited rights to appeal in federal court. Finally, the FDIC manages the resolution.

The Dodd-Frank Act provides the FDIC with receivership powers, modeled on its bank receivership powers, with some differences, such as requirements that the FDIC consult with the primary regulator. As receiver, the FDIC can manage assets, sign contracts, terminate claims, collect obligations, and perform management functions. The Dodd-Frank Act sets priorities among classes of unsecured creditors, with senior executives and directors coming last before shareholders in order of priority. It requires that similarly situated creditors be treated similarly, unless doing so would increase the cost to the government. The FDIC is allowed to create bridge companies, as a way to divide good and bad assets, for a limited period of time to facilitate the resolution. Unlike FHFA's resolution regime, the Dodd-Frank regime does not allow for conservatorship.

The Dodd-Frank Act calls for shareholders and creditors to bear losses and management "responsible for the condition of the company" to be removed. The FDIC is allowed to use its funds to provide credit to the firm while in receivership if funding cannot be obtained from private credit markets. Unlike the resolution regime for banks, there is no least cost resolution requirement and the regime is not pre-funded (the FDIC may borrow from Treasury to finance it). Instead, costs that cannot be recouped in the process of resolution must be made up after the fact through assessments on counterparties (to the extent that their losses were smaller under receivership than they would have been in a traditional bankruptcy process) and risk-based assessments on financial firms with assets exceeding $50 billion. Since the rationale for limiting losses to counterparties is to prevent systemic risk, it is unclear how those counterparties could be assessed after the fact without also posing some systemic risk. A lack of pre-funding means that a firm's resolution will, in effect, be financed by its competitors (i.e., firms with assets exceeding $50 billion) instead of itself. The FDIC is limited to providing assistance in the resolution up to 10% of the failed firm's total consolidated assets in the first 30 days of the resolution; thereafter the limit becomes 90% of total consolidated assets available for repayment.

The FDIC has stated,

> the most promising resolution strategy [under Title II] from our point view will be to place the parent company into receivership and to pass its assets, principally investments in its subsidiaries, to a newly created bridge holding company. This will allow subsidiaries that are equity solvent and contribute to the franchise value of the firm to remain open and avoid the disruption that would likely accompany their closings ... .
>
> Equity claims of the firm's shareholders and the claims of the subordinated and unsecured debt holders will be left behind in the receivership....

> Therefore, initially, the bridge holding company will be owned by the receivership. The next stage in the resolution is to transfer ownership and control of the surviving franchise to private hands....
>
> The second step will be the conversion of the debt holders' claims to equity. The old debt holders of the failed parent will become the owners of the new company....[128]

This approach has been dubbed "Single Point of Entry," and the FDIC proposed a rule implementing it in December 2013.[129] A *BGOV* study argues that Single Point of Entry will only mitigate moral hazard if the holding company holds sufficient common equity and debt that can absorb losses in resolution at the parent level; otherwise, investors will anticipate that public funds will be used to absorb losses.[130]

SELECTED LEGISLATION IN THE 113TH CONGRESS

S.Amdt. 689 to the FY2014 budget resolution (S.Con.Res. 8) creates a non-binding budget reserve fund that allows for future legislation "related to any subsidies or funding advantage relative to other competitors received by bank holding companies with over $500 billion in total assets.... " It was adopted by the Senate on March 22, 2013.

H.Con.Res. 25, as amended and passed by the Senate on October 16, 2013, creates a non-binding budget reserve fund that allows for future legislation "related to any subsidies or funding advantage relative to other competitors received by bank holding companies with over $500 billion in total assets.... "

S. 2270, as passed the Senate on June 5, 2014, would allow regulators to exempt insurers from the "Collins Amendment" to the Dodd-Frank Act[131]—bank capital requirements that would otherwise apply because the insurers are bank holding companies or have been designated as systemically important. It also exempts such insurers from preparing financial statements according to Generally Accepted Accounting Principles (GAAP). Title I of H.R. 5461, which passed the House on September 16, 2014, contains the same language as S. 2270. It also includes three unrelated titles.

H.R. 4881, as ordered to be reported by the House Financial Services Committee on June 20, 2014, would place a one-year moratorium on FSOC designations of non-bank SIFIs upon enactment.

H.R. 5016, the Financial Services and General Government Appropriations Act, contained a provision introduced by H.Amdt. 1096 that

> None of the funds made available by this Act may be used to (1) designate any nonbank financial company as "too big to fail"; (2) designate any nonbank financial company as a "systemically important financial institution"; or (3) make a determination that material financial distress at a nonbank financial company, or the nature, scope, size, scale, concentration, interconnectedness, or mix of the activities of such company, could pose a threat to the financial stability of the United States.

It passed the House on July 16, 2014.

S. 798, the Terminating Bailouts for Taxpayer Fairness Act, would require a leverage ratio of at least 8% "equity capital" to "consolidated assets" for any bank or bank holding company with at least $50 billion of consolidated assets and a capital surcharge of at least 15% for any bank or bank holding company with at least $500 billion of consolidated assets. For other banks, it calls for leverage ratios comparable to leverage ratios in place as of May 1, 2013.[132] The leverage ratio for banks with at least $50 billion in assets and capital surcharge for banks with at least $500 billion in assets would apply to non-bank affiliates and subsidiaries, with the exception of subsidiaries or affiliates that are functionally regulated by the SEC or state insurance regulators. The bill would prevent "further implementation" of the Basel III agreement, which modifies safety and soundness regulation of small and large banks. The new capital requirements would supersede the ratios used under existing capital requirements that determine whether a bank is well-capitalized and the enhanced capital requirements in the Dodd-Frank Act for BHCs with at least $50 billion in assets and non-banks designated as systemically important (SIFIs). The bill allows, but does not require, regulators to establish risk-based capital requirements for financial institutions with at least $20 billion in assets if the regulators unanimously agree that the bill's other provisions are insufficient to prevent excessive risk concentration. The bill bans financial assistance to non-bank firms, subsidiaries, and affiliates from the federal government, Treasury's Exchange Stabilization Fund, the FDIC, or the Fed (through its discount window or Section 13(3) emergency powers). It also strikes from Section 806 of the Dodd-Frank Act access for financial market utilities (FMUs) to Federal Reserve account services, borrowing privileges, and interest payments. It also strikes the FDIC's systemic risk exception to least cost resolution under its bank resolution powers. The bill would modify the Federal Reserve's Small Bank Holding Company Policy Statement, which permits bank holding companies with consolidated assets of $500 million or less to acquire debt levels higher than permitted larger bank holding companies, by making the policy applicable to companies with assets of $5 billion or less. Under Dodd-Frank, bank holding companies subject to the Small Bank Holding Company Policy Statement are exempt from Basel III. The bill has other provisions, including exemptions from certain regulations for small or rural banks.

H.R. 3711/S. 1282, the 21st Century Glass-Steagall Act, would separate depository institutions from insurance companies, security entities, swap entities, and investment advisors. This legal separation includes banks affiliating with, owning, or having board members from such companies; operating in the same financial holding company; and holding an interest in a financial subsidiary. It would prohibit depository institutions from engaging in insurance activities, securities activities (including underwriting; market making; acting as a broker-dealer, futures commission merchant, investment adviser, or investment company; and making investments in hedge funds or private equity funds), swap activities (including acting as a swap dealer and major swap participant), agency transactional services, management consulting and counseling activities, proprietary trading, or prime brokerage activities. It would require banks to terminate non-bank affiliations, financial holding companies, and financial subsidiaries within five years, although federal bank regulators could require early termination or six-month extensions under certain circumstances. It would allow depository institutions to purchase securities on behalf of customers and for their own accounts, subject to restrictions. It would allow depository institutions to purchase swaps only to hedge a documented activity against specified risks. It would prohibit federal savings associations from investing in investment companies. The bill would also repeal provisions of the bankruptcy code that allow for qualified financial contracts, including repos, swaps, and master netting agreements, to avoid a stay or be liquidated, terminated, or accelerated.

S. 100, the Terminating the Expansion of Too Big to Fail Act, would repeal the provisions in the Dodd-Frank Act granting FSOC authority to designate non-bank SIFIs and Fed authority to subject them to enhanced prudential regulation, and all references to non-bank SIFIs in the Dodd-Frank Act. It would also repeal Title VIII of the Dodd-Frank Act, which provides for enhanced prudential supervision of payment, clearing, and settlement systems designated by FSOC as systemically important ("financial market utilities"). It has been referred to committee.

H.R. 1450/S. 685, Too Big to Fail, Too Big to Exist Act, would require the Secretary of the Treasury to produce a list of financial firms it believes are too big to fail, and break up those firms "so that their failure would no longer cause a catastrophic effect on the United States.... " It has been referred to committee.

H.R. 129/S. 985 Return to Prudent Banking Act, would prohibit affiliations between depositories and investment banks or securities firms. It has been referred to committee.

H.R. 613, Systemic Risk Mitigation Act, would require BHCs with at least $50 billion in assets to issue long-term subordinated debt equal to at least 15% of the bank's assets. If the average daily closing price of a credit default swap using the subordinated debt as a reference entity exceeds 0.5 percentage points, the Fed would require the BHC to increase its Tier 1 capital. If the closing price exceeds 0.75 percentage points, the Fed may suspend the BHC's dividend payments. If the closing price exceeds 1 percentage point, the company would be placed into receivership under the Orderly Liquidation Authority. The bill repeals the Fed's authority to implement enhanced prudential regulation of banks with $50 billion or more in assets and non-bank SIFIs designated by FSOC. It also repeals the Volcker Rule ban on proprietary trading and hedge fund sponsorship. The bill was referred to committee.

H.R. 2266, Subsidy Reserve Act, would require the Fed to estimate the implicit subsidy enjoyed by BHCs with more than $500 billion in assets and non-banks designated as SIFIs by the FSOC, and would require those firms to set aside that amount in a "subsidy reserve" account.

H.R. 4060, Systemic Risk Designation Improvement Act, would require FSOC to designate BHCs as SIFIs through the same process used to designate non-banks as SIFIs beginning one year after enactment. It would prohibit FSOC from designating any BHC with less than $50 billion in assets. It would repeal the section of the Dodd-Frank Act that subjects all BHCs with more than $50 billion in assets to enhanced supervision. H.R. 3036 is a similar bill.

H.R. 4532 would change the mandatory threshold for enhanced Fed supervision for banks from $50 billion to $250 billion in assets. For banks with total assets between $50 billion and $250 billion, FSOC would be required to determine that the bank posed systemic risk in order for the bank to be subject to enhanced supervision. Other provisions of the Dodd-Frank Act applying to banks with more than $50 billion in assets are also modified to apply only to banks that are subject to enhanced supervision.

Representative Dave Camp's Tax Reform Act of 2014 discussion draft includes an excise tax of 0.035% on bank and non-bank SIFIs levied on the

SIFI's total consolidated assets (as reported to the Federal Reserve) in excess of $500 billion.[133]

CONCLUSION

Contagion stemming from problems at TBTF (or too interconnected to fail) firms is widely regarded to have been one of the primary sources of systemic risk during the recent financial crisis. To avoid contagion, a series of ad hoc government interventions were undertaken that protected creditors and counterparties—in a few cases, also managers and shareholders—of large and interconnected firms from losses. Economic theory suggests that these interventions exacerbated the moral hazard implications of TBTF, reducing the incentive for creditors and counterparties to safeguard against extreme outcomes, and increased the incentive to become larger and more interconnected going forward. Competing theories blame the lack of regulatory authority and failed regulation for the role of TBTF in the recent crisis. The failures of both highly regulated banks and lightly regulated non-banks suggest that neither lack of regulation nor failed regulation were solely responsible for TBTF.

Policy before the financial crisis could be characterized as an implicit market discipline approach with ambiguity about which firms policy makers considered to be TBTF and how the imminent failure of a systemically important firm might be addressed. This ambiguity was defended on the grounds that it would result in less moral hazard than if TBTF firms were explicitly identified, since the ambiguity would promote market discipline. As the crisis unfolded, policy quickly shifted to an implicit government assistance approach where Bear Stearns, Fannie Mae, Freddie Mac, and AIG received direct government support and several emergency programs were instituted to ensure that other financial firms remained liquid and solvent. Not every large failing firm received assistance, however, with Lehman Brothers being the notable exception. Both before and during the crisis, policy could be characterized as ad hoc because arguably no general approach or principles were articulated that clearly signaled to firms or investors how a systemically important firm could expect to be treated in different scenarios. Some believe that this policy uncertainty made the crisis worse.

The rapid shift from market discipline to government assistance during the crisis undermines the future credibility of the pre-crisis policy approach. If policy makers wanted to return to a market discipline approach, making that approach effective would arguably require statutory changes that bolster policy makers' credibility by "tying their hands" to make assistance more difficult in the event of a future TBTF failure. This could be accomplished by eliminating broad, open-ended authority that was invoked during the last crisis, such as Section 13(3) of the Federal Reserve Act and the FDIC's systemic risk exception to least cost resolution. Policy makers cannot be prevented from enacting future legislation allowing assistance, however, much as TARP was enacted expeditiously when the crisis worsened in September 2008. If investors do not believe that market discipline will be maintained because policy makers face short-term incentives to provide government assistance in times of crisis, then a "no bailouts" promise would not prevent moral hazard.

One view is that the genie cannot be put back in the bottle—market participants now believe that the government will provide assistance to TBTF firms based on the 2008 experience, in which case they face little incentive to monitor or respond to excessive risk taking. If so, the policy options to mitigate moral hazard are to regulate TBTF firms or use government policy to reduce the systemic risk posed by TBTF firms.

In theory, a special regulatory regime for TBTF firms could set safety and soundness standards at a strict enough level to neutralize moral hazard effects. The complexity and interconnectedness of large firms complicates their effective regulation, however. Moreover, a special regulatory regime for TBTF firms could backfire if regulatory capture occurs. Special regulation makes explicit which firms are TBTF, removing any ambiguity that might promote market discipline. As market discipline wanes, the burden on regulators to mitigate moral hazard increases. If regulators are unwilling or unable to apply regulatory standards that negate the benefits of being TBTF, then being subject to the special regulatory regime could give TBTF firms a competitive advantage over their industry rivals. The experience of Fannie Mae and Freddie Mac points to the dangers of this approach. Those two firms were subject to their own regulatory regime prior to the crisis and were able to borrow at lower interest rates than other financial firms, presumably because of the implicit government guarantee of their obligations.

Systemic risk stemming from TBTF can also be mitigated by reducing potential spillover and contagion effects. Examples of proposals to reduce contagion effects include a special resolution regime for failing systemically important firms and placing limits on counterparty exposure to large firms. Events in 2008, however, demonstrate the challenge in eliminating systemic risk posed by TBTF firms because it is unlikely that policy makers will correctly anticipate all of the channels of contagion in a crisis. Moreover, in determining whether to use government resources to limit losses to creditors, the receiver faces the same short-term incentives to spare creditors from losses that lead to moral hazard. Critics point to the open-ended assistance to Fannie Mae and Freddie Mac since 2008 as a cautionary tale, although this was through government conservatorship, rather than receivership.

Some argue for eliminating TBTF directly by reducing the size or scope of the largest firms. It is uncertain what size limit would eliminate TBTF—given that interconnectedness is a nebulous concept—and success can only be confirmed by observing what occurs after a firm fails. Weighed against the benefits of eliminating the TBTF problem, the benefits to the financial system that would be lost by eliminating large firms are also disputed. In the case of reducing scope, some large firms would remain, and they would be less diversified against risk. Fannie Mae and Freddie Mac are examples of large, narrowly focused firms that many nonetheless viewed as TBTF.

A comprehensive policy is likely to incorporate more than one approach because different approaches are aimed at different parts of the problem. Some approaches focus on preventive measures (keeping TBTF firms out of trouble), whereas others are reactive (addressing what to do in the event of a TBTF failure). Some policy approaches are complementary—others could undermine each other. A market discipline approach is arguably most likely to succeed if coupled with size limits—although size limits thwart market-based profit incentives and outcomes. Policies that involve identification of TBTF firms, such as a special regulatory regime, are less compatible with a market discipline approach. Efforts to minimize spillover effects could be more effective if the TBTF firms are regulated for safety and soundness, so that spillover effects can more easily be identified ahead of time. Policy makers have historically coped with the moral hazard associated with deposit insurance through a combination of safety and soundness regulation, a resolution regime, and limits on spillover effects (e.g., limits on counterparty exposure). (Market discipline's role is limited by deposit insurance, but it plays a role with uninsured depositors and other creditors.) Yet TBTF poses some additional challenges to the bank regulation model, such as the difficulties of imposing a strict least cost resolution requirement on a resolution regime and effectively regulating firms with complex and wide-ranging activities.

Each of these policy approaches to coping with TBTF has strengths and weaknesses; there is no silver-bullet solution to the problem because future policy makers face incentives to deviate from the approach to avoid crises, please interest groups, increase financial innovation and the availability of credit, and so on. Judging the relative merits of each policy approach depends in part on which approach future policy makers can best commit to and effectively carry out.

The Dodd-Frank Act devised a strategy to end TBTF that, to varying degrees, incorporated each approach discussed in this report. Ultimately, the only definitive test of whether the strategy succeeds is whether the failure of a large firm can be managed without a "bailout" and whether large firms stay healthy in a financial downturn—events that may not occur for years or even decades. Until then, perceptions of whether the TBTF problem still exists may develop (and be observable in market data), which could subsequently be proven true or false.

Although TBTF was one cause of systemic risk in the recent crisis, it was not the only one. The Dodd-Frank Act also attempted to address other sources of systemic risk. Although the broader issue of systemic risk is beyond the scope of this report, some policy options discussed in this report may be more effective at mitigating systemic risk if applied more broadly than to TBTF firms exclusively. Otherwise, some sources of systemic risk may migrate to firms not regulated for safety and soundness, without increasing the stability of the overall financial system. If systemic risk mainly stems from certain activities, regardless of size, a policy focus on large institutions could risk creating a false sense of security.

Risk is central to financial activity, so an optimal system is probably not one where large firms never fail. An optimal system is one in which a large firm can fail without destabilizing the financial system. The only system that can guarantee that large firms will not cause systemic risk is one without large firms, but a system without large firms may be less efficient. Other approaches seek to limit systemic risk to acceptable levels. Creating a more stable financial system by mitigating the moral hazard associated with TBTF may result in credit becoming more expensive and less available in the short run, but the availability of credit could be less volatile over time. Some policy makers would consider a tradeoff of less credit for a more stable financial system to be a tradeoff worth taking, considering that the recent crisis resulted in the deepest and longest recession since the Great Depression. Arguably, part of the cause of the crisis was that credit became too readily available, at least in some sectors (e.g., the housing bubble). At least partly offsetting the higher costs of capital for firms designated as systemically important would be relatively lower costs of capital for other firms.

APPENDIX. SELECTED HISTORICAL EXPERIENCES WITH "TOO BIG TO FAIL"

Before the Recent Crisis

There have always been large financial firms in the United States, but concentration within the banking sector and non-bank financial sector has increased in recent decades. This growth is a reflection of both policy changes that made growth easier and market changes that made growth more profitable. For example, technological change altered the types of financial products that could be offered and the relative costs of offering them, and investments in information technology may be subject to economies of scale.

Two important policy changes that allowed financial firms to become larger since the Great Depression were the erosion of the separation of banking from other financial services (such as investment banking) and the erosion of prohibitions on interstate banking.

The Glass-Steagall Act forbade commercial banks from underwriting or trading in certain types of securities and affiliating with a business engaged principally in investment banking. It forbade investment banks from accepting deposits and forbade the same company from owning a commercial bank and an investment bank. The Bank Holding Company Act prohibited banks from affiliating with companies engaging in insurance underwriting and defined the activities closely related to banking that banks were allowed to engage in.[134] Implementation of these restrictions relied upon regulators' judgment and interpretation, which evolved over time. Regulators interpreted which securities commercial banks were eligible to purchase, which activities fell within the "business of banking," and how closely affiliated commercial banks could be with investment banks. From the 1970s on, regulators began to interpret Glass-Steagall more loosely, and differences between commercial banks and investment banks began to erode.[135]

The Gramm-Leach-Bliley Act (GLBA) of 1999 repealed the prohibition on affiliations between commercial banks and investment banks or insurance companies, and created a financial holding company (FHC) structure to facilitate those affiliations. Within a FHC or BHC, firewalls are required to prevent financial problems at non-depository subsidiary from affecting a depository subsidiary. (GLBA kept intact the provisions of Glass-Steagall preventing investment banks from accepting deposits.) While GLBA made it easier for firms in diverse lines of business to operate under a holding company structure, it also formalized Federal Reserve supervision and regulation of complex financial firms. GLBA formalized the Fed's role as "umbrella regulator" of bank holding companies and financial holding companies and the Office of Thrift Supervision as umbrella regulator of thrift holding companies, and allowed the regulators to set consolidated capital standards at the holding company level. The Fed's role as umbrella regulator gave it very limited powers, however, to regulate or examine subsidiaries that already had a functional regulator, such as investment firms and insurers.[136]

Traditionally, banks were chartered to operate in one state. Interstate banking by national banks was allowed with a state's consent under the McFadden Act of 1927 (P.L. 69-639). The absence of state consent prevented widespread interstate banking for the next several decades, curbing the growth in nationwide banks. A series of legislative and regulatory changes led to the spread of interstate banking in the 1980s and 1990s. The Riegle-Neal Interstate Banking and Branching Efficiency Act of 1994 (P.L. 103-328) further liberalized interstate banking.[137] The Riegle-Neal Act prevented mergers resulting in a BHC exceeding 10% of national deposits and 30% of a state's deposits.

The history of government bailouts on TBTF grounds before 2008 is largely limited to the cases of a few banks. In cases where government intervention to prevent the failure of non-banks on TBTF grounds was urged (Long-Term Capital Management), the government ultimately decided not to intervene financially to save the companies, and the spillover effects were limited. The **Appendix** does not review cases where federal assistance was provided on other than systemic risk grounds. Most of the economic arguments of how financial firms are prone to contagion and runs do not apply to non-financial firms. Examples include assistance to non-financial firms such as Lockheed in 1970, Chrysler in 1980, and Chrysler and GM in 2008, where assistance was justified on the grounds of avoiding negative effects on the region or industry.[138]

Resolution of Banks before and after the Federal Deposit Insurance Corporation Improvement Act

Currently, the two main methods for resolving failed banks are "depositor payoff" (winding down the bank and paying off depositors) and "purchase and assumption" (selling parts of failed banks, such as deposits and sound assets, to healthy banks).[139] In either method, uninsured depositors and creditors are compensated according to the priority of their claims to the extent that the proceeds of the sale or liquidation allow; only insured depositors are guaranteed to be fully compensated. In practice, it was standard for the acquiring bank to take on the accounts of the uninsured depositors in the case of a purchase and assumption, resulting in no losses for the latter.[140] According to Stern and Feldman, "Reliance on [purchase and assumption] led the deposit insurer to cover all depositors. The FDIC covered more than 99 percent of uninsured depositors from 1985 to 1991, a period in which roughly 1,200 commercial banks failed."[141]

In the past, an alternative option for resolving troubled banks was open bank assistance. Under open bank assistance, the FDIC could make loans to banks that could no longer obtain funding from the private sector in order to keep banks operating as an ongoing concern as an alternative to resolving them. Banks receiving open bank assistance were often required by the FDIC to replace management and dilute shareholders, but creditors and depositors would be unaffected. In 1950, Congress granted the FDIC the ability to give open bank assistance to troubled banks if the bank's "continued existence was determined to be 'essential' to providing adequate banking services in the community," leaving the determination of "essential" to the FDIC.[142] "Essentiality" was invoked 10 times between 1971 and 1991, the largest example of which was for Continental Illinois, which is discussed below in detail.[143] In 1982, the Garn-St. Germain Act broadened the FDIC's ability to provide open bank assistance to include cases where the FDIC determined that it would cost less than liquidation.

Open bank assistance was not used until the 1970s, and was not used frequently until the Savings and Loan Crisis in the 1980s. Between 1980 and 1992, it was used for 133 banks, which were larger on average than banks resolved under the other methods. 70 of the 133 instances were for banks within two specific bank holding companies, BancTexas and First City Bancorporation of Texas. While these two were not among the largest banks in the country, the FDIC provided them with open bank assistance on the grounds that their failure would lead to contagion throughout Texas banks, which had been weakened by the energy bust.[144]

Open bank assistance could be used because a bank was deemed TBTF, but it could also be used for other reasons, including regional difficulties, which were more acute before interstate banking. Some of the banks to which it was applied were large by state standards, but were not particularly large at a national level (which few banks were, at the time). Furthermore, prior to various legislation in the 1980s, the purchase and assumption method was relatively more costly and often resulted in litigation, making open bank assistance relatively more attractive from regulators' perspective. Thus, it is difficult to establish how many of these 133 cases were motivated by TBTF concerns, or how much this experience had led banks, creditors, and counterparties to conclude that large banks would not be allowed to fail.

Regulators could also avoid resolving a bank through regulatory forbearance. An example of regulatory forbearance is allowing banks to temporarily operate with capital below required levels. Regulators could choose to allow regulatory forbearance on TBTF grounds, although in practice, it often occurred with small thrifts in the 1980s.[145]

Many economists criticized the handling of bank resolutions in the 1980s, arguing that regulatory forbearance worsened the moral hazard problem, because a troubled bank allowed to remain in operation had even more incentive to take risks. Legislation in 1991 reduced the potential for regulatory forbearance by requiring prompt corrective action and least cost resolution of troubled banks.[146] These legislative changes and others made open bank assistance less likely, and according to FDIC data, open bank assistance was not used between 1993 and 2008.[147] (Purchase and assumption continued to be the main method of resolution after 1991, but bids involving only insured deposits became more common.) Current law, as amended by the 1991 legislation, allows the FDIC to waive the least cost resolution method if the Treasury Secretary (in consultation with the President, Federal Reserve, and FDIC) believes that least cost resolution would cause systemic risk, however.[148] TBTF is potential grounds for invoking this systemic risk exception. Thus, while the 1991 legislation is perceived to have reduced moral hazard at small banks, it is not clear whether it had a significant effect on the TBTF problem.

Penn Central Railroad

After unsuccessfully seeking financial assistance from Congress and the Fed, Penn Central Railroad filed for bankruptcy in June 1970. At that time, it had $82 million in commercial paper outstanding, and when it filed for bankruptcy, the Fed feared its bankruptcy would cause disruption in the commercial paper market for all borrowers. The Fed temporarily removed legal interest rate ceilings to avoid a credit crunch and "made clear that the Federal Reserve discount window would be available to assist banks in meeting the needs of businesses unable to roll over maturing commercial paper."[149] In other words, the Fed was willing to assist the counterparties to prevent contagion from a perceived TBTF failure, rather than preventing the firm from failing. In any case, the perceived contagion from that source did not materialize—data do not indicate an unusual amount of discount window lending by the Fed in 1970.[150]

Beginning in 1974, the federal government provided financial assistance to maintain the viability of passenger rail service in the wake of Penn Central's bankruptcy. This assistance was not provided to prevent bankruptcy or to maintain financial stability, and is therefore beyond the scope of this report.

Franklin National

Franklin National, the nation's 20th-largest bank, experienced financial difficulties in 1974. Fearing that its failure would destabilize money markets, the Fed purchased its foreign exchange balances and futures contracts and provided it loans through the discount window to keep it afloat. When Franklin was resolved later that year, the FDIC assumed Franklin's $1.7 billion unpaid discount window loan.[151]

Continental Illinois

Continental Illinois was the nation's seventh-largest bank in 1984.[152] Continental Illinois losses have been tied to its aggressive growth in commercial lending beginning in the late 1970s.[153] Continental Illinois' problems began in 1982 with the failure of a correspondent bank, and came to a head in 1984 with a run by some uninsured depositors. Despite being subject to the FDIC's resolution regime, the Comptroller of the Currency at the time testified that Continental Illinois could not be allowed to fail because it would have caused the failure of more than 100 banks with deposits at Continental Illinois, and dozens of corporate customers.[154] It began receiving federal assistance in 1984 in the form of discount window loans from the Fed that peaked at $8 billion and a guarantee by the FDIC of all uninsured depositors and creditors. Eventually, policy makers decided a more permanent solution was needed. Instead of taking Continental Illinois into receivership, the FDIC purchased $3.5 billion of problem loans and $1 billion of preferred shares, and repaid $3.5 billion in loans from the Federal Reserve. The final cost to FDIC was $1.1 billion.[155] The chairman of the board and chief executive officer were replaced, and the FDIC received an option to acquire Continental Illinois' stock to cover potential losses.

Continental Illinois was regulated for safety and soundness, operating in an era before many financial regulations were liberalized by the Gramm-Leach-Bliley Act and other legislative and regulatory changes.[156] One problem identified was the pace with which regulators addressed Continental's problems—the bank failed in September; the previous May, OCC had stated that the bank's capital ratios "compared favorably to those of other multinational banks."[157] Had regulators addressed Continental Illinois' financial problems sooner, the ultimate cost to taxpayers may have been lower. Continental Illinois also led to a more explicit TBTF policy, at least for banks. At a congressional hearing, Comptroller of the Currency Todd Conover testified that "the federal government won't currently allow any of the nation's 11 largest banks to fail," but did not name those banks.[158] One study found that after this testimony, the 11 largest banks received higher ratings on their bonds and borrowed at lower costs.[159]

Long-Term Capital Management

In 1998, the hedge fund Long-Term Capital Management (LTCM) experienced a liquidity crisis as a result of large leveraged trading losses resulting from an unanticipated widening of credit spreads. To avoid a failure that the Fed thought could be destabilizing to the financial system as a whole, the New York Fed organized a group of large financial institutions to offer LTCM private assistance in the form of a $3.6 billion capital injection, without the use of any public funds or guarantees. The Fed was concerned that liquidating LTCM's large trading positions could destabilize financial markets and impose large losses on counterparties. In the weeks before the capital injection, LTCM's capital had been rapidly depleted by losses, but its net asset value was still positive, albeit small, at the time of the intervention.[160] The Fed's actions in this case could be described as helping the rescuing firms (who were also LTCM counterparties) to overcome the collective action problem—the firms involved were better off recapitalizing the firm than liquidating it, but unless they could act collectively, it was in no firm's individual interest to recapitalize it alone. Critics claimed the Fed's intervention was unnecessary, as an alternative offer from another group of investors to purchase the firm on less attractive terms was also made.[161]

As in 2007, overall markets came under unusual stress and became illiquid in 1998. Unlike 2007, the stress passed and markets recovered quickly in 1998. Although it is unknown what would have happened had LTCM been allowed to fail, this experience seemed at the time to provide a framework for coping with problems at a TBTF firm—preventing LTCM's failure prevented contagion from spreading to other institutions or markets, and conditions were able to quickly normalize. Since the government did not offer financial assistance, it could continue to claim that TBTF firms would not be bailed out. LTCM's problems did not cause investors to doubt the health of similar firms, as happened in the recent crisis. A lesson that many drew from this episode was that market mechanisms and existing policy tools could contain the contagion effects resulting from liquidity problems at a highly leveraged and interconnected firm that was not regulated for safety and soundness.

Firms in 2008

Several large firms experienced difficulty in 2008, and these problems were resolved in a number of ways. Bear Stearns and AIG were rescued from failure through government assistance. Lehman Brothers filed for bankruptcy. Fannie Mae and Freddie Mac entered government conservatorship. Wachovia and Washington Mutual were acquired by other banks without government assistance.

As the name implies, "too big to fail" requires both size and the prospect of failure. Part of the reason the policy issue came to the forefront in 2008 and not earlier is because the crisis led to so many failures of large and small firms. The probability of a large (or small) firm failing in 2008 was much higher than in the decades of financial stability leading up to 2008. More contentious is the argument made by some that the probability of failure was also higher in 2008 because large firms were taking greater risks than in previous decades. Evidence presented in support of this argument includes the rise over time in financial firms' use of leverage (debt-to-equity ratios),[162] unstable sources of liquidity, and complex financial instruments such as credit default swaps (which could be used by a firm to reduce or increase certain forms of risk).

Bear Stearns

In the recent crisis, the investment bank Bear Stearns was the first TBTF firm to receive government assistance to avert failure.[163] Bear Stearns was not a bank holding company regulated for safety and soundness, nor subject to the FDIC's resolution regime.[164] It came under severe liquidity pressures in early March 2008, when creditors refused to roll over short-term debt and counterparties withdrew funds, in what observers have coined a non-bank run. An SEC press release a few days before its takeover indicated that Bear Stearns had $17 billion of cash and other liquid assets—an amount that was quickly depleted by the run.[165] The run was set off by concerns that Bear Stearns held a large portfolio of illiquid, "troubled" assets that investors believed would continue losing value in the future and deplete its remaining capital.

By the weekend of March 15, it had become clear that Bear Stearns could not survive the run by creditors. Although Bear Stearns was not indisputably "too big to fail" (it was the 138th-largest firm by revenues in 2007 on *Fortune Magazine*'s Fortune 500 list),[166] some policy makers argued for government intervention on the grounds that Bear Stearns was "too interconnected to fail," meaning too many counterparties and markets would be disrupted by a traditional bankruptcy filing.[167] The Fed sought a healthy firm to acquire Bear Stearns, but was unable to find a willing partner without financial assistance. Over the weekend of March 15, the Fed arranged and assisted in the takeover of Bear Stearns by J.P. Morgan Chase at a very low purchase price (originally $2 per share, subsequently increased to $10 per share), which Bear Stearns' board of directors agreed to accept instead of pursuing a bankruptcy filing. The takeover led to replacement of some of Bear Stearns' management and the low share price meant that shareholders were effectively diluted, although they likely fared better than they would have in a bankruptcy proceeding. J.P. Morgan Chase agreed to honor all of Bear Stearns' contractual obligations, however, which meant that creditors and counterparties were fully compensated, creating moral hazard problems.

The main stumbling block for J.P. Morgan Chase was Bear Stearns' large portfolio of troubled assets. As part of the agreement, the Fed agreed to purchase up to $30 billion of Bear Stearns' assets through Maiden Lane I, a new Limited Liability Corporation (LLC) based in Delaware that it created and controlled. J.P. Morgan Chase would bear up to $1.15 billion in future first losses, based on assets valued at $29.97 billion at marked-to-market prices by Bear Stearns on March 14, 2008.[168] About half of these assets were collateralized mortgage obligations. The Fed has gradually sold off the assets, in order "to minimize disruption to financial markets and maximize recovery value."[169] This transaction exposed the Fed to significant credit risk on its balance sheet for the first time in decades. By 2012, Maiden Lane had received more from asset sales than the Fed had contributed to their purchases. Principal and interest were recouped, and some assets remained that could provide the Fed with additional future profits when sold. CBO estimated at the time of inception that the Maiden Lane transaction was not subsidized since the assets were bought at market prices.[170] In addition, during the JP Morgan Chase takeover, Bear Stearns had an average of $13.9 billion loans outstanding from the Primary Dealer Credit Facility from March 17 to June 23, 2008, and $1.5 billion loans outstanding from the Term Securities Lending Facility from March 28 to May 9, 2008.[171] These facilities were broadly based emergency Fed programs created during the crisis. These loans were repaid in full with interest.

Had Bear Stearns been a bank holding company, it might have been able to boost its liquidity with collateralized loans from the Fed. It also would have been subject to prudential regulation by the Fed that might have required it to pursue a more conservative business strategy. Since it was not a bank holding company, the Fed relied on emergency lending powers not used to lend to non-banks since the Great Depression. Since these powers limited the Fed to lending, the Fed was required to set up the LLC structure to make the asset purchases possible.

Although Bear Stearns' liquidity problems were driving it into bankruptcy had the government not interceded, it is unclear whether it was insolvent. Before that weekend, Bear Stearns was not insolvent by two common measurements: its stock price (representing the current market valuation of the firm's net worth) was still $30 per share, and its primary regulator, the Securities and Exchange Commission (SEC), issued a press release on March 11 that stated that Bear Stearns was adequately capitalized according to its net capital rule.[172] Even after the crisis, existing shares were valued positively in the J.P. Morgan Chase takeover, and no capital was provided to Bear Stearns as part of the Fed's assistance (since the assets bought by Maiden Lane were purchased at market value, according to the Fed). On the other hand, J.P. Morgan stated that the equity in Bear Stearns was exhausted and J.P. Morgan Chase took additional losses from costs associated with the Bear Stearns acquisition.[173]

Unlike the LTCM experience, the rescue of Bear Stearns arguably did not cause investors to conclude that Bear Stearns was an isolated "bad apple." Instead, speculation persisted over the next few months that other investment banks would suffer the same fate—speculation that came to a head with the wave of financial firm failures in September 2008.

Ban on Naked Short Selling in July 2008

As financial turmoil worsened in the summer of 2008, the stock value of many large financial firms fell quickly. The SEC responded on July 15, 2008, by announcing that investors would no longer be able to "naked short sell" the stocks of 19 large financial firms, an investment strategy that would pay off if the firms' stock price fell further.[174] The firms chosen were Fannie Mae, Freddie Mac, and the primary dealers (large financial firms that conduct open market operations with the Federal Reserve).[175] Some market participants perceived this announcement as an explicit list of the firms that the government considered too big to fail. If this announcement was intended to rescue troubled firms, either by making short selling more difficult or by making too big to fail status more explicit, it did not work in all cases—in September 2008, Lehman Brothers entered bankruptcy, while Fannie Mae and Freddie Mac entered government conservatorship. Nor did the list closely correspond to which firms would or would not receive government assistance subsequently—American International Group (AIG) received assistance although it was not one of the 19 firms listed, while Lehman Brothers did not receive although it was included on the list.

The July ban was superseded by an SEC rule issued on September 18, 2008, that temporarily banned all short-selling of the stocks of 700 financial firms and an October 1, 2008, rule that imposed a permanent ban on naked short-selling.

Fannie Mae and Freddie Mac

Not only were Fannie Mae and Freddie Mac very large, their TBTF status was also influenced by their unusual status as government sponsored enterprises (GSEs). Because of unusual features such as their congressional charter, line of credit with the Treasury, dominance of the home mortgage secondary market, and original status as government agencies, investors perceived them as more likely to be backed by the government than other firms, although their securities had no explicit government guarantee. This perception allowed them to consistently borrow at a lower cost than other financial firms, despite holding relatively little capital. Before conservatorship, Fannie Mae and Freddie Mac were the only firms regulated by their federal regulator, whose independence and powers were limited compared to other regulators.[176] These institutional features led critics to argue that the GSEs enjoyed the benefits of "regulatory capture." Their regulator found them to meet the statutory definition of well capitalized as recently as July 2008.[177]

Holding mainly mortgage-backed securities and mortgages in their portfolios, they were uniquely vulnerable to the decline in the housing market and MBS prices. In July 2008, investor concern about persistent losses and the potential for future losses led to a sharp decline in stock prices and cast doubt on their ability to roll over maturing debt. Treasury Secretary Paulson argued that the solution to this problem was for Congress to grant him what he referred to as a "bazooka"—the authority for Treasury to provide the GSEs with unlimited funding. He argued that the bazooka would calm investor fears, and as a result would not need to be used. Congress provided this authority in the Housing and Economic Recovery Act (P.L. 110-289).

By September 2008, the government decided to take the GSEs into conservatorship following further losses.[178] Conservatorship means that the government has assumed the normal powers of the officers, board of directors, and shareholders, but the GSEs would continue business operations. In addition, the government would purchase their MBS and inject as much capital as needed to keep the firms solvent. In return, the government received warrants to purchase 79.9% of the companies' common stock, which would dilute existing shareholders when exercised. Management was also replaced and dividends on preferred shares were eliminated, but creditors, including subordinated debt holders, and counterparties suffered no losses.

One rationale for placing the GSEs in conservatorship was that their dominant role in mortgage-backed securities markets could not have been replaced quickly by the private sector given the housing downturn. Without them, mortgage credit would have become less available, placing further downward pressure on the housing market. Another rationale was the potential for contagion to counterparties and creditors given the large amount of GSE debt and GSEguaranteed MBS outstanding.

To bridge the gap between the companies' assets and liabilities, the government provided $187.5 billion to the companies in exchange for preferred shares between 2008 and 2012. The government received $55 billion of dividends on those shares through 2012. Since then, the GSEs' assets have matched their liabilities and no further preferred share issuance has been needed. Under the existing agreement, the GSEs' profits (after dividend payments) would have accumulated in their coffers.[179] Treasury announced in August 2012 that, "(a)cting upon the commitment ... that the GSEs will be wound down and will not be allowed to retain profits, rebuild capital, and return to the market in their prior form," the preferred share agreements had been amended to replace the dividend and commitment fee with a "net income sweep" that would remit all profits to the Treasury.[180] Regardless of the amount remitted, the terms of the sweep do not allow for a reduction in the preferred shares outstanding. Thus, while Treasury has not recouped any principal, it earned a cumulative $202.8 billion in income through the first quarter of 2014—more than it outlayed.

In economic terms, the subsidy to the GSEs, which takes into account future losses and the opportunity cost inherent in the GSEs' ability to borrow at below market rates, was estimated by CBO to be $291 billion through 2009. Since this estimate was made in August 2009, the state of the housing market has improved considerably, which could reduce expected defaults and thus the size of the subsidy, were CBO to update its estimate. In addition, CBO assumes that the companies will continue to do business at below-market costs in the future that will lead to future subsidies from the government.[181]

Between December 2008 and March 2010, the Fed purchased $67 billion of debt issued by Freddie Mac and $67 billion issued by Fannie Mae as part of its "Large Scale Asset Purchases" (popularly known as quantitative easing). While the asset purchases were intended to provide support to mortgage markets and to stimulate overall economic conditions, another effect of these purchases was to reduce the GSEs' borrowing costs, all else equal. As these assets have matured, the Fed's holdings have declined over time. The Fed faces no default risk on its GSE holdings as long as the Treasury continues to stand behind the GSEs, and will not experience capital losses (or gains) as long as it continues to hold the securities to maturity. The Treasury and Fed have also purchased debt and MBS issued by the GSEs since 2008. The MBS purchases were made at market prices on the secondary market, so the purchases conferred no direct benefit to the GSEs, but had the effect of indirectly raising the price received by the GSEs for their MBS.

Lehman Brothers

Shortly after the failures of Fannie Mae and Freddie Mac, the investment bank Lehman Brothers experienced a liquidity crisis. Lehman Brothers was the 47th-largest firm by revenues in 2007 on *Fortune Magazine*'s Fortune 500 list.[182] Lehman Brothers was not a bank holding company regulated for safety and soundness, nor subject to the FDIC's resolution regime. Lehman Brothers was a unitary thrift holding company under OTS umbrella supervision; OTS was focused mainly on the health of the depository subsidiaries. It also complied with an SEC net capital rule.[183] Policy makers decided to allow Lehman Brothers to file for bankruptcy when it became clear that no other firm was willing to acquire the firm without government assistance. According to Bankruptcydata.com, Lehman Brothers was the largest firm by assets ever to file for bankruptcy.[184]

Lehman Brothers was larger than Bear Stearns and was involved in similar business lines. Bear Stearns had been saved with government assistance, and many market participants were surprised that a similar arrangement was not made for Lehman Brothers. Unlike Bear Stearns, Lehman Brothers had access to Fed lending facilities (created after the Bear Stearns crisis), but did not have enough collateral under the terms of the Fed program to borrow enough to meet its liquidity needs at the time of its failure. (This problem did not arise when the Fed rescued AIG the next day.) Policy makers argued that markets should not have expected government assistance because they had stressed since the Bear Stearns intervention that similar assistance could not be expected in the future and that failures were necessary to prevent moral hazard problems. Policy makers also argued that Lehman Brothers had plenty of time to defend themselves from the fate suffered by Bear Stearns by raising more capital and long-term liquidity. (Lehman Brothers did raise some in the summer of 2008.) Policy makers believed that they and counterparties were now well enough prepared for a counterparty failure that systemic risk could be contained.[185]

Some point to the complex, lengthy nature of Lehman Brothers' bankruptcy proceedings as evidence that Lehman Brothers was too big to fail, while others argue that bankruptcy proceedings have gone relatively smoothly and are successfully resolving the claims of creditors and counterparties in an orderly fashion.[186] A New York Fed study finds that creditors received an unusually low recovery rate from the Lehman bankruptcy.[187]

Where Lehman Brothers' failure proved more disruptive to financial markets was through its effects on money market mutual funds (MMF) and the commercial paper market. On September 16, 2008, a MMF called the Reserve Fund "broke the buck," meaning that the value of its shares had fallen below face value. This occurred because of losses it had taken on short-term debt issued by Lehman Brothers, which filed for bankruptcy on September 15, 2008. Money market investors had perceived "breaking the buck" to be highly unlikely, and its occurrence set off a run on money market funds, as investors simultaneously attempted to withdraw an estimated $250 billion of their investments—even from funds without exposure to Lehman Brothers.[188] MMFs are major investors in commercial paper, so this run greatly decreased the demand for new commercial paper.[189] Firms rely on the ability to issue new debt to roll over maturing debt to meet their liquidity needs. A blanket federal guarantee of MMFs and three Federal Reserve commercial paper programs were created to restore calm to these markets.[190]

Contagion from Lehman Brothers' failure also spread to its three remaining independent "bulge bracket" investment bank rivals, Merrill Lynch, Morgan Stanley, and Goldman Sachs. All three experienced liquidity strains following Lehman Brothers' failure, which all three survived, but only after fundamental changes to their business models. Merrill Lynch merged with Bank of America under financial strain, which would cause problems for Bank of America in the ensuing months. Goldman Sachs and Morgan Stanley changed their charters to become bank holding companies, under the umbrella supervision of the Federal Reserve. All three relied heavily on broadly based federal facilities to weather the storm. Borrowing from the Fed's Primary

Dealer Credit Facility peaked at $48 billion for Morgan Stanley and $40 billion for Merrill Lynch on September 26, 2008, and at $17 billion for Goldman Sachs on October 10, 2008. All three firms also accessed the Fed's Term Securities Lending Facility throughout the fall and its Commercial Paper Funding Facility beginning in late October. Morgan Stanley and Goldman Sachs each received $10 billion in exchange for preferred shares through TARP's Capital Purchase Program on October 28, 2008, and $10 billion of CPP funds for Merrill Lynch were received by Bank of America after their merger.

Although the Fed was not willing to rescue Lehman Brothers, it provided Lehman Brothers with liquidity for a short time to ease the bankruptcy process.[191] Lehman Brothers borrowed an average of $23 billion each day from the Fed's Primary Dealer Credit Facility, a broadly based emergency facility, from September 15, the day it filed for bankruptcy, to September 17, 2008.[192] Lehman Brothers also borrowed from the Fed's Term Securities Lending Facility frequently from March 2008 to September 12, 2008.

AIG

At the same time as the failure of Lehman Brothers, American International Group (AIG) ran into liquidity problems as a result of collateral calls on its credit default swaps and securities lending program.[193]

AIG is a large financial firm operating domestically and abroad; at the time of the crisis, its insurance operations were the fifth largest in the world. While AIG is often thought of as an insurance company, it was a complex financial institution with many different types of subsidiaries, such as AIG Financial Products, which Fed Chairman Bernanke reportedly likened to a hedge fund.[194] Its overall legal structure was a unitary thrift regulated by the Office of Thrift Supervision (OTS), although its thrift operations were relatively small. AIG's insurance subsidiaries were regulated at the state level. Losses were centered in the Financial Products subsidiary and its securities lending program; as its umbrella regulator, OTS was focused mainly on the health of the depository subsidiaries. OTS has testified that it did not fully foresee the potential losses that transactions undertaken by AIG Financial Products posed to the holding company.[195]

Unlike Lehman Brothers, policy makers decided that the systemic risk implications of an AIG failure were too great. AIG was listed as the 10th-largest firm by revenues in 2007 on *Fortune Magazine*'s Fortune 500 list.[196] On September 16, 2008, the Fed announced that it was taking action to support AIG. Using emergency authority, this support took the form of a secured two-year line of credit with a value of up to $85 billion and a high interest rate (set at 8.5 percentage points above the London Interbank Offered Rate). Although the Fed denied assistance to Lehman Brothers on the grounds that it lacked acceptable collateral, the loan to AIG was collateralized by the general assets of AIG.[197] In addition, the government received warrants to purchase up to 79.9% of the equity in AIG.

Once the determination to assist AIG had been made, assistance arguably became open-ended, and more government assistance was provided on several subsequent occasions. On October 8, 2008, the Fed announced that it would lend AIG up to an additional $37.8 billion against securities held by its insurance subsidiaries. These securities had been previously lent out and were not available as collateral at the time of the original intervention, increasing AIG's cash flow problems. In October 2008, AIG also announced that it had applied to the Fed's general Commercial Paper Facility and was approved to borrow up to $20.9 billion at the facility's standard terms.

The financial support for AIG was restructured in early November 2008. The restructured financial support included up to a $60 billion loan from the Fed, with the term lengthened to five years and the interest rate reduced by 5.5 percentage points; $40 billion in preferred share purchases through the TARP through a new program created for AIG called the "Systemically Significant Failing Institutions Program"; up to $52.5 billion total in asset purchases by the Fed through two Limited Liability Corporations (LLCs) known as Maiden Lane II and Maiden Lane III. AIG contributed an additional $6 billion for the LLCs and will bear the first $6 billion in any losses on the asset values. By 2012, the Maiden Lanes had received more from asset sales than the Fed had contributed to their purchases. Principal and interest were recouped, and further gains from these LLCs were shared between the Fed and AIG.

The 79.9% common equity position of the government in AIG remained essentially unchanged after the restructuring of the intervention, although assistance was increased. Additional restructurings were announced in March 2010 and September 2010. In the latter restructuring, the Federal Reserve loan was repaid in full and the preferred shares were converted into common equity. This increases the risk and potential reward for the government from its AIG holdings since the common equity can rise or fall in value based on market conditions and the future financial performance of AIG. Warrants initially valued at $1.2 billion were also issued to AIG's private shareholders at this time, transferring value from the government to shareholders. The government sold its common equity stake between May 2011 and December 2012.

With each restructuring, costs were reduced for AIG and risks were shifted away from AIG to the government. Policy makers initially provided loans with very high interest rates out of moral hazard concerns, but found that punitive conditions decreased the ongoing viability of the company (and, hence, the probability that the assistance would be repaid). Therefore, when assistance was revised, conditions typically became less punitive. Since the government held 92.6% of the common stock in AIG at the peak, however, a case can be made that the benefits of any restructuring that improves AIG's future profitability mostly accrues to the government.

On a cash-flow basis, the Fed and Treasury combined ultimately received $23 billion more than they outlayed to AIG. Whether this resulted in an economic profit for the federal government or a subsidy to AIG depends on the opportunity cost of those funds, based on the risks that the government undertook and the time value of money. CBO has made such a calculation, and estimates that the TARP portion of the assistance to AIG will have a net cost of $15 billion over the lifetime of the assistance.[198] At the time of the Fed's intervention, CBO estimated a $2 billion subsidy for the Fed portion of the assistance; since the Fed's intervention turned out to be cash-flow positive and CBO has revised downward its estimates of TARP subsidies over time, that amount could be re-estimated downward if CBO were to update it.

Washington Mutual and Wachovia

Two large banks, Washington Mutual and Wachovia, were successfully resolved by the FDIC through mergers during the 2008 crisis, at no cost to the taxpayers.

Washington Mutual was a thrift holding company. Its depository subsidiary experienced depositor runs in 2008 following losses. It was the 81st-largest firm by revenues in 2007 on *Fortune Magazine*'s Fortune 500 list and the largest thrift holding company.[199] Depositors withdrew $9.4 billion between July 12 and July 30, and $15 billion between September 11 and 26—the closest the 2008 crisis saw to a traditional bank run.[200] On September 25, the thrift was taken into receivership by the FDIC. It was resolved through a purchase and assumption agreement with J.P. Morgan Chase. As part of the agreement, J.P. Morgan Chase paid $1.9 billion to assume the claims of uninsured depositors, counterparties with qualified financial contracts, and secured creditors; it did not assume the claims of unsecured creditors or equity holders.[201] The remainder of the company filed for bankruptcy on September 26. Thus, the receivership required no federal funds, and the moral hazard problem was mitigated since unsecured creditors and equity holders suffered losses. J.P. Morgan Chase's willingness to pay to assume other liabilities implies that it believed the remaining assets were sufficient to honor those liabilities.

Washington Mutual received a $1 billion, 28-day loan from the Federal Reserve's Term Auction Facility on September 11, 2008. The bank was closed by the FDIC on September 25, 2008, and the loan was repaid after its merger. Since the loan was fully collateralized and the Fed receives priority ahead of other creditors, it appears to have posed little risk to the taxpayers in the face of receivership. Nonetheless, the loan appears to have been a departure from Fed policy since the Fed's broadly based lending programs were intended to provide liquidity to solvent firms.

Washington Mutual could be seen as an example of a TBTF bank that experienced an orderly resolution through the FDIC's resolution regime at no cost to the taxpayers. Or it could be seen as too small to be relevant to the TBTF debate.

Wachovia (the 46th-largest firm on *Fortune Magazine*'s Fortune 500 list in 2007) faced runs soon after Washington Mutual failed. According to Federal Reserve testimony,

> The day after the failure of WaMu, Wachovia Bank depositors accelerated the withdrawal of significant amounts from their accounts. In addition, wholesale funds providers withdrew liquidity support from Wachovia. It appeared likely that Wachovia would soon become unable to fund its operations.[202]

According to the Fed, problems at Wachovia were unforeseen, making the bank both a victim and a potential transmitter of contagion:

> At the time, Wachovia was considered "well capitalized" by regulatory standards and until very recently had not generally been thought to be in danger of failure, so there were fears that the failure of Wachovia would lead investors to doubt the financial strength of other organizations in similar situations, making it harder for those institutions to raise capital and other funding.[203]

On September 27 and 28, Wells Fargo and Citigroup placed competing bids to acquire Wachovia. Initially, those bids were contingent on federal assistance. FDIC assistance under the systemic risk exception to least cost resolution had been approved.[204] Later, Wells Fargo revised its offer, acquiring Wachovia without federal assistance and averting a receivership.

Neither the Washington Mutual nor the Wachovia acquisitions were found to breach the RiegleNeal 10% nationwide deposit cap. JP Morgan Chase's acquisition of Washington Mutual's deposits and other assets occurred through an FDIC purchase and assumption arrangement. The 10% deposit cap does not apply to an FDIC purchase and assumption. In its approval of Wells Fargo's acquisition of Wachovia, the Fed noted that using the most current data, the merged entity would be above the 10% deposit limit. The Fed then argued that since that data were released with a lag, projections of *current* deposit data indicated that the merger would probably fall below the 10% cap.[205]

Although the Fed's Term Auction Facility was intended for healthy firms, Wachovia received nine Term Auction Facility loans between September 11, 2008, and February 26, 2009, including $5 billion on September 25, 2008, one day before the run on Wachovia began. Its merger with Wells Fargo was announced on October 3, 2008.

TARP, Citigroup, Bank of America, and the Stress Tests

The first and largest program initiated under the Troubled Asset Relief Program (TARP) was the Capital Purchase Program (CPP).[206] The purpose of the CPP was to provide banks and bank holding companies (BHC) with preferred shares to increase their capital buffers against future losses at a time when it was difficult for banks to access private capital. The CPP was intended for healthy banks of all sizes and unsuitable candidates were rejected. Therefore, it does not closely match the definition of bailout used in this report, which implies assistance to unhealthy firms, or TBTF assistance. Nevertheless, CPP funds went to banks that later failed (14 mostly small banks, as of December 2011)[207] and the first recipients were the nine largest BHCs, all of whom had fully repaid CPP shares by 2010. If limited to healthy banks and purchased at market rates, preferred shares impose limited risk on taxpayers. Despite the handful of losses on CPP investments in small banks, CBO has estimated that the government will ultimately earn an overall economic profit (i.e., earn an above market rate of return) from the CPP from dividends and warrants. In October 2012, CBO estimated that profit to be $18 billion.[208]

After the initial disbursement of CPP funds, Citigroup and Bank of America received additional TARP capital injections and asset guarantees for their balance sheet holdings through a special TARP program with no other recipients. The additional capital paid a higher dividend rate than the CPP shares. Other TARP programs included programs to assist AIG (discussed above) and the automakers. As will be discussed, the program for automakers was used to provide special assistance to two financial firms, Chrysler Financial and GMAC (later renamed Ally Financial).

Following the additional TARP capital injections, Citigroup remained well capitalized according to regulatory standards.[209] It appears that without TARP funds Citigroup would have fallen to slightly below the Fed's minimum Tier 1 Leverage requirements of 4% at the end of 2008, assuming they had not raised private capital in the absence of TARP funds.[210] Regulations require BHCs to submit a plan to the Fed in a timely manner if they fall below minimum capital requirements.[211] In February 2009, Citigroup and the federal government reached an agreement to convert up to $27.5 billion of Citigroup's TARP preferred shares into common equity. This agreement had the result of boosting Citigroup's common equity ratios and ending dividend payments to the government.[212] It also exposed the government to greater risk and potentially greater return on its investments, since common equity can rise and fall in value, unlike the TARP preferred shares. Citigroup was the largest financial firm in the country and eighth-largest firm overall on *Fortune Magazine*'s 2007 Fortune 500 list.[213]

Bank of America's financial problems centered mainly on its acquisitions of Countrywide and another very large financial firm, the investment bank Merrill Lynch. At the time of the Lehman Brothers crisis, Merrill Lynch also came under financial pressure as a result of its similar business model, forcing it to seek a merger partner. Merrill Lynch (the 22nd-largest firm on *Fortune Magazine*'s Fortune 500 list in 2007) was larger than either of those firms. In September 2008, Bank of America and Merrill Lynch reached an agreement in principle to merge. As financial conditions deteriorated further, Bank of America considered pulling out of the merger. To prevent this, according to the Treasury Secretary at the time, the government agreed to purchase another $20 billion of preferred shares through TARP and enter into a federal asset guarantee agreement.[214] The merger was finalized in January 2009, and Bank of America received the additional TARP shares shortly thereafter; the asset guarantee was never finalized. In its March 2009 call report, Bank of America remained well capitalized according to regulatory standards.[215] It appears that even without TARP funds Bank of America would have remained above the Fed's minimum Tier 1 leverage requirements of 4% in that quarter.[216]

In May 2009, the Federal Reserve released the results of the Supervisory Capital Assessment Program, its "stress tests" for the 19 largest bank holding companies.[217] The stress tests were meant to determine whether these banks would remain well capitalized in the event of a downside economic scenario. The tests required banks to be able to maintain Tier 1 Risk-Based Capital of

6% and Tier 1 Common Capital of 4% in this scenario. Of the participants, 10 of 19 were found to be well capitalized against future losses; of those 10, the 9 participating in TARP bought back their preferred shares and exited the program shortly thereafter. Of the other nine that required additional capital to withstand hypothetical losses under the adverse scenario, seven (including Bank of America, which was required to raised $33.9 billion) were able to raise the needed capital without government funds; GMAC required TARP funds (through the Automotive Industry Financing Program) to raise the needed capital; and Citigroup, which was required to raise $5.5 billion, met the threshold for Tier 1 Common Capital in part by converting more of its existing CPP preferred shares into common shares. After the preferred shares were converted to common equity, the government owned about one-third of the company.[218]

In December 2009, Citigroup bought back $20 billion of TARP preferred securities outstanding, replacing those shares with private capital, and terminated the government's asset guarantee for a fee. In March 2010, the Treasury announced plans to dispose of its common shares in Citigroup by the end of the year. The government ultimately sold these shares for $31.9 billion, or $6.9 billion more than the initial assistance extended. Treasury reports that for the three programs assisting Citigroup combined, it had a positive cash flow of $13.4 billion.[219]

In December 2009, Bank of America repurchased all of its TARP preferred shares, replacing those shares with private capital, and paid a fee to cancel the asset guarantee that was negotiated but never entered into.

The experience with Bank of America and Citigroup is quite different from the experience with AIG and the GSEs. While TARP funds kept Bank of America's and Citigroup's capital levels above the minimally required level, neither firm is believed to have been close to insolvency—although it is unknown what would have happened to Merrill Lynch had Bank of America not acquired it. Bank of America repaid TARP funds in full in December 2009, and the government fully divested from Citigroup in 2010. CBO has estimated that the government earned an economic profit, calculated using a risk-adjusted discount rate, of $8 billion from its special assistance to the two companies.[220]

GMAC

While Congress authorized TARP to "purchase, and to make and fund commitments to purchase, troubled assets from any financial institution, on such terms and conditions as are determined by the Secretary, and in accordance with this Act and the policies and procedures developed and published by the Secretary," TARP funding was also used to facilitate the bankruptcy process for GM and Chrysler.[221] Economists have generally focused on financial firms as being TBTF because of the interconnectedness inherent in financial intermediation; determining whether automakers can be TBTF is beyond the scope of this report.

In conjunction with the automakers, two financial firms related to the automakers, GMAC and Chrysler Financial, also received TARP assistance. Chrysler Financial was a relatively small financial firm, and it repaid its $1.5 billion TARP loan in full with interest by July 2009. GMAC received several rounds of TARP funding in order to return its capital levels to acceptable levels. After converting to a bank holding company during the crisis, GMAC was the 10th-largest bank holding company, with $180 billion in assets, in the first quarter of 2009. It dominated dealer floorplan financing for GM and Chrysler, and reportedly had three times the market share of its five largest competitors in auto financing.[222]

TARP first purchased $5 billion of GMAC preferred shares in December 2008 and lent $884 million to GM, which was later transferred to GMAC, as part of the initial assistance provided to the automakers. As discussed above, GMAC was one of the nine bank holding companies that were required to raise additional capital under the May 2009 stress tests. It was the only one of those nine that raised the capital through additional TARP disbursements, rather than through private markets. The government purchased an additional $7.5 billion of preferred shares and converted the $884 million loan into 35.4% of GMAC's common equity in May 2009. The government then purchased $2.54 billion of trust preferred securities and an additional $1.25 billion of preferred shares in December 2009. At the same time, it converted $3 billion in preferred shares for 20.9% of GMAC's common equity. In December 2010, it converted an additional $5.5 billion of preferred shares into 17.5% of GMAC's common equity; $5.9 billion of preferred shares remain outstanding, and the government has sold the trust preferred securities to private investors at face value. This made recoupment of funds for the government dependent on the future value of GMAC (renamed Ally Financial).[223] To date, the government has sold its preferred shares back to GMAC and some of its common stock to private investors. Although the government still holds shares, the proceeds from share sales plus income received less writeoffs to date has slightly exceeded its total initial outlays. CBO does not estimate a separate subsidy cost for the government's assistance to GMAC, but estimates "a small net cost" for assistance to GMAC and Chrysler Financial combined.[224]

End Notes

[1] For more information, see CRS Report R41073, *Government Interventions in Response to Financial Turmoil*, by Baird Webel and Marc Labonte.

[2] For an overview, see CRS Report R41350, *The Dodd-Frank Wall Street Reform and Consumer Protection Act: Background and Summary*, coordinated by Baird Webel. For more information on systemic risk provisions, see CRS Report R41384, *The Dodd-Frank Wall Street Reform and Consumer Protection Act: Systemic Risk and the Federal Reserve*, by Marc Labonte.

[3] For more information on the FSOC, see CRS Report R42083, *Financial Stability Oversight Council: A Framework to Mitigate Systemic Risk*, by Edward V. Murphy.

[4] Information on designated firms can be accessed here: http://www.treasury.gov/initiatives /fsoc/designations/Pages/ default.aspx.

[5] MetLife, press release, September 4, 2014, https://www.metlife.com/about/press-room/index.html?compID=140852. See also U.S. Treasury, press release, September 4, 2014, http://www.treasury.gov/press-center/press-releases/Pages/ jl2621.aspx.

[6] Financial Stability Board, "2013 Update of Global Systemically Important Banks," November 11, 2013, http://www.financialstabilityboard.org/publications/r_131111.pdf; Financial Stability Board, "Global Systemically Important Insurers and the Policy Measures That Will Apply to Them," July 18, 2013, http://www.financialstabilityboard.org/publications /r_130718.pdf. The Financial Stability Board is an international forum of which the United States is a member. A list of the U.S. firms can be found in the section below entitled "Regulating TBTF."

[7] See, for example, Government Accountability Office, *Large Bank Holding Companies – Expectations of Government Support*, GAO-14-621, July 2014.

[8] Data from National Information Center, http://www.ffiec.gov/nicpubweb/nicweb/Top50 Form.aspx. This list includes any type of institution that includes a depository subsidiary. These data exaggerate changes in the relative importance of large banks since they do not take into account inflation or growth in the economy.

[9] Federal Reserve Bank of Chicago, *Top Banks and Holding Companies*, period ending December 31, 2012, available at http://www.chicagofed.org/webpages. In addition, the top five savings and loan holding companies hold 68% of total assets and the top five state-member banks hold 47% of total assets; banks in those categories are considerably smaller in absolute terms than bank holding companies, however.

[10] Andrew Haldane and Robert May, "Systemic Risk in Banking Ecosystems," *Nature*, vol. 469, January 2011, p. 351.

[11] Organization of Economic Cooperation and Development, *Bank Competition and Financial Stability*, 2011, Figure 1.1.

[12] Many of these large institutions that focus on non-banking activities are chartered as bank holding companies or savings and loan holding companies.

[13] For more information, see CRS Report R43345, *Shadow Banking: Background and Policy Issues*, by Edward V. Murphy and Tobias Adrian, Adam Ashcraft, and Zoltan Pozsar,

"Shadow Banking," Federal Reserve Bank of New York, working paper, December 31, 2009.

[14] Tobias Adrian, Christopher Burke, and James McAndrews, *The Federal Reserve's Primary Dealer Credit Facility*, Federal Reserve Bank of New York, Current Issues in Economics and Finance, vol. 15, no. 4, New York, NY, August 2009.

[15] According to one estimate, mergers and acquisitions during the crisis increased the assets of the four largest banks from 30% to 44% of total bank assets. Richard Fisher, "Two Areas of Present Concern," speech before the Senior Delegates' Roundtable of the Fixed Income Forum, Federal Reserve Bank of Dallas, July 23, 2009.

[16] Data can be accessed at http://money.cnn.com/magazines. The lack of financial firms in the top 10 by revenue does not appear to be driven by the effects of the financial crisis. For example, there were two predominantly financial firms in the top 10 by revenue in 2006.

[17] One study of the ten most concentrated industries did not include any financial firms. See Andrea Alegria *et al*, "Highly Concentrated: Companies that Dominate Their Industries," *IBISWorld*, February 2012, http://www.ibisworld.com/Common/MediaCenter/Highly%20 Concentrated%20Industries.pdf.

[18] An alternative perspective is that the simultaneous failure or emergency experienced by many firms during the crisis was primarily caused by a lack of diversified risk that led to many firms experiencing losses on similar investments (in this case, mortgage-related investments), as opposed to losses being caused by counterparty exposure. This perspective does not necessarily require a TBTF problem to explain the crisis. For example, see Daniel Tarullo, "Regulating Systemic Risk," speech at 2011 Credit Markets Symposium, Charlotte, North Carolina, March 31, 2011, http://www.federalreserve.gov/newsevents/speech /tarullo20110331a.htm.

[19] Hereafter, for convenience, this report will use the terms "too big to fail" and "too interconnected to fail" interchangeably.

[20] International Monetary Fund, United States—Selected Issues, July 13, 2009, p. 24.

[21] See, for example, Financial Crisis Inquiry Commission, *Final Report,* Ch. 18, http://fcic-static.law.stanford.edu/ cdn_media/fcic-reports/fcic_final_report_full.pdf. For an alternative perspective on the importance of Lehman Brothers, see "Dissenting Views" in the same report.

[22] For more information on the events of 2008, see the Appendix.

[23] In the case of Fannie Mae and Freddie Mac, this was arguably the policy goal—Fannie Mae's and Freddie Mac's low-borrowing costs were seen by some as desirable insofar as it led to lower borrowing costs for homeowners. A key feature of the housing bubble was overinvestment in housing, spurred by the over-availability of mortgage credit.

[24] Evidence that larger banks are consistently riskier than smaller banks is mixed. For example, one measure of riskiness is leverage (the proportion of liabilities to equity held by a bank). One study found that large U.S. commercial banks were less leveraged than small banks on average during the past decade, but the median large bank was modestly more leveraged than the median small bank. Large banks also had more off-balance-sheet activities, which some believe made banks appear to be less risky than they turned out to be. The study also found that investment banks were much more leveraged than commercial banks, and large investment banks were more leveraged than small ones. Source: Sebnem Kalemli-Ozcan, Bent Sorensen, Sevcan Yesiltas, "Leverage Across Firms, Banks, and Countries," National Bureau of Economic Research, working paper no. 17354, August 2011. Anecdotal evidence points to a number of large banks whose risky behavior resulted in failure or rescue during the crisis, but most failing banks over the past few years were small banks.

[25] Economists refer to this as a "principal-agent" problem.

[26] Studies using empirical evidence to estimate the TBTF funding advantage are reviewed in Financial Crisis Inquiry Commission, "Governmental Rescues of 'Too Big To Fail' Financial Institutions," Preliminary Staff Report, August 2010, ch. 3, http://fcic-static.law.stanford.edu/cdn_media Randall Kroszner, "A Review of Bank Funding Cost Differentials," University of Chicago, working paper, November 2013, https://www.stern.nyu.edu/sites/default/files/assets Thomas Hoenig, Testimony before the Committee on Financial Services, U.S. House of Representatives, June 26, 2013, Attachment 3, http://financialservices.house.gov/uploadedfiles/hhrg-113-ba00-wstate-thoenig-20130626.pdf.

[27] See Goldman Sachs, "Measuring the TBTF Effect on Bond Pricing," *Global Markets Institute*, May 2013.

[28] Government Accountability Office, *Large Bank Holding Companies – Expectations of Government Support*, GAO-14-621, July 2014, p. 40-55.

[29] Government Accountability Office, *Large Bank Holding Companies – Expectations of Government Support*, GAO-14-621, July 2014, p. 24 and Financial Stability Oversight Council, *Annual Report*, 2014, p. 117.

[30] Financial Crisis Inquiry Commission, "Governmental Rescues of 'Too Big To Fail' Financial Institutions," Preliminary Staff Report, August 2010, ch. 3, http://fcic-static.law.stanford.edu/cdn_media Governmental-Rescues.pdf.

[31] An alternative perspective is that there was no explicit TBTF policy because changes in market structure over time— namely, the emergence of large, complex banks and non-bank financial firms—did not trigger legislative changes to create a TBTF policy.

[32] Thrifts, credit unions, and banks that did not have holding company structures were not subject to prudential oversight by the Fed. In this sense, some large banks were regulated differently than some small banks before the crisis, although not all bank holding companies were large and not all thrifts were small.

[33] Since there was no explicit TBTF policy, it is speculative as to whether the Fed considered all of the banks it identified as large complex banking institutions to be TBTF. Prior to the crisis, there was not authority to set higher quantitative prudential standards for TBTF banks, although regulators do enjoy discretion in their supervision. See Federal Reserve, *Framework for Risk-Focused Supervision of Large Complex Institutions*, Handbook, August 1997, http://www.federalreserve.gov/boarddocs/srletters/1997/sr9724a1.pdf.

[34] For more information, see Mark Greenlee, "Historical Review of 'Umbrella Regulation' by the Board of Governors of the Federal Reserve System," Federal Reserve Bank of Cleveland, working paper 08-07, October 2008.

[35] For more information, see "Selected Historical Experiences With "Too Big To Fail"

[36] For more information on the GSEs, see CRS Report RL34657, *Financial Institution Insolvency: Federal Authority over Fannie Mae, Freddie Mac, and Depository Institutions*.

[37] As discussed above, due to the nature of financial intermediation, financial firms can never hold enough liquidity to survive a run. Nevertheless, critics have argued that the Fed's response to turmoil enabled firms to take on excessive liquidity risk. This policy is sometimes referred to as the "Greenspan put," referring to the fact that the Fed's willingness to provide liquidity in times of trouble provided firms with a hedge against liquidity risk.

[38] 12 USC 1823(c). In total, GAO reports that the FDIC's systemic risk exception was invoked five times during the crisis. See Government Accountability Office, *Federal Deposit Insurance Act:Regulators' Use of Systemic Risk Exception*, GAO-10-100, April 2010.

[39] Information on government assistance provided during the crisis can be found in CRS Report R41073, *Government Interventions in Response to Financial Turmoil*, by Baird Webel and Marc Labonte.

[40] A GAO evaluation found that while the largest banks received a majority of the assistance from the Fed's broadly based emergency programs in dollar terms, they had the lowest ratio of assistance to total assets, whereas the smallest banks had the highest ratio. By contrast, the largest banks had the highest ratio of guaranteed debt to assets in the FDIC's TGLP and the highest ratio of capital to assets in TARP while participating. Government Accountability Office, *Government Support for Bank Holding Companies*, GAO-14-18, November 2013, Table 4, 5, and 6.

[41] See, for example, Financial Crisis Inquiry Commission, *Final Report,* Ch. 18, http://fcic-static.law.stanford.edu/ cdn_media/fcic-reports/fcic_final_report_full.pdf; Congressional Oversight Panel, *An Overall Assessment of TARP and Financial Stability*, 112th Cong., 1st sess., March 4, 2011, S.Hrg.112-3. For an overview of government assistance during the crisis, see CRS Report R43413, *Costs of Government Interventions in Response to the Financial Crisis: A Retrospective*, by Baird Webel and Marc Labonte.

[42] An alternative perspective is that government intervention worsened the crisis by creating policy uncertainty. See, for example, John Taylor, "The Financial Crisis and the Policy Responses: An Empirical Analysis of What Went Wrong," November 2008, working paper, http://www.stanford.edu/~johntayl/FCPR.pdf.

[43] As will be discussed in the section below entitled "Resolving a Large, Interconnected Failing Firm," the failure could be resolved by the bankruptcy process or a special receivership regime, similar to how banks are resolved. If the latter is used, then issues arise as to what government support becomes available to creditors through the receiver.

[44] Economists refer to this as a "time inconsistency" problem. See Gary Stern and Ron Feldman, *Too Big to Fail*, Brookings Institute Press, Washington, D.C., 2004, ch. 2.

[45] Congressional Oversight Panel, *March Oversight Report*, March 16, 2011, p. 153, http://frwebgate.access.gpo.gov/cgi-bin/getdoc.cgi?dbname=112_senate_hearings&docid =f:64832.pdf.

[46] See, for example, John Taylor, "The Financial Crisis and the Policy Responses: An Empirical Analysis of What Went Wrong," November 2008, working paper, http://www.stanford.edu/~johntayl/FCPR.pdf.

[47] For more information, see the Appendix.

[48] For example, CBO expected TARP alone to have a subsidy cost of $190 billion in January 2009. See Congressional Budget Office, *The Budget and Economic Outlook*, January 2009, p. 25.

[49] CRS Report R43413, *Costs of Government Interventions in Response to the Financial Crisis: A Retrospective*, by Baird Webel and Marc Labonte.

[50] Congressional Budget Office, *Report on the Troubled Asset Relief Program*, April 2014. There is no recent estimate of the economic costs for programs outside of TARP. Economic gains on assistance to AIG outside of TARP partly or wholly offset economic costs to AIG through TARP.

[51] An alternative perspective is that government intervention worsened the crisis by creating policy uncertainty. See, for example, John Taylor, "The Financial Crisis and the Policy Responses: An Empirical Analysis of What Went Wrong," November 2008, working paper, http://www.stanford.edu/~johntayl/FCPR.pdf.

[52] One variation on this approach would be to cap borrowing, so that a firm would face no size limit when financing its activities through capital, but in effect could not grow past a specified threshold through the use of leverage.

[53] Federal Deposit Insurance Corporation, "Continental Illinois and 'Too Big to Fail'," *History of the Eighties*, Ch. 7, http://www.fdic.gov/bank/historical/history. For more information, see the section below on Continental Illinois in the Appendix.

[54] See, for example, Anat R. Admati *et* al, "Fallacies, Irrelevant Facts, and Myths in the Discussion of Capital Regulation: Why Bank Equity is Not Expensive," working paper, March 23, 2011, https://gsbapps.stanford.edu/ researchpapers/library/RP2065R1&86.pdf.

[55] The evidence on the existence of economies of scale is reviewed in Inci Otker-Robe et al, "The Too-Important-to Fail Conundrum," International Monetary Fund, *Staff Discussion Note SGN/11/12*, May 2011, available at http://www.imf.org/external/pubs/ft/sdn/2011/sdn 1112.pdf. See also David Wheelock and Paul Wilson, "Do Large Banks Have Lower Costs? New Estimates of Returns to Scale for U.S. Banks," Federal Reserve Bank of St. Louis, Working Paper 2009-054E, May 2011, http://research.stlouisfed.org/wp/2009/2009-054.pdf.

[56] According to Hamilton Place Strategies, the largest syndicated loan in 2012 involved underwriting by the four largest U.S. banks and two foreign banks. See Hamilton Place Strategies, "Banking on Our Future," *HPSinsight*, February 2013.

[57] These benefits are also discussed in Hamilton Place Strategies, "Banking on Our Future," *HPSinsight*, February 2013.

[58] Financial Stability Oversight Council, *Study and Recommendations Regarding Concentration Limits on Large Financial Companies*, January 2011, http://www.treasury.gov/initiatives /Documents/ Study%20on%20Concentration%20Limits%20on%20Large%20Firms%2001-17-11.pdf.

[59] See Thorsten Beck, "Bank Competition and Financial Stability, Friends or Foes?," in *Competition in the Financial Sector*, Bank Indonesia and Banco de Mexico, 2008; Antonio Ruiz-Porras, "Banking competition and financial fragility: Evidence from panel-data, *Estudios Economicos*, vol. 23, no. 1, 2008.

[60] See Renee Haltom, "Why Was Canada Exempt From the Financial Crisis?, *Economic* Focus, Fourth Quarter, 2013, p. 22.

[61] See Jeremy Stein, "Regulating Large Financial Institutions," speech at the International Monetary Fund, April 17, 2013.

[62] Financial Stability Oversight Council, *Study and Recommendations Regarding Concentration Limits on Large Financial Companies*, January 2011, p. 8, http://www.treasury.gov /initiatives/Documents/
Study%20on%20Concentration%20Limits%20on%20Large%20Firms%2001-17-11.pdf.

[63] It can be accessed at http://federalreserve.gov/newsevents/press/bcreg/20140508a.htm.

[64] For more information, see the Appendix.

[65] Tobias Adrian and Adam Ashcraft, "Shadow Banking: A Review of the Literature," Federal Reserve Bank of New York, Staff Report no. 580, October 2012.

[66] The Financial Stability Oversight Council has grappled with coming up with developing metrics for these concepts in its rulemaking (12 CFR Part 1310, RIN 4030-AA00). Different perspectives on defining the concepts can be found in the public comments to the rulemaking. See also International Monetary Fund, Bank for International Settlements, Financial Stability Board, *Guidance to Assess the Systemic Importance of Financial Institutions, Markets and Instruments*, report, October 2009, available at http://www.imf.org/external/np/g20/pdf/100109.pdf.

[67] Reinstating the Glass-Steagall Act in its entirety would involve many other policy areas as well that have changed significantly over time. Proponents of reinstating Glass-Steagall are usually understood to be focused on four key provisions. For more information, see CRS Report R41181, *Permissible Securities Activities of Commercial Banks Under the Glass-Steagall Act (GSA) and the Gramm-Leach-Bliley Act (GLBA)*, by David H. Carpenter and M. Maureen Murphy.

[68] Under current law, there are still limits on the types of business activities that banking subsidiaries can undertake, but non-banking subsidiaries within the same holding company may operate in different lines of financial business.

[69] Financial Stability Oversight Council, *Study and Recommendations on Prohibitions on Proprietary Trading*, January 2011, http://www.treasury.gov/initiatives/Documents/Volcker%20sec%20%20619%20study%20final%201%2018%2011%20rg.pdf.

[70] Thomas Hoenig and Charles Morris, "Restructuring the Banking System to Improve Safety and Soundness," Federal Reserve Bank of Kansas City, working paper, December 2012.

[71] Independent Commission on Banking, *Interim Report*, United Kingdom, April 2011.

[72] High-level Expert Group on Reforming the Structure of the EU banking Sector Chaired by Erkki Liikanen, *Final Report*, European Union, October 2, 2012.

[73] In the United States, some have argued that each subsidiary within a holding company should be made legally and operationally separate. See, for example, Sheila Bair, *Bull by the Horns*, Simon and Schuster, (New York, NY: 2012), p. 329; Brad Miller, "Use Stand-Alone Subsidiaries to Break Up Megabanks," *Wall Street Journal*, October 21, 2012.

[74] The term swaps refers to over-the-counter derivatives. It is statutorily defined in 7 USC 1a(47).

[75] Cady North, "Volcker Rule Risk Concentrated in 25 Banks," Bloomberg Government, October 14, 2011, p. 5.

[76] See American Bankers Association, *Letter to Alastair Fitzpayne: Information on the FSOC Notice 2010-0002*, November 3, 2010, http://www.aba.com/aba/documents/news/VolckerTrust11410.pdf; SIFMA, *Volcker Rule*, http://www.sifma.org/issues

[77] For more information, see CRS Report R41298, *The "Volcker Rule": Proposals to Limit "Speculative" Proprietary Trading by Banks*, by David H. Carpenter and M. Maureen Murphy.

[78] Available at http://federalreserve.gov/newsevents/press/bcreg/20131210a.htm.

[79] For more information, see CRS Report R41398, *The Dodd-Frank Wall Street Reform and Consumer Protection Act: Title VII, Derivatives*, by Rena S. Miller and Kathleen Ann Ruane.

[80] Available at http://federalreserve.gov/newsevents/press/bcreg/20130605a.htm.

[81] The potential for each type of financial firm to be a source of systemic risk is evaluated in Douglas Elliot, "Regulating Systemically Important Financial Institutions That Are Not Banks," Brookings Institution, working paper, May 9, 2013, available at http://www.brookings.edu/research/papers/2013/05/09-regulating-financial-institutions-elliott.

[82] Whether all non-bank firms or only TBTF ones performing a given financial activity are important sources of systemic risk is beyond the scope of this report, but if all were, a case could be made that a prudential regulatory regime should be applied uniformly to all such firms, and not just large ones.

[83] See Office of Financial Research, *Asset Management and Financial Stability*, September 2013, http://www.treasury.gov/initiatives/ofr/research/Documents/OFR_AMFS_FINAL.pdf; Douglas Elliott, "Systemic Risk and the Asset Management Industry," Brookings Institution, May 2014.

[84] This is discussed in more detail in the Appendix. See also Arthur Wilmarth, "The Dodd-Frank Act: A Flawed and Inadequate Response to the Too-Big-To-Fail Problem," *Oregon Law Review*, vol. 89, April 6, 2011, p. 951.

[85] Dafna Avraham, et al., "Peeling the Onion: A Structural View of U.S. Bank Holding Companies," *Liberty Street Economics*, July 20, 2012, available at http://libertystreeteconomics.newyorkfed.org/2012/07/peeling-the-onion-astructural-view-of-us-bank-holding-companies.html#.U-TnELFgi68.

[86] See, for example, Thomas Hoenig, "Back to Basics: A Better Alternative to Basel Capital Rules," Federal Deposit Insurance Corporation, speech delivered to the American Banker Regulatory Symposium, September 14, 2012.

[87] This issue was discussed by the Attorney General at a 2013 hearing. See U.S. Congress, Senate Judiciary Committee, *Oversight of the U.S. Department of Justice*, 113th Cong., 1st sess., March 6, 2013.

[88] During the debate of the Dodd-Frank Act, policy makers considered keeping the identities of regulated firms confidential, but they concluded that this would be impractical.

[89] Congressional Budget Office, *Measuring the Capital Positions of Fannie Mae and Freddie Mac*, June 2006.

[90] For an in-depth discussion, see the section in the Appendix entitled "Fannie Mae and Freddie Mac."

[91] Office of Federal Housing Enterprise Oversight, "Fannie Mae and Freddie Mac Capital," *Mortgage Market Note 08- 2*, July 17, 2008.

[92] Assuming that the overall supply of credit remained constant, raising the cost of capital at TBTF firms would reduce the amount of credit supplied to those firms, thereby increasing the supply of credit available to other firms. Economic theory predicts that the greater supply of credit available to other firms would reduce their cost of capital.

[93] FSOC issued a final rule in April 2012. It can be accessed at http://www.treasury.gov /initiatives/fsoc/rulemaking/Documents/Authority%20to%20Require%20Supervision%20 and%20Regulation%20of%20Certain%20Nonbank%20Financial%20 Companies.pdf.

[94] Financial Stability Oversight Council, "Council Names Two Companies for Consolidated Supervision and Enhanced Prudential Standards," *press release*, July 9, 2013.

[95] MetLife, press release, September 4, 2014, https://www.metlife.com/about/press-room/index.html?compID=140852.

[96] A current list of top 50 depositories by asset size is available at http://www.ffiec.gov/nicpubweb/nicweb/ Top50Form.aspx. Some of the firms on this list are not bank holding companies. Other types of depositories, such as savings and loan holding companies, with more than $50 billion in assets are not subject to the final rule, but the Fed has indicated that it intends to propose rulemaking in the future that apply to them. There are no official data on the largest financial firms that are not depositories.

[97] CRS was not able to locate an official list of banks subject to Title I enhanced supervision. About 130 banks (foreign and domestic) have submitted resolution plans ("living wills") pursuant to Title I, however. See Martin Gruenberg, testimony before the Senate Committee on Banking, Housing, and Urban Affairs, September 9, 2014, p. 5.

[98] The rule can be accessed at http://federalreserve.gov/newsevents/press/bcreg/20140218a.htm.

[99] Many provisions of the Basel III Accord were adopted in rulemaking in July 2013. The 2013 final rule does not include the capital surcharge for G-SIBs, which regulators have announced will be proposed at a later date. For more information, see http://federalreserve.gov/bankinforeg/basel/USImplementation.htm.

[100] Bank for International Settlements, *Basel III Summary Table*, http://www.bis.org/bcbs/basel3/b3summarytable.pdf.

[101] The final rule can be accessed here: http://federalreserve.gov/newsevents/press/bcreg/bcreg20140903a1.pdf.

[102] Financial Stability Board, "Policy Measures to Address Systemically Important Financial Institutions," November 4, 2011, http://www.financialstabilityboard.org/publications/r_111104bb.pdf. The identification methodology is described in Basel Committee on Banking Supervision, "Global Systemically Important Banks: Assessment Methodology," *Consultative Document*, July 2011, http://www.bis.org/publ/bcbs201.pdf.

[103] Financial Stability Board, "2013 Update of Global Systemically Important Banks," November 11, 2013, http://www.financialstabilityboard.org/publications/r_131111.pdf.

[104] The rule applies to all banks with more than $700 billion in assets, and was set at that level to include all banks designated as G-SIBs. The rule can be viewed at http://federalreserve.gov/newsevents/press/bcreg/20140408a.htm.

[105] Financial Stability Board, "Global Systemically Important Insurers and the Policy Measures That Will Apply to Them," July 18, 2013, http://www.financialstabilityboard.org/publications/r_130718.pdf. The Financial Stability Board is an international forum of which the United States is a member. A list of the U.S. firms can be found in the section below entitled "Regulating TBTF."

[106] Financial Stability Board, "Assessment Methodologies for Identifying Non-Bank Non-Insurer Global Systemically Important Financial Institutions," January 8, 2014, http://www.financialstabilityboard.org/publications/r_140108.htm.

[107] Hon. Jeb Hensarling et al, "Letter to Secretary Lew, Chair White, and Chair Yellen," May 9, 2014.

[108] Gary Stern and Ron Feldman, *Too Big to Fail* (Washington, DC: Brookings Institution Press), 2004.

[109] An alternative view is that Lehman Brothers' bankruptcy was more disruptive because the rescue of Bear Stearns led creditors to conclude that other large investment banks would also be rescued.

[110] The Fed has issued a proposed rule to implement these standards, which can be accessed at http://www.federalreserve.gov/newsevents/press/bcreg/bcreg20111220a1.pdf.

[111] For more information, see CRS Report R41398, *The Dodd-Frank Wall Street Reform and Consumer Protection Act: Title VII, Derivatives*, by Rena S. Miller and Kathleen Ann Ruane.

[112] For more information, see CRS Report R41529, *Supervision of U.S. Payment, Clearing, and Settlement Systems: Designation of Financial Market Utilities (FMUs)*, by Marc Labonte.

[113] For more information, see CRS Report R40530, *Insolvency of Systemically Significant Financial Companies (SSFCs): Bankruptcy vs. Conservatorship/Receivership*, by David H. Carpenter.

[114] See CRS Report RL34657, *Financial Institution Insolvency: Federal Authority over Fannie Mae, Freddie Mac, and Depository Institutions*, by David H. Carpenter and M. Maureen Murphy.

[115] For more information on purchase and assumption and other resolution methods, see the section below entitled "Resolution of Banks Before and After the Federal Deposit Insurance Corporation Improvement Act."

[116] For more information, see the section below entitled "Fannie Mae and Freddie Mac."

[117] See, for example, Sheila Bair, "We Must Resolve to End Too Big to Fail," remarks at the 47th Annual Conference on Bank Structure and Competition, Federal Reserve Bank of Chicago, May 5, 2011, http://www.fdic.gov/bank/ analytical/quarterly/2011_vol5_2 /Article1.pdf.

[118] For more information, see CRS Report RS22950, *Fannie Mae and Freddie Mac in Conservatorship*, by Mark Jickling.

[119] For more information, see "Washington Mutual and Wachovia." The Fortune list can be accessed at http://money.cnn.com/magazines

[120] The FDIC gives a detailed explanation of how the failure of a firm like Lehman Brothers could have been managed more smoothly under a resolution regime in "The Orderly Liquidation of Lehman Brothers Holdings Under the Dodd-Frank Act," *FDIC Quarterly*, vol. 5, no. 2, 2011, p. 31, http://www.fdic.gov/bank/analytical/quarterly/2011_vol5_2/ lehman.pdf.

[121] See, for example, Jeffrey Lacker and John Weinberg, "Now How Large is the Safety Net?" *Economic Brief 10-06*, June 2010, http://www.richmondfed.org/publications/research /economic_brief/2010/pdf/eb_10-06.pdf.

[122] See, for example, Kenneth Scott and John Taylor, "How to Let Too Big to Fail Banks Fail," *Wall Street Journal*, May 16, 2013, p. A15; Hoover Institute, Resolution Project publications, available at http://www.hoover.org/ taskforces/economic-policy/resolution-project/publications. For a comparison, see Sabrina Pellerin and John Walter, "Orderly Liquidation Authority as an Alternative to Bankruptcy," Federal Reserve Bank of Richmond, *Economic Quarterly*, vol. 98, no. 1, First Quarter 2012, p. 1.

[123] International Monetary Fund, "Resolution of Cross-Border Banks – A Proposed Framework for Enhanced Coordination," June 2010, available at http://www.imf.org/external/np/pp/eng /2010/061110.pdf.

[124] For more information, see CRS Report RL34623, *Housing and Economic Recovery Act of 2008*, coordinated by N. Eric Weiss.

[125] For more information, see CRS Report RL34657, *Financial Institution Insolvency: Federal Authority over Fannie Mae, Freddie Mac, and Depository Institutions*, by David H. Carpenter and M. Maureen Murphy. Before HERA, Fannie Mae's and Freddie Mac's regulator had more limited powers of conservatorship and no powers of receivership.

[126] HERA required that the GSE be put into receivership if it became insolvent. Transfers from Treasury since 2008 to maintain solvency have had the effect of avoiding the receivership requirement.

[127] This finding does not require the firm to have been previously designated as systemically important for Title I's purposes of heightened prudential regulation.

[128] Martin J. Gruenberg, Acting Chairman of the Federal Deposit Insurance Corporation, Remarks to the Federal Reserve Bank of Chicago Bank Structure Conference; Chicago, IL, May 10, 2012.

[129] It can be accessed here: http://www.gpo.gov/fdsys/pkg/FR-2013-12-18/pdf/2013-30057.pdf. For more information on the FDIC as receiver under Title II, see http://www.fdic.gov/resauthority/.

[130] Christopher Payne and Tony Costello, "Will Orderly Resolution Work?," *BGOV Analysis*, May 19, 2014.

[131] For background on the Collins Amendment, see the section above entitled "Regulating TBTF."

[132] The current Tier 1 leverage ratio is 4%. The bill provides a definition of equity and assets that make the quantitative ratios under the bill not directly comparable to ratios under current law, however.

[133] The discussion draft is posted here: http://waysandmeans.house.gov/uploadedfiles/statutory_text_tax_reform_act_of_2014_discussion_draft__022614.pdf.

[134] 70 Stat. 133.

[135] For more information on the erosion of Glass Steagall, see CRS Report R41181, *Permissible Securities Activities of Commercial Banks Under the Glass-Steagall Act (GSA) and the Gramm-Leach-Bliley Act (GLBA)*, by David H. Carpenter and M. Maureen Murphy.

[136] For more information, see Mark Greenlee, "Historical Review of 'Umbrella Regulation' by the Board of Governors of the Federal Reserve System," Federal Reserve Bank of Cleveland, working paper 08-07, October 2008.

[137] For more information, see CRS Report 94-744, *The Riegle-Neal Interstate Banking and Branching Efficiency Act of 1994*, by M. Maureen Murphy. (This report is out of print, but available by request.)

[138] See General Accounting Office, *Guidelines for Rescuing Large Failing Firms and Municipalities*, GAO Report GGD-84-34, March 29, 1984; CRS Report R41401, *General Motors' Initial Public Offering: Review of Issues and Implications for TARP*, by Bill Canis, Baird Webel, and Gary Shorter; CRS Report R41940, *TARP Assistance for Chrysler: Restructuring and Repayment Issues*, by Baird Webel and Bill Canis.

[139] For more information on the resolution process, see CRS Report RL34657, *Financial Institution Insolvency: Federal Authority over Fannie Mae, Freddie Mac, and Depository Institutions*, by David H. Carpenter and M. Maureen Murphy.

[140] Federal Deposit Insurance Corporation, *Managing The Crisis*, Part 1, Chapter 3, August 1998, http://www.fdic.gov/ bank/historical/managing/history1-03.pdf.

[141] Gary Stern and Ron Feldman, *Too Big to Fail*, (Washington, D.C.: Brookings Institution Press), 2004, p. 151.

[142] Federal Deposit Insurance Corporation, *Managing The Crisis*, Part 1, Chapter 5, August 1998, p. 153, http://www.fdic.gov/bank/historical/managing/history1-05.pdf.

[143] Federal Deposit Insurance Corporation, "Continental Illinois and 'Too Big to Fail'," *History of the Eighties*, Ch. 7, http://www.fdic.gov/bank/historical/history

[144] Besides FDIC resolutions, there were a large number of thrift resolutions in the 1980s. Since these institutions tended to be small, this experience is not central to the TBTF issue.

[145] FDIC, "The Savings and Loan Crisis and Its Relationship to Banking," *History of the Eighties – Lessons for the Future*, December 1997, Ch. 4, http://www.fdic.gov/bank /historical/history

[146] The Federal Deposit Insurance Corporation Improvement Act, P.L. 102-242. Previously, the FDIC had to demonstrate that its resolution method was less costly than an insured deposit payoff; that requirement could be waived in the case of the "essentiality" exception noted above.

[147] FDIC data on bank failures can be accessed at http://www2.fdic.gov/hsob/Select Rpt.asp?EntryTyp=30.

[148] 12 U.S.C 1823(c).

[149] Federal Reserve annual report quoted in Anna Schwartz, "The Misuse of the Fed's Discount Window," *Federal Reserve Bank of St. Louis Review*, September/October 1992, p. 58.

[150] For more information on the Fed's response to the Penn Central failure, see Mark Carlson and David Wheelock, "The Lender of Last Resort: Lessons from the Fed's First 100 Years," Federal Reserve Bank of St. Louis, working paper 2012-056B, February 2013.

[151] Mark Carlson and David Wheelock, "The Lender of Last Resort: Lessons from the Fed's First 100 Years," Federal Reserve Bank of St. Louis, Working Paper 2012-056B, February 2013.

[152] Federal Deposit Insurance Corporation, "Continental Illinois National Bank and Trust Company," *Managing The Crisis*, Part 2, Chapter 4, August 1998, http://www.fdic.gov /bank/historical/managing/history2-04.pdf.

[153] Federal Deposit Insurance Corporation, "Continental Illinois and 'Too Big to Fail'," *History of the Eighties*, ch. 7, http://www.fdic.gov/bank/historical/history

[154] The claim that more than 100 banks would have failed has been disputed in Larry Wall, "Too Big to Fail After FDICIA," *Federal Reserve Bank of Atlanta Economic Review*, no. 78, January/February 1993, p. 1.

[155] Federal Deposit Insurance Corporation, "Continental Illinois National Bank and Trust Company," *Managing The Crisis*, Part 2, Chapter 4, August 1998, http://www.fdic.gov /bank/historical/managing/history2-04.pdf.

[156] The role of regulatory supervision in Continental Illinois' failure is discussed in Federal Deposit Insurance Corporation, "Continental Illinois and 'Too Big to Fail'," *History of the Eighties*, Ch. 7, http://www.fdic.gov/bank/ historical/history/235_258.pdf.

[157] Office of the Comptroller of the Currency, "Statement on Continental Illinois," news release 84-45, May 10, 1984.

[158] Tim Carrington, "U.S. Won't Let 11 Biggest Banks in Nation Fail," *Wall Street Journal*, September 20, 1984, p. 1.

[159] Donald Morgan and Kevin Stiroh, *Too Big to Fail After All These Years*, Federal Reserve Bank of New York, Staff Report Number 220, New York, NY, September 2005.

[160] For more details, see U.S. General Accounting Office, *Long-Term Capital Management*, GGD-00-3, October 1999, http://www.gao.gov/archive/2000/gg00003.pdf.

[161] Kevin Dowd, *Too Big to Fail? Long-Term Capital Management and the Federal Reserve*, Cato Institute, Briefing Paper Number 52, Washington, DC, September 1999, http://www.cato.org/pubs/briefs/bp52.pdf.

[162] The increase in leverage was more pronounced at investment banks than commercial banks. See, for example Sebnem Kalemli-Ozcan, Bent Sorensen, Sevcan Yesiltas, "Leverage Across Firms, Banks, and Countries," working paper, August 2011.

[163] For more detailed information, see CRS Report RL34427, *Financial Turmoil: Federal Reserve Policy Responses*, by Marc Labonte.

[164] Bear Stearns complied with an SEC net capital rule, but was not subject to safety and soundness supervision. For more information, see CRS Report R43087, *Who Regulates Whom and How? An Overview of U.S. Financial Regulatory Policy for Banking and Securities Markets*, by Edward V. Murphy.

[165] Securities and Exchange Commission, "Statement of SEC Division of Trading and Markets Regarding The Bear Stearns Companies," press release 2008-44, March 11, 2008, http://www.sec.gov/news/press/2008/2008-44.htm.

[166] List can be accessed at http://money.cnn.com/magazines

[167] Greg Ip, "Central Bank Offers Loans to Brokers, Cuts Key Rate," *Wall Street Journal*, March 17, 2008, p. A1.

[168] Federal Reserve Bank of New York, "New York Fed Completes Financing Arrangement Related to JPMorgan Chase's Acquisition of Bear Stearns," press release, June 26, 2008.

[169] Federal Reserve Bank of New York, "Statement on Financing Arrangement of JPMorgan Chase's Acquisition of Bear Stearns," press release, March 24, 2008.

[170] Congressional Budget Office, *The Budgetary Impact and Subsidy Costs of the Federal Reserve's Actions During the Financial Crisis*, May 2010.

[171] Lending records can be accessed at http://www.federalreserve.gov/newsevents/reform

[172] Securities and Exchange Commission, "Statement of SEC Division of Trading and Markets Regarding The Bear Stearns Companies," press release 2008-44, March 11, 2008, http://www.sec.gov/news/press/2008/2008-44.htm.

[173] J.P. Morgan Chase, Annual Report, 2008, p. 9, http://files.shareholder.com/downloads/ONE/2506919982x0x283416/66cc70ba-5410-43c4-b20b-181974bc6be6/2008_AR_Complete_AR.pdf.

[174] Short selling consists of borrowing shares and selling them, in the hope that the short seller can buy back the borrowed shares at a lower price in the future. A short sale is "naked" if the seller does not actually borrow shares for delivery to the buyer. For more information, see CRS Report RS22099, *Regulation of Naked Short Selling*, by Mark Jickling.

[175] Kara Scannell and Tom Lauricella, "SEC Extends Short-Selling Rules," *Wall Street Journal*, July 30, 2008, p. C. 1.

[176] Limits on OFHEO's powers and independence are discussed in CRS Report RL32069, *Improving the Effectiveness of GSE Oversight: Legislative Proposals in the 108th Congress*, by Loretta Nott and Mark Jickling.

[177] Office of Federal Housing Enterprise Oversight, Statement of OFHEO Director James B. Lockhart, July 10, 2008.

[178] For more information, see CRS Report RL34661, *Fannie Mae's and Freddie Mac's Financial Problems*, by N. Eric Weiss.

[179] For more information, see Federal Housing Finance Agency, U.S. Treasury Support for Fannie Mae and Freddie Mac," Mortgage Market Note, no. 10-1, Jan. 20, 2010.

[180] U.S. Treasury, "Treasury Department Announces Further Steps to Expedite Wind Down of Fannie Mae and Freddie Mac," press release, August 16, 2012. The agreement allows the GSEs to build a capital reserve of $3 billion.

[181] Congressional Budget Office, *The Budgetary Cost of Fannie Mae and Freddie Mac*, Testimony before the Committee on the Budget, U.S. House of Representatives, June 2011.

[182] List can be accessed at http://money.cnn.com/magazines

[183] For more information, see CRS Report R43087, *Who Regulates Whom and How? An Overview of U.S. Financial Regulatory Policy for Banking and Securities Markets*, by Edward V. Murphy.

[184] http://www.bankruptcydata.com/Research/Largest_Overall_All-Time.pdf.

[185] For example, see Chairman Ben Bernanke, "Lessons from the Failure of Lehman Brothers," testimony before the Committee on Financial Services, U.S. House of Representatives, April 20, 2010, http://www.federalreserve.gov/ newsevents/testimony/bernanke20100420a.htm. Thomas Baxter, testimony before the Financial Crisis Inquiry Commission, September 1, 2010, http://fcic-static.law.stanford.edu/cdn_media

[186] See CRS Report R40928, *Lehman Brothers and IndyMac: Comparing Resolution Regimes*, by David H. Carpenter.

[187] Michael Fleming and Asani Sarkar, "The Failure Resolution of Lehman Brothers," Federal Reserve Bank of New York, *Economic Policy Review*, vol. 20, no. 2, March 2014.

[188] Figure cited in Fed Chairman Ben Bernanke, "Financial Reform to Address Systemic Risk," speech at the Council on Foreign Relations, March 10, 2009, http://www.federalreserve.gov/newsevents/speech/bernanke20090310a.htm.

[189] There is debate over whether the money market run triggered by Lehman Brothers' bankruptcy should be considered to be caused by Lehman Brothers being TBTF. The view that attributes the run to TBTF interprets the run as triggered by concerns about the exposure of Lehman Brothers counterparties. The alternative view is that the run was triggered by concerns about holding paper issued by any financial firm with exposure to

"toxic" MBS. Neither view is inconsistent with the fact that many of the funds that experienced runs were not holding paper issued by Lehman Brothers. See, for example, Daniel Tarullo, "Regulating Systemic Risk," speech at 2011 Credit Markets Symposium, Charlotte, North Carolina, March 31, 2011, http://www.federalreserve.gov/newsevents/speech/ tarullo20110331a.htm.

[190] This section draws on information from CRS Report R41073, *Government Interventions in Response to Financial Turmoil*, by Baird Webel and Marc Labonte.

[191] Thomas Baxter, testimony before the Financial Crisis Inquiry Commission, September 1, 2010, http://fcicstatic.law.stanford.edu/cdn_media

[192] Data from http://www.federalreserve.gov/newsevents/reform

[193] See CRS Report R40438, *Federal Government Assistance for American International Group (AIG)*, by Baird Webel

[194] Craig Torres and Hugh Son, "Bernanke Says Insurer AIG Operated Like a Hedge Fund," *Bloomberg*, March 3, 2009.

[195] Scott Polakoff, Testimony before the Subcommittee on Capital Markets, Insurance, and Government Sponsored Enterprises, House Committee on Financial Services, U.S. House of Representatives, March 18, 2009, http://www.house.gov/apps/list/hearing/financial

[196] List can be accessed at http://money.cnn.com/magazines

[197] Chairman Ben Bernanke, Testimony Before the House Committee on Financial Services, March 24, 2009.

[198] Congressional Budget Office, *Report on the Troubled Asset Relief Program*, April 2014, Table 3.

[199] List can be accessed at http://money.cnn.com/magazines. Scott G. Alvarez, "The Acquisition of Wachovia Corporation by Wells Fargo & Company," Testimony Before the Financial Crisis Inquiry Commission, Washington, D.C., September 1, 2010.

[200] Kirsten Grind, "WaMu's Final Days," *Puget Sound Business Journal*, Friday, September 25, 2009, http://seattle.bizjournals.com/seattle/stories/2009/09/28/story1.html?page=1.

[201] Federal Deposit Insurance Corporation, "JPMorgan Chase Acquires Banking Operations of Washington Mutual," Press Release PR-85-2008, September 25, 2008.

[202] Scott G. Alvarez, "The Acquisition of Wachovia Corporation by Wells Fargo & Company," Testimony Before the Financial Crisis Inquiry Commission, Washington, D.C., September 1, 2010, http://www.federalreserve.gov/ newsevents/testimony/alvarez20100901a.htm.

[203] *Ibid.*

[204] *Ibid.*

[205] Federal Reserve, "Statement by the Board of Governors of the Federal Reserve System Regarding the Application and Notices by Wells Fargo and Company to Acquire Wachovia Corporation," October 12, 2008, p. 7, http://www.federalreserve.gov/newsevents/press /orders/orders20081021a1.pdf.

[206] For more information on all TARP programs, see CRS Report R41427, *Troubled Asset Relief Program (TARP): Implementation and Status*, by Baird Webel.

[207] U.S. Department of Treasury, *TARP Monthly 105(a) Report – December 2011*, January 2012. The largest failure was CIT Group, with $76 billion in consolidated assets in the first quarter of 2009.

[208] Congressional Budget Office, *Report on the Troubled Asset Relief Program*, October 2012.

[209] In their regulatory call reports, banks report capital ratios for three measures: Total Risk-Based Capital, Tier 1 Risk-Based Capital, and Tier 1 Leverage. For large BHCs, the Fed sets a minimum Tier 1 leverage requirement of 3% of total assets for banks receiving the highest regulatory rating and 4% of total assets for all other firms (12 CFR 225 Appendix

D). The regulatory rating that firms receive is confidential. For Tier 1 Risk-Based Capital and Total Risk-Based Capital, respectively, the Fed sets minimum requirements of 4% and 8% of risk-weighted assets.

[210] At the holding company level, Citigroup reported $118.8 billion of Tier 1 Capital in its December 2008 call report; of this total, $45 billion was from TARP. An estimate for the other two regulatory capital ratio measures cannot be easily calculated.

[211] 12 CFR Part 225, Subpart J.

[212] Citigroup, "Citi to Exchange Preferred Securities for Common, Increasing Tangible Common Equity to as Much as $81 Billion," press release, February 27, 2009, http://www.citigroup.com/citi/press/2009/090227a.htm.

[213] List can be accessed at http://money.cnn.com/magazines

[214] Henry Paulson, Testimony before the Committee on Oversight and Government Reform, U.S. House of Representatives, July 16, 2009, posted at http://online.wsj.com/public /resources PaulsonTestimony.pdf.

[215] The first quarter of 2009 was the first call report to incorporate TARP shares and the Merrill Lynch merger. In their regulatory call reports, banks report capital ratios for three measures: Total Risk-Based Capital, Tier 1 Risk-Based Capital, and Tier 1 Leverage. For large BHCs, the Fed sets a minimum Tier 1 leverage requirement of 3% of total assets for banks receiving the highest regulatory rating and 4% of total assets for all other firms (12 CFR 225 Appendix D). The regulatory rating that firms receive is confidential. For Tier 1 Risk-Based Capital and Total Risk-Based Capital, respectively, the Fed sets minimum requirements of 4% and 8% of risk-weighted assets.

[216] At the holding company level, Bank of America reported $117.9 billion of Tier 1 Capital in its December 2008 call report; of this total, $45 billion was from TARP. An estimate for the other two capital ratio measures cannot easily be calculated.

[217] Federal Reserve, *The Supervisory Capital Assessment Program: Overview of Results*, May 7, 2009. For an evaluation, see Special Inspector General for Troubled Asset Relief Program, *Exiting TARP: Repayments by the Largest Financial Institutions*, SIGTARP report 11-005, September 29, 2011.

[218] Citigroup, *Supervisory Capital Assessment Program Results – Update on Exchange Offer*, May 7, 2009, http://www.citigroup.com/citi/fin/data/p090507a.pdf.

[219] U.S. Treasury, "Treasury Prices Sale of Citigroup Subordinated Notes for Proceeds of $894 Million," press release, February 5, 2013.

[220] Congressional Budget Office, *Report on the Troubled Asset Relief Program*, April 2014.

[221] More information can be found in out-of-print CRS Report R40003, *U.S. Motor Vehicle Industry: Federal Financial Assistance and Restructuring*, coordinated by Bill Canis, available upon request.

[222] Congressional Oversight Panel, *January Oversight Report*, January 13, 2011, p. 82.

[223] CRS Report R41846, *Government Assistance for GMAC/Ally Financial: Unwinding the Government Stake*, by Baird Webel and Bill Canis.

[224] Congressional Budget Office, *Report on the Troubled Asset Relief Program*, April 2014, p. 6.

INDEX

A

B

C

G

H

I

J

L

M

N

O

P

Q

R